Holocaust Representations in Animated Documentaries

Holocaust Representations in Animated Documentaries
The Contours of Commemoration

Liat Steir-Livny

EDINBURGH
University Press

Edinburgh University Press is one of the leading university presses in the UK. We publish academic books and journals in our selected subject areas across the humanities and social sciences, combining cutting-edge scholarship with high editorial and production values to produce academic works of lasting importance. For more information visit our website: edinburghuniversitypress.com

© Liat Steir-Livny, 2024, 2025

Grateful acknowledgement is made to the sources listed in the List of Illustrations for permission to reproduce material previously published elsewhere. Every effort has been made to trace the copyright holders, but if any have been inadvertently overlooked, the publisher will be pleased to make the necessary arrangements at the first opportunity.

Edinburgh University Press Ltd
13 Infirmary Street,
Edinburgh, EH1 1LT

First published in hardback by Edinburgh University Press 2024

Typeset in Garamond MT Pro
by Cheshire Typesetting Ltd, Cuddington, Cheshire

A CIP record for this book is available from the British Library

ISBN 978 1 3995 2399 8 (hardback)
ISBN 978 1 3995 2400 1 (paperback)
ISBN 978 1 3995 2401 8 (webready PDF)
ISBN 978 1 3995 2402 5 (epub)

The right of Liat Steir-Livny to be identified as the author of this work has been asserted in accordance with the Copyright, Designs and Patents Act 1988, and the Copyright and Related Rights Regulations 2003 (SI No. 2498).

Contents

List of Figures	vii
Preface	ix
Introduction	1

Part I: "Unimating" the Holocaust

Chapter 1: Standing up to the Nazis	19
Chapter 2: Resourcefulness	37
Chapter 3: Ghettos and Camps	65
Chapter 4: The Exceptional—Representing the Horrors	103

Part II: The Life After 60

Chapter 5: The Face of Post-Trauma	135

Part III: Secondary Trauma, Postmemory, and Wishful Postmemory

Chapter 6: Struggling with the Parents' Memories	171
Chapter 7: The Memories Don't Let Go	197
Conclusion	217
Bibliography	223
Filmography	239
Index	240

Figures

1.1	*Grandma Mimi* (Shirley Prishkolnik, 2016)	21
1.2	*Yehudit* (Daniel Geron, 2015)	26
1.3	*Red Fox—The Story of Zippora Feibelevich* (Daniella Koffler, 2020)	35
2.1	*Nyosha* (Liran Kapel and Yael Dekel, 2012)	44
2.2	*The German Nurse—The Story of Elka Bornstein* (Daniella Koffler, 2020)	46
2.3	*Bettine Le Beau—A Lucky Girl* (Martin O'Neill and Andrew Griffin, 2015)	49
2.4	*A Thousand Kisses* (Richard Goldgewicht, 2017)	54
2.5	*Overnight Stay* (Übernachtung, Daniela Sherer, 2009)	60
3.1	*Silence* (Silvie Bringas and Orly Yadin, 1998)	69
3.2	*Luck: The Story of Israel Kleinmann* (Anat Kosty, 2020)	81
3.3	*Nana* (Ali Kellner, Canada, 2017)	86
3.4	*The Dress* (Hadar Huber, 2013)	88
3.5	*My Good Fortune in Auschwitz* (Reber Dosky, 2012)	91
3.6	*Facing the Sea—The Story of Saul Oren (Horenfeld)* (Daniella Koffler, 2020)	93
3.7	*Another Planet* (Amir Yatziv, 2017)	101
4.1	*Noch Am Leben* [*Still Alive*] (Anita Lester, 2017)	104
4.2	*Kol Nidrei* (Shira Meishar, 2020)	111
4.3	*Eva Kor: The Holocaust Survivor Who Forgave the Nazis* (Anna Humphries and Amelia Chiew, 2020)	113
4.4	*7 Minutes in the Warsaw Ghetto* (Johan Oettinger, 2012)	127
5.1	*Broken Branches* (Ayala Sharot, 2014)	145
5.2	*A Trip to the Other Planet* (Israel, Tom Kless, 2014)	163
6.1	*I Was a Child of Holocaust Survivors* (Ann Marie Fleming, 2012)	180
6.2	*German Shepherd* (Nils Bergendal, Sweden, 2014)	182
6.3	*Waltz with Bashir* (Ari Folman, 2009)	187
7.1	*2nd World War 3rd Generation* (Elad Eisen, Gil Laron, and Shahar Madman, 2013)	203
7.2	*Sketches from München* (Shahaf Ram, 2013)	205
7.3	*Compartments* (Daniella Koffler and Uli Seis, 2017)	209

Preface

Animated documentaries date back to 1918. In animated documentaries, real people play themselves even when they are not filmed. Their stories are presented through their voiceovers, written testimonies, or oral testimonies. In this sense, advertising, scientific, educational, and public service movies cannot be considered animated documentaries.[1]

For many years, documentary movies were considered real and objective, whereas animation was perceived as fiction or simply a form of children's entertainment. Thus, from its inception in 1918, animated documentary was marginalized and delegitimized as a documentary genre. However, since the late 1990s, this binary division between live action and animated documentaries has tended to fade. Today, animated documentaries are produced and screened in festivals, shown on primetime TV, and the genre is taught, researched, and produced in university film departments. Nevertheless, its portrayal of the "real" remains a topic of concern and is highly contested.

Short animated documentaries dealing with the Holocaust began appearing in the late 1990s. In the last two decades, dozens have been produced in the Western world, thus constituting a new phenomenon and inaugurating a new field of Holocaust commemoration. To date, however, there is very little research on these movies or their place in Holocaust remembrance.[2]

---

[1] Definitions vary. For example, Annabelle Honess Roe, *Animated Documentary* (London: Palgrave Macmillan, 2013, 4) argues that documentaries integrating animated elements and scenes should not be defined as animated documentaries. Other researchers refer to them as "hybrid movies." This book analyzes a number of examples of so-called hybrid movies. See for example Jeffrey Skoller, "Introduction to the Special Issue Making It (Un)real: Contemporary Theories and Practices in Documentary Animation," *Animation: An Interdisciplinary Journal* 6, no. 3 (2011): 207–214.

[2] Walden discusses the movies *I Was a Child Holocaust Survivor* and *Silence*. See: Victoria Grace Walden, "Animation: Textural Difference and the Materiality of Holocaust Memory," *Animation Studies Online Journal*, December 31, 2014, https://bit.ly/3k293Re accessed February 2, 2015. Orly Yadin, the director of *Silence*, also wrote about her movie. See Orly Yadin, "But is it Documentary?" in Toby Haggith & Newman Joanna, *Holocaust, and the Moving Image: Representations in Film and Television since 1933* (London & New York: Wallflower, 2005), 168–172; Orly Yadin and Sylvie

Holocaust Representations in Animated Documentaries: The Contours of Commemoration is the first comprehensive analysis of animated Holocaust documentaries. It explores movies produced in the USA, Canada, Australia, Europe, and Israel. Out of the 123 animated Holocaust movie titles in the Yad Vashem multimedia archive, twenty-five Holocaust animated documentaries were selected that epitomize the esthetic and thematic features of Holocaust animated documentaries in the Western World.[3]

Based on theories developed in the fields of animated documentary, Holocaust studies, trauma studies, and memory studies, this book discusses the ways in which animated Holocaust documentaries create a new layer of Holocaust microhistory, their advantages and disadvantages over live action movies, and their problematic features. It shows how these movies can visualize subject matter that previously eluded live action documentaries, such as the unfilmed past and people's inner worlds of fantasies, dreams, and emotions. In so doing, they deepen the audience's understanding of the emotional states of the victims during the Holocaust, their post-trauma, and its effects on their descendants' postmemory. Although these innovative modes of representation contribute to Holocaust remembrance, the book shows that Holocaust animated documentaries also have specific shortcomings and have generated a new set of problems relating to Holocaust memory and representation, since the vast majority marginalize the horrors and instead focus on small incidents that reflect bravery, resilience, solidarity, and hope. Many recycle idiomatic Holocaust icons instead of creating new trajectories

---

Bringas, "Silence," *Opticon1826*, no. 9 (Autumn 2010), https://bit.ly/3C8YJNH. *Silence* is also discussed in the following articles: Ruth Lingford and Tim Webb, "Silence: The Role of the Animators," in Toby Haggith & Newman Joanna, *Holocaust and the Moving Image: Representations in Movie and Television since 1933* (London & New York: Wallflower, 2005), 173–174; Brian Winston, "'Ça va de soi': The Visual Representation of Violence in the Holocaust Documentary," in Joram Ten Brink and Joshua Oppenheimer (eds.), *Killer Images: Documentary Movie, Memory and the Performance of Violence* (London: Wallflower, 2012), 97–119; Jessica Copley, "Modes of Representing"; Kerner, *Film and the Holocaust*, 243–260, and in Annabelle Honess Roe, *Animated Documentary* (London: Palgrave Macmillan), 146–169. *Seven Minutes in the Warsaw Ghetto* was reviewed in Richard Raskin's "Art and the Holocaust: Positioning *Seven Minutes in the Warsaw Ghetto*," *Short Film Studies Journal* 4, no. 2 (October 2014): 223–226; Richard Raskin, "An Interview with Johan Oettinger on *Seven Minutes in the Warsaw Ghetto*," *Short Film Studies Journal* 4, no. 2 (October 2014): 191.

[3] This book focuses on Holocaust animated documentaries and does not include animated video clips that relate to the Holocaust, such as "Aaron Razel – The Holy Hunchback," *YouTube*, March 31 2019, https://bit.ly/2Xe8cUv, Holocaust movies for children like "Anne Frank's Diary – An Animated Feature Movie," *YouTube*, May 3, 2020, https://bit.ly/3k1UGfF, animated documentaries which deal with the Allies and not the Holocaust such as "The Sand Mine," https://bit.ly/3Ek8HOf, or fiction animation such as "The Execution of Memory," *YouTube*, May 14, 2020, https://bit.ly/2Xdpn8F.

of representation, and many minimize Jewry and Judaism to universalize the Holocaust.

This book analyzes why and how animation can enhance Holocaust representations and the ways in which these movies can provide an important and new way to teach, document, and commemorate. At the same time, it stresses how animated documentaries can oversimplify and distort Holocaust memory. These topics are discussed in the light of first-person testimony that often intersects with the directors' postmemory of these events.

The Introduction presents an overview of the scholarly debate on animated documentaries, Holocaust animated documentaries, and the mediation of trauma. The book is divided into three main parts, each of which analyzes a different topic.

Part I, *"Unimating" the Holocaust*, is made up of four chapters that analyze movies dealing with the Nazi period (1933–1945). It explores the techniques employed to deal with the unfilmed past of Holocaust events and ways of visualizing the inner world of the victims. It shows how these documentaries bring the past to life and allow viewers to enter specific sites, as well as experience events and feelings that were not and cannot be captured on camera. However, it exposes how even though these movies were made in different countries by directors who did not discuss esthetics, thematic and narrative strategies, the vast majority deal with small incidents and fractured moments focusing on positive features such as resilience, human kindness, resourcefulness, and redemption. The section analyzes these trends while confronting it with the scholarly debate on this type of narrative.[4] This section also presents research on the place of infamous Holocaust symbols[5] in movies and the relationships between the Jewish and Universal aspects[6] of these movies.

Chapter 1: **Standing up to the Nazis**: This chapter shows that focusing on personal stories of resilience or standing up to the Nazis does not mean representing the atrocities of the Holocaust. These acts of bravery indeed took place, and their representation sheds more light on girls' and young women's behavior under Nazi rule. However, at the same time, these acts dominate the movies and marginalize the atrocities. The movies analyzed in this chapter are

---

[4] Lawrence Langer, "Redemptive and Unredemptive Holocaust Memory," in: *The Afterdeath of the Holocaust* (London: Palgrave Macmillan, 2021), 37–61. See especially 38–44; Yehuda Bauer, *Teaching the Holocaust in the Corona Era*, Zoom Conference, June 2, 2020.

[5] Oren Baruch Stier, *Holocaust Icons: Symbolizing the Shoah in History and Memory* (New Brunswick: Rutgers University Press, 2015), 2–3.

[6] Dan Michman, "Particularist and Universal Interpretations of the Holocaust: Complex Relationships," *Moreshet* 17, no. 100 (December 2019): 223–243.

Grandma Mimi (Shirley Prishkolnik, 2016),[7] *Yehudith* (Daniel Geron, 2015),[8] and *Red Fox—The Story of Zippora Feibelevich* (Daniella Koffler, 2020).[9]

Chapter 2: **Resourcefulness**: Another form of bravery depicted in several movies is the victims' resourcefulness. These movies tell the stories of girls, teenagers, and young women and broaden the visualization of women's responses to the Holocaust. However, their acts are not defined as gender-related.[10] They center on incidents that suggest "a ray of light in the darkness" of that era but obfuscate the atrocities in doing so. The movies analyzed in this chapter are *Nyosha* (Liran Kapel and Yael Dekel, 2012),[11] *Bettine Le Beau—A Lucky Girl* (Martin O'Neill and Andrew Griffin, 2015),[12] *The German Nurse—The Story of Elka Bornstein* (Daniella Koffler, 2020),[13] *A Thousand Kisses* (Richard Goldgewicht, 2017)[14] and *Overnight Stay* (Übernachtung, Daniela Sherer, 2009).[15]

Chapter 3: **Ghettos and Camps**: Movies that depict ghettos, concentration camps, labor camps, and extermination camps do not necessarily show the atrocities at the dreadful sites where Jews were starved, tortured, violently abused, and murdered. This chapter explores how the vast majority of

---

[7] "Grandma Mimi," *Facebook*, May 8, 2016, accessed May 8, 2016, https://bit.ly/3z3Z5Di

[8] "Yehudit—English Subtitles," Cinema and Animation Department, Tel-Hai College, *YouTube*, December 30, 2015, accessed January 1, 2016, https://bit.ly/3tMQcNy

[9] "Red Fox—The Story of Zippora Feibelevich," *YouTube*, April 16, 2020, https://bit.ly/3hFhZdU

[10] For another view of gender and the Holocaust see: Marion Kaplan (New York University), "Gendering Holocaust Studies Looking Back and Forward," *YouTube*, March 14, 2021, https://bit.ly/2XzAQj2

[11] "Nyosha", *Vimeo*, https://vimeo.com/43928582. The movie has been screened in fifty international film festivals, has been covered widely in newspapers, TV and Holocaust conferences, and received highly positive reviews. "Conference Future of Holocaust Testimonies lll – Nyosha—Animated Movie Based on Holocaust Survivor Testimony," *YouTube*, June 1, 2014, https://bit.ly/3tQOLgY; David Shamah, "Animated Holocaust Movie uses Spielberg Online Witness Archive," *The Times of Israel*, April 18, 2012, accessed April 19, 2012, https://bit.ly/3EIXjeW

[12] Griff, "Bettine Le Beau—A Lucky Girl," *Vimeo*, 2015, https://vimeo.com/118019503

[13] "The German Nurse," https://bit.ly/2Z843m5

[14] "A Thousand Kisses," vimeo.com/258300600

[15] "*Overnight Stay*," My Hero Films Community, https://bit.ly/3CxstUF. The movie has been screened in various festivals including the 2010 Annecy International Animated Movie Festival, the 2010 Hiroshima Animated Movie Festival, the CFC World Wide Short Movie Festival in Toronto, Silverdocs, and the Florida Movie Festival. It received a bronze award at the USC First Look Student Movie Festival, and a 3rd place BAFTA/LA award. In addition to the Haifa IFF, the movie was included in the 2010 DOK Leipzig, and the Chicago Children's Movie Festival. See: Ayelet Dekel, "Overnight Stay/Übernachtung at Haifa IFF," *Midnight East*, September 18, 2010, https://bit.ly/39n19Mm

directors refrain from representing horror even though they can capitalize on the ability of animation to represent the unfilmed past from the victims' point of view, rather making sure nothing is presented as too alarming or shocking. In so doing, they deprive viewers who do not have a background on the topic of an understanding of the true nature of these spaces. The movies analyzed in this chapter are *Silence* (Silvie Bringas and Orly Yadin, 1998),[16] *My Good Fortune in Auschwitz* (Reber Dosky, 2012), *The Dress* (Hadar Huber, 2013),[17] *Nana* (Ali Kellner, Canada, 2017),[18] *Another Planet* (Amir Yatziv, 2017), *Facing the Sea—The Story of Saul Oren (Horenfeld)*[19] (Daniella Koffler, 2020), and *Luck: The Story of Israel Kleinmann* (Anat Kosty, 2020).[20] Comparative examples from the hybrid documentaries *Dear Fredy* (Rubi Gat, 2016) and *Kishon* (Eliav Lilty, 2017) will also be examined.

Chapter 4: **The Exceptional—Representing the Horrors**: A handful of movies have taken advantage of the power of animated documentary to deal with horrific events without recourse to graphic or pornographic violence. The movies analyzed in this chapter are *Noch Am Leben [Still Alive]* (Anita Lester, 2017),[21] *7 Minutes in the Warsaw Ghetto* (Johan Oettinger, 2012), *2nd World War 3rd Generation* (Elad Eisen, Gil Laron, and Shahar Madmon, 2013),[22] *Kol Nidrei* (Shira Meishar, 2020),[23] and *Eva Kor: The Holocaust Survivor who Forgave the Nazis* (Anna Humphries and Amelia Chiew, 2020).[24] This chapter also discusses segments of the feature-length hybrid documentaries *Karski and the Lords of Humanity* (Slawomir Grünberg, Poland, 2015), *Dear Fredy* (Rubi Gat, 2016), and *Sabotage* (Noa Aharoni, 2022).[25]

Part II, *The Life After*, consists of a single chapter, **The Face of Post-Trauma**. It draws on the research on Post-Traumatic Stress Disorder (PTSD)[26]

---

[16] "Silence: – příběh z období holocaustu" (Eng, Czech subtitles), *YouTube*, January 31, 2009, https://bit.ly/3mi0lhz

[17] Hadar Huber, "The Dress," *Vimeo*, https://vimeo.com/71809187

[18] Ali Kellner, "Nana," *Alikelner*, https://bit.ly/3D4wtwc

[19] "In Front of the Sea—The Story of Saul Oren," *YouTube*, April 16, 2020, https://bit.ly/2WwcsyV

[20] "Luck: The Story of Israel Kleinmann", *YouTube*, April 16, 2020, https://bit.ly/3l1zffw

[21] A. D. Lester, "Noch Am Leben (Still Alive)," *Vimeo*, https://bit.ly/3L8oG5J or "JFI Presents: Noch Am Leben (Still Alive)," *YouTube*, October 1, 2018, https://bit.ly/3S4cLIp

[22] Ina Toker, "The Y Generation makes Holocaust Movies," *YNET*, April 24, 2017, https://bit.ly/3Vmpvwh

[23] "Kol Nidrei—The Story of Moshe Kaptain," *YouTube*, 16 April 2020, https://bit.ly/3A93XYa

[24] "Eva Kor: The Holocaust Survivor who Forgave the Nazis | BBC Ideas," *YouTube*, February 20, 2020, https://bit.ly/3DaoNZo

[25] "Sabotage," https://bit.ly/3FMjt2b

[26] Judith. L. Herman, *Trauma vehachlama [Trauma and Healing]*, (Tel-Aviv: Am Oved, 1994)

and its manifestations in Holocaust survivors[27] to discuss how animated documentary can visualize the components of post-trauma in Holocaust survivors. The chapter analyzes how animated documentaries attempt to visualize the inner world of post-traumatic survivors and their manifestations of PTSD. Aesthetic strategies are essential to depicting these facets of the trauma's after-effects in all their complexity and ambiguity. The chapter presents different modes of dealing with the past, testimonies, and their representation. It shows how animated documentaries can serve as a vehicle for fostering new relationships between the viewer and the documentary text.

The chapter specifically examines representations of strategies of survival. It deals with lost identities and the way they re-emerge later in life. It analyzes movies that highlight the lives of the survivors after the Holocaust and their traumatic memory. It aligns with research on the subjective meaning of the events for the witnesses, since the survivors build their behaviors and lives around this interpretation.[28] The movies analyzed in this chapter convey a rich and consistent representation of PTSD symptoms by showing what cannot be seen by the naked eye.[29] The movies analyzed are *Silence* (Silvie Bringas and Orly Yadin, 1998); *Broken Branches* (Ayala Sharot, 2014),[30] *A Trip to the Other Planet* (Tom Kless, 2014),[31] and *Kishon* (Eliav Lilty, 2017), as well as parts of *Noch Am Leben [Still Alive]* (Anita Lester, 2017) and *Eva Kor: The Holocaust Survivor who Forgave the Nazis* (Anna Humphries and Amelia Chiew, 2020).

Part III—*Secondary Trauma, Postmemory, and Wishful Postmemory* is dedicated to the representation of descendants of survivors. The post-Holocaust generations are exposed to stories and recollections of trauma they did

---

[Hebrew]; Cathy Caruth, *Unclaimed Experience: Trauma, Narrative, and History* (Baltimore: Johns Hopkins University Press, 2016); "PTSD," *Diagnostic and Statistical Manual of Mental Disorders* (5th ed.) (Arlington: American Psychiatric Publishing, 2013), 271–280.

[27] See for example: Dov Shmotkin, Amit Shrira, Shira C. Goldberg and Yuval Palgi, "Resilience and Vulnerability Among Aging Holocaust Survivors and Their Families: An Intergenerational Overview," *Journal of Intergenerational Relationships* 9, no. 1 (2011): 7–21; Inbar Levkovitz, "Bein hosen vepgiut: nizolei shoah mizdaknim beisrael" ["Between Strength and Venerability: Aging Holocaust Survivors in Israel"], *Hebrew Psychology*, April 18, 2012, accessed October 1, 2018, https://bit.ly/3zfqlip

[28] Dan Bar-On, *Hapsychologia shel hashoah [The Psychology of the Holocaust]* (Ra'anana: Open University Press, 2006).

[29] Ohad Landesman and Roy Bendor, "Animated Recollections and Spectatorial Experience in Waltz with Bashir," *Animation: An Interdisciplinary Journal* 6, no. 3 (2011): 353–370.

[30] Trailer: "Broken Branches," https://bit.ly/3QN75L6. The movie has been screened internationally at many festivals and has won awards. See: "Broken Branches," 2015, https://bit.ly/3L83n4f

[31] "A Trip to the Other Planet", *YouTube*, https://bit.ly/3Y8HsyT

not experience and can only imagine.³² Based on a wide range of scholarly research on second and third generations and their postmemory,³³ Part III explores the way animated documentaries represent various aspects of secondary traumatic stress in the descendants of survivors.³⁴ It shows how, by combining the range of aesthetics of animated documentaries and by visualizing the unfilmed past and the inner worlds and various modes of "witness to the witness,"³⁵ animated documentaries can lead to greater comprehension of the transgenerational transfer of the trauma.³⁶ It analyzes how animated documentaries point outward and visualize the unfilmed childhood of the descendants, while at the same time pointing inwards and plunging into the unconscious in scenes that evoke, rather than represent, experiences and feelings. This part is divided into two chapters:

Chapter 6: **Struggling with the Parents' Memories:** This chapter deals with the representation of the second generation. The term "second-generation" was coined by Canadian psychoanalysts as a clinical concept, and today is commonly used to denote the children of Holocaust survivors. Marianne Hirsch suggested that the Holocaust, as represented in the works of second-generation survivors, is an indirect affinity structured on imagination and memory that is inherited. This is what she termed "postmemory," which characterizes the experience of those controlled by events that happened before they were born, and who apply their imagination to places they cannot remember.³⁷ "Prosthetic memory" was defined by Alison Landsberg

---

32 For example, Victoria Aarons and Alan L. Berger, *Third-Generation Holocaust Representation: Trauma, History, and Memory* (Evanston: Northwestern University Press, 2017), 3–39.

33 Marianne Hirsch coined this term, which characterizes the experience of those controlled by events that occurred before they were born, and who apply their imagination to places they cannot remember. See: Marianne Hirsch, "Past Lives, First Memories in Exile," *Poetics Today* 17, no. 4 (1996): 659–667.

34 Charles Figley, ed., *Compassion Fatigue: Secondary Traumatic Stress Disorders from Treating the Traumatized* (New York: Brunner/Mazel, 1995), esp. 1–20.

35 An idiom coined by Dori Laub to describe the interviewer of the Holocaust survivor. See Dori Laub, "Bearing Witness on the Vicissitudes of Listening," in *Testimony: Crises of Witnessing in Literature, Psychoanalysis and History*, Shoshana Felman and Dori Laub (London: Routledge, 1992), 57–74.

36 See for example: Nurith Gertz, *A Different Choir: Holocaust Survivors, Aliens, and Others in Israeli Cinema and Literature* (Tel-Aviv: Am Oved and Open University, 2004) [Hebrew], 78–102; Liat Steir-Livny, *Two Faces in the Mirror: The Representation of Holocaust Survivors in Israeli Cinema* (Jerusalem: Eshkolot-Magnes, 2009), 96–204; Yosefa Loshitzky, *Identity Politics on the Israeli Screen* (Austin: University of Texas Press, 2002), 32–71; Aaron Kerner, *Movie and the Holocaust* (London: Bloomsbury, 2001), 195–242; Brad Prager, *After the Fact: The Holocaust in Twenty-First Century Documentary Movie* (London: Bloomsbury, 2015).

37 Marianne Hirsch, "Past Lives, First Memories in Exile," *Poetics Today* 17, no. 4 (1996): 659–667.

as characterizing memories of historical events that people adopt as their own even though they did not actually experience them.[38] These expressions have been examined in a range of cultural texts that represent the children of Holocaust survivors.[39] This chapter deals with the ways animated documentaries create another layer of representation of postmemory and prosthetic memory by visualizing what eluded live action documentaries: the unfilmed past and the inner worlds of the second generation, by visualizing the stream of consciousness, unconscious elements, dreams, and the imaginary. The movies analyzed are *I Was a Child of Holocaust Survivors* (Ann Marie Fleming, 2012),[40] *German Shepherd* (Nils Bergendal, Sweden, 2014), and *Waltz with Bashir* (Ari Folman, 2009).

Chapter 7: **The Memories Don't Let Go:** This chapter deals with the representation of the third generation. The third generation began to be studied in the 1980s, when psychologists in the United States who were treating a seven-year-old boy, the grandson of Holocaust survivors, claimed that the effects of the Holocaust had strongly affected him and that the issue deserved comprehensive treatment in the psychiatric community.[41] Since then, psychologists and psychiatrists have debated the term "third-generation" and its characteristics. Some researchers claim that the trauma of the Holocaust is transferred to the second and third generations. Some claim that the third generation, as a group, does not have distinguishing traits relative to trauma and that there is no difference between the biological grandchildren of Holocaust survivors and other groups whose grandparents are not Holocaust survivors. Others note the wide spectrum of reactions to trauma, which does not justify viewing the third generation as one group. Various books and movies in the last two decades draw on third-generation narratives from several continents and highlight the diversity of inherited memory and the transgenerational transfer of trauma, as well as the elements shared by members of this group.[42] This chapter highlights the ways the Holocaust is remembered, misremembered, and debated in various contexts, and the way it shaped the lives of the grandchildren and their relationships not only with the surviving grandparents but also with their parents—the second generation. The movies analyzed are *2nd World War 3rd Generation*

---

[38] Alison Landsberg, *Prosthetic Memory: The Transformation of American Remembrance in the Age of Mass Culture* (New York: Columbia University Press, 2004).

[39] For an overview of research see: Liat Steir-Livny, *Remaking Holocaust Memory: Documentary Cinema by Third-Generation Survivors in Israel* (Syracuse: Syracuse University Press, 2019).

[40] "I Was a Child of Holocaust Survivors," https://bit.ly/3PmN9Go

[41] Perihan Aral Rosenthal and Stuart Rosenthal, "Holocaust Effects in the Third Generation: Child of Another Time," *American Journal of Psychotherapy* 34, no. 4 (1980): 572–580.

[42] See Steir-Livny, *Remaking Holocaust Memory*, 20–22.

(Elad Eisen, Gil Laron, and Shahar Madmon, 2013), *Noch Am Leben* [*Still Alive*] (Anita Lester, 2017), *Sketches from München* (Shahaf Ram, 2013),[43] and *Compartments* (Daniella Koffler and Uli Seis, 2017).

Overall, this first book-length study of animated Holocaust documentaries reveals their unique epistemological potential as well as their shortcomings and problematic features. It exemplifies how animated documentaries can broaden and deepen the range of representations and provide an enhanced perspective on reality, truth, memory, and subjectivity.[44] It also critiques the ways the Holocaust is represented in animated documentaries and underscores its pitfalls. This extensive analysis of the many facets of animated Holocaust documentaries constitutes a comprehensive examination of this new cultural field of Holocaust representation in the postmillennial era and contributes to the investigation of contemporary Holocaust memory.

---

[43] "Sketches from Munich," https://bit.ly/3UWSKEu
[44] Honess Roe, "Absence, Excess and Epistemological Expansion: Towards a Framework for the Study of Animated Documentary," *Animation: An Interdisciplinary Journal* 6, no. 3, 2011, 215–231.

Introduction

Animation dates back to the advent of cinema and informed many early approaches to moviemaking. For years, however, it was considered an inferior genre, due perhaps to the success of the Disney studios (founded in 1923), which made animation synonymous with the Disney style. Until the 1990s, there was scant acknowledgment of animation in cinema research. Since then, however, cinematic studies have not only analyzed animation theoretically, but have legitimized it as an important and influential esthetic genre in its own right.[1]

Animated documentaries appeared as early as 1918,[2] but were ignored or disparaged for years. This genre was seen as undermining the principles of the documentary form by destabilizing its claim to the real and objective through its use of stylistic devices associated with inauthentic and/or juvenile movies.[3] Nevertheless, this dismissal of animation has also gradually evolved over the years. Since the 1960s, numerous cinema specialists have questioned the notion of the "truth" conveyed in documentary cinema. Theoreticians have made the case that documentary movies are not in fact descriptive of reality, but rather are "a creative treatment of reality," as John Grierson put it, that use ingredients from the real world to tell a story about reality. Subjective choices related to directing, moviemaking, and editing are made consciously, and reality is compressed into a narrative.[4] At the same time there has been

---

[1] Paul Wells, *Understanding Animation* (London & New York: Routledge, 1998), 1–9; Alan Cholodenko, "Introduction," in Alan Cholodenko (ed.), *The Illusion of Life: Essays on Animation* (Sydney: Power Publications, 1991), 9–30.

[2] *The Sinking of the Lusitania* (Winsor McCay, 1918) is considered to be one of the earliest animated documentaries, if not the first. See: Joseph A. Kraemer, "*Waltz with Bashir* (2008): Trauma and Representation in the Animated Documentary," *Creativeclay Animations*, April 3, 2017, accessed May 3, 2017, https://bit.ly/3Ef5gYP

[3] Annabelle Honess-Roe, "Absence, Excess and Epistemological Expansion: Towards a Framework for the Study of Animated Documentary," *Animation: An Interdisciplinary Journal* 6, no. 3 (2011): 215–231.

[4] Hardy Forsyth (ed.), *Grierson on Documentary* (London: Faber & Faber, 1966); Erik Barnouw, *Documentary: A History of the Non Fiction Movie* (Oxford: Oxford University Press, 1993); Richard Barsam, *Nonfiction Movie: A Critical History* (Indiana: Indiana University Press, 1992);

a growing call to recognize that no historical text[5] can be an authentic reflection of the past, but instead is constructed through the prism of ideologies and emplotment, and is always a story, not the presentation of objective knowledge.[6]

The contemporary success of animated documentaries is also due in large part to rapid advances in computer technology. Today animation is no longer solely defined by frame-by-frame cell, cut-out, or stop-motion pixilation, and the number of advanced animation techniques is staggering (flash animation and 3D CGI, and many more).[7]

This acknowledgment that the truth value of documentaries is problematic, the advances in technology, the mimetic capabilities of computer imaging software, and postmodernist theories have altered the perception of what constitutes truth and blurred what once was perceived as the frontier between the high art of documentary cinema and the mass entertainment lowbrow art of animation. In addition, cross-disciplinary approaches to cinema have recast the ways animated documentary is viewed and interpreted.[8] Today, various sub-genres of documentary movies such as pseudo-documentaries, mockumentaries, and others are eliciting research and commentary.[9] In today's digital age, live action footage is only one of

---

John Corner, *The Art of Record: A Critical Introduction to Documentary* (Manchester: Manchester University Press, 1996); Charles Warren (ed.), *Beyond Document: Essays on Nonfiction Film* (Hanover & London: University of New England Press, 1996); Bill Nichols, *Introduction to Documentary* (Indiana: Indiana University Press, 2001); Michael Renov, *The Subject of Documentary* (Minnesota: University of Minnesota Press, 2004); Brian Winston, Gail Vanstone, and Wang Chi, *The Act of Documenting: Documentary Film in the 21st Century* (London: Bloomsbury Academic, 2017).

[5] Hayden White, "The Historical Text as Literary Artifact," in *Tropics of Discourse: Essays in Cultural Criticism*, ed. Hayden White (Baltimore: Johns Hopkins University Press, 1978), 221–236. Republished in Geoffrey Roberts (ed.), *The History and Narrative Reader* (London: Routledge, 2001); Peter Novick, *That Noble Dream: The "Objectivity Question" and the American Historical Profession* (Cambridge: Cambridge University Press, 1988), 573–629.

[6] Victoria Walden, "Animation: A Different Way of Looking at the Past," *Animation Studies* 2.0, November 26, 2014, accessed November 1, 2015, https://bit.ly/3C39AbO

[7] Skoller, "Introduction," 209, 213, Tess Takahashi, "Experiments in Documentary Animation: Anxious Borders, Speculative Media," *Animation: An Interdisciplinary Journal*, 6, no. 3 (2011): 231–245 (esp. 234).

[8] Steve Fore, "Reenacting Ryan: The Fantasmatic and the Animated Documentary," *Animation: An Interdisciplinary Journal* 6, no. 3 (2011), 277–292.

[9] Gary D. Rhodes and John Parris Springer (eds.), *Docufictions: Essays on The Intersection of Documentary And Fictional Moviemaking* (Jefferson: McFarland, 2006); Craig Hight, "Mockumentary: A Call To Play," in Thomas Austin and Wilma de Jong (eds.), *Rethinking Documentary: New Perspectives, New Practices* (Berkshire: Open University Press, 2008), 204–216.

many ways of documenting the world. Animated documentaries are increasingly seen as being on a par with live action documentaries because neither are indexical, "objective," or "authentic."[10]

Overall, the boundaries used to define genre and formal categories now seem anachronistic and of little value for understanding contemporary movies. Animated documentary is increasingly perceived as a legitimate genre[11] that mixes "realistic" themes with fantastic stylistic devices and can make powerful claims about reality. It is now clear that what is abstract and/or non-naturalistic in form does not have to be fictional in content, but rather can represent "reality" and "truth."[12] In the last two decades, animated documentaries have become an integral part of documentary movie festivals, and feature-length animated documentaries now have mainstream theatrical releases and are shown on primetime television. There are more conferences that deal with this specific genre, and research on animated documentaries has flourished.[13]

ANIMATED HOLOCAUST DOCUMENTARIES

Debates on whether the Holocaust can be represented in art or in popular culture go back to the 1940s. This controversy may never be satisfactorily resolved, although the Holocaust has been represented in a wide range of cultural media—and also in cinema—for over seventy-five years.[14]

---

[10] Nea Ehrlich, "Animated Documentaries as Masking," *Animation Studies Online Journal* 6 (2011), accessed January 6, 2015, https://bit.ly/3Cba8MZ; Fore, "Reenacting Ryan," 277–278.

[11] Skoller, "Introduction," 207.

[12] Landesman and Bendor, "Animated Recollection," 353–370; Ward, "Animated Realities"; Ehrlich, "Animated Documentaries."

[13] To name a few: Sybil DelGaudio, "If Truth Be Told, can 'Toons' Tell it? Documentary and Animation," *Movie History* 9, no. 2 (1997): 189–199; Paul Ward, "Animated Realities: The Animated Movie, Documentary, Realism," in *Reconstruction: Studies in Contemporary Culture* 8, no. 2 (2008), accessed June 1, 2010, https://bit.ly/3z0yPK0; Paul Wells, "The Beautiful Village and the True Village: A Consideration of Animation and the Documentary Aesthetic," in Paul Wells (ed.), *Art and Animation* (London: Academy Editions, 1997), 40–45; Honess Roe, *Animated Documentary* (London: Palgrave Macmillan, 2013), 231–246; Ehrlich, "Animated Documentaries"; Jayne Pilling (ed.), *Animating the Unconscious* (London & New York: Columbia University Press, 2012); *Animation: An Interdisciplinary Journal* 6, no. 3 (2011) (the entire special issue was devoted to animated documentary); Gunnar Strøm, "The Animated Documentary," *Animation Journal* 11 (2003), 46–63; Walden, "Animation: Textural Difference"; Karen Beckman, *Animating Movie Theory* (Durham: Duke University Press, 2014); Annabelle Honess Roe, "Against Animated Documentary?".

[14] There is a heated, longstanding debate on these issues. See, for example, Theodor W. Adorno, *Negative Dialectics* (London: Routledge, 2000); Naomi Mandel, *Against the*

In a cultural world which considered animation as juvenile, very few animated movies[15] on the Holocaust were produced between the aftermath of World War II and the late 1990s (for exceptions, see *Pérák a SS* [*Springman and the SS*] [Jiří Trnka and Jiří Brdečka, Czechoslovakia, 1946],[16] *Sarah/The Seventh Match* [Yoram Gross, Australia, 1975], and *l'Empreinte* [*Imprint*] [Jacques Armand Cardon, France, 1975]). These rare movies were animated fiction.

This change was driven by developments in another genre. The Holocaust was seldom depicted in comics until the 1980s. Like animation, comics were considered juvenile and inappropriate for such a serious topic.[17] The international success of the graphic novel *Maus: A Survivor's Tale* (Art Spiegelman, 1986)[18] became the springboard for the development of

---

Unspeakable: Complicity, the Holocaust, and Slavery in America (Charlottesville: University of Virginia Press, 2007); Mark Godfrey, *Abstraction and the Holocaust* (New Haven: Yale University Press, 2007); Shoshana Felman and Dori Laub, *Edut* [Testimony] (Tel-Aviv: Resling 2008); Elie Wiesel, "Art and the Holocaust: Trivializing Memory," *The New York Times*, June 11, 1989, accessed October 2, 2010, https://nyti.ms/3z96rFz; Saul Friedlander (ed.), *Probing the Limits of Representation: Nazism and the "Final Solution"* (Cambridge & London: Harvard University Press, 1992); Ziva Amishai-Maisels, *Desciption and Interpretation – The Influence of the Holocaust on the Visual Arts* (Pergamon: Oxford, 1993); Libi Saxton, *Haunted Images: Movie, Ethics, Testimony and the Holocaust* (London & New York: Wallflower Press, 2008); Alvin Rosenfeld, *The End of the Holocaust* (Bloomington & Indianapolis: Indiana University Press, 2013).

[15] The first time the Nazis were depicted in an animation movie was during World War II. Disney Studios contributed to the war effort by producing short animation movies starring Donald Duck and other famous cartoon characters, which became part of a series of humorous anti-Nazi propaganda movies. The best-known is *The Face of the Fuhrer*, which describes a grueling day in a Nazi factory called "Naziland." See: "Donald Duck—Der Fuehrer's Face | eng sub," *YouTube*, https://bit.ly/3tCTanv; Yonathan Tomkins, "Donald Duck in Reserve: Animation Propaganda during WWII," *Slil* 2 (2008), 5–27 [Hebrew], https://bit.ly/3tFrKgL

[16] See: "The Springman and the S.S. (1946) – B&W / 14:18 Mins," *YouTube*, August 17, 2016, https://bit.ly/2Xh1CMY. The movie is also known as *The Chimney Sweep* in the USA. See: "Jiří Trnka," *A Medium Corporation*, accessed July 1, 2015, https://bit.ly/3k5BwFR

[17] Ya'aoba Sechrduti, *Nigun hagoral: hasoah bacomics 1942–1958* (*The Playback of Destiny: Holocaust in Comics 1942–1954*) (Tel-Aviv: New World, 2019) (Hebrew).

[18] Numerous articles have been written about *Maus*. See, for example, Terrence Des Press, "Holocaust Laughter?", in *Writing and the Holocaust*, ed. Lang Berl (New York: Holmes and Meier, 1988), 216–233; Andreas Huyssen, "Of Mice and Mimesis: Reading Spiegelman with Adorno," in Barbie Zelizer (ed.), *Visual Culture and the Holocaust* (London: Rutgers University Press, 2001), 28–44; Ewert, Jeanne, "Art Spiegelman's Maus and the Graphic Narrative," in Marie-Laure Ryan, *Narrative Across Media: The Languages of Storytelling* (Nebraska: University of Nebraska Press, 2004), 180–193; Deborah R. Geis (ed.), *Considering Maus: Approaches to Art Spiegelman's "Survivor's tale" of the Holocaust* (Alabama: University Alabama Press, 2007); Erin McGlothlin, "'When Time Stands Still': Traumatic Immediacy and Narrative Organization

animated documentaries about the Holocaust. In *Maus*, Art Spiegelman addresses the trauma experienced by his father Vladek, and his complex relationship with him and the past as a second-generation Holocaust survivor. It portrays Jews as mice and Nazis as cats, and Spiegelman even dared to incorporate black humor into the narrative. When it was released, *Maus* was heavily criticized for its use of comic book figures. Very quickly, however, critics came to praise Spiegelman's bold artistic decision, and *Maus* became the first comic book to win a Pulitzer Prize (1992). In 1992, Spiegelman published a sequel, entitled *Maus II: And Here My Troubles Began*. More than 100 books and essays have been written on these two texts, which constituted a paradigm shift in scholarly discourse and turned comics from "lowbrow culture" into "highbrow culture." *Maus* proved that a serious and complex subject like the Holocaust could be documented through a medium that was perceived as juvenile, fictional, and frivolous. Linguistically it changed the practice of referring to such books as "comics," with the term "graphic novels" now preferred, and paved the way for numerous Holocaust-related graphic novels—some of which were based on first person testimony[19]—and later encouraged the emergence of animated Holocaust documentaries. The connection between the two formats is clear, as Jessica Copley pointed out when commenting that the comic book has an almost cinematic quality.[20]

There were a few animated scenes in the early hybrid documentary *Everything's for You* (Abraham Ravett, 1989), in which director Ravett deals with his complicated life as a second-generation Holocaust survivor and his relationship with his Holocaust survivor father. Especially since the 2000s, more Holocaust documentaries have incorporated animated scenes, thus turning the "documentary" into a "hybrid movie" (for example, *Pictures from my Life* [Yoram Gross, 2014], *The Dark Side* [Natalie Assouline Travilio, 2015], *Dear Freddy* [*Fredy hayakar*, Rubi Gat, 2017], and others).

---

in Art Spiegelman's *Maus* and *In the Shadow of Two Towers*," in: Samantha Baskind and Ranen Omer-Sherman (eds.), *The Graphic Novel: Critical Approaches* (New Brunswick: Rutgers, 2008), 94–110.

[19] Assaf Gamzou, "Third-Generation Graphic Syndrome: New Directions in Comics and Holocaust Memory in the Age after Testimony," *The Journal of Holocaust Research* 33, no. 3 (2019): 224–237, https://bit.ly/392BLeI

[20] Jessica Copley, "Modes of Representing the Holocaust." Holocaust survivor Yoram Gross became an animator after World War II and immigrated to Australia in 1967. Among other works, he produced a very successful cartoon TV show for children entitled *The Adventures of Blinky Bill* (1993–1995, 2004–2005), which tells the story of Blinky the koala in a small Australian town. Gross interpolated autobiographical events from his life during the Holocaust into the story, such as the fact that he saved his sister, and lost his mother but found her after the war, et cetera. See the documentary: *Blinky and Me* (Tomasz Magierski, 2011).

Since the late 1990s, many purely animated documentaries have been produced. *Silence* (11 min, UK, Silvie Bringas and Orly Yadin, 1998) was the first fully animated Holocaust documentary. The movie tells the story of Tana Ross, who survived the Holocaust as a child, and explored her learned and self-imposed silences. *Silence* has won many awards[21] and has been shown on TV, at movie festivals, in schools, and in museums. In Sweden, it is now an integral part of high school educational programs.[22] Since then, dozens of animated Holocaust documentaries of various lengths have been produced in Israel, Europe, the USA, and Canada. They vary considerably in style, type of animation, their representation of reality, and choice of topics. These movies provide new perspectives on representational modes, testimonial strategies, reality, subjectivity, truth, mediation, and the avenues of exploration made possible when the Holocaust is represented through this genre.[23]

ANIMATED DOCUMENTARIES AND ANIMATED HOLOCAUST DOCUMENTARIES: STRENGTHS AND WEAKNESSES

Research on animated documentaries since the 1990s has shown how this genre can inform and enhance audiences' grasp of issues. Studies have also discussed how this genre can overcome the specific problems of live action documentaries and enrich the scope of the documentary realm.

Animated documentary is often considered the most honest form of documentary moviemaking. Because of its obvious unrealistic aesthetic, it is clear to viewers that it does not purport to be an indexical record of events presenting a purported transparency between event and image.[24] Orly Yadin, who directed *Silence*, argued that choosing to tell a Holocaust story through animated documentary is an ethical and not only an esthetic choice. In her opinion, the power of the photographic image is so great that even the most sophisticated of viewers can easily forget that no documentary is a transparent record of life, but rather a moviemaker's interpretation of it. The honesty of animation lies in the fact that the moviemaker is completely clear about his or her intervention.[25]

---

[21] "'Silence' by Orly Yadin & Sylvie Bringas," *Animated Documentray.com*, No Date, accessed June 1, 2015, https://bit.ly/3C7ySFS
[22] Yadin, "But is it Documentary?".
[23] Saxton, *Hunted Images*, 3, 6. In his 2001 book Aaron Kerner analyzed *Silence* in a section titled "Experimental Movies." Today animated Holocaust documentaries are no longer considered experimental, but rather as one of the main genres within Holocaust cinema. See Aaron Kerner, *Film and the Holocaust*, 243–260.
[24] Orly Yadin, "But is it Documentary?"; Walden, "Animation."
[25] Orly Yadin, "But is it Documentary?"

When viewers watch an animated documentary, they know that the person/event is a fabricated construction.[26] This enables them to explore temporal and spatial realms beyond the reflection of reality.[27] Specifically, for spectators, the viewing experience in an animated documentary is characterized by a heightened awareness of the presence of the moviemaker's attitudes and beliefs in the visuals. The cards are on the table, since by choosing this genre the director "declares" in advance that the events have a genuine historical basis but do not visually reside in the original space and time of those events.[28] Since the movies' visual "artificiality" is clear, this encourages the viewers to question the layering of what is considered the "real" and its many concealed or invisible aspects.[29] This honesty enables the viewing of the familiar world in a different light and, as a result, invokes contemplation that rejects the problematic perception by many viewers of live action documentary as a statement of fact, or as a clear window onto the past to what "really happened."[30]

Ohad Landesman and Roy Bendor suggested that animation serves as a vehicle for fostering a new relationship between the viewer and the documentary text. This relationship moves away from *faith* in the image to *trust* that the documentary text is making truthful claims that reflect the world in sophisticated ways.[31]

Tobias Ebbrecht argued that the many cultural representations of the Holocaust in Western popular culture have turned the Holocaust into a "master paradigm"; i.e., a series of well-known, repetitive Holocaust narratives and visuals that have appeared so often that they have almost become clichés[32] and similar esthetic tropes.[33] Animated Holocaust documentaries can avoid these clichés and depict the Holocaust through new visualizations.

Animated documentary can also enable the presentation of traumatic experiences because of the "distancing" inherent to animation. These movies

---

[26] Paul Ward, "Animating with Facts: The Performative Process of Documentary Animation in *The Ten Tark* (2010)," *Animation: An Interdisciplinary Journal* 6, no. 3, 296.

[27] Honess Roe, *Animated Documentary*, 40.

[28] Fore, "Reenacting Ryan," 281, 288–289.

[29] Ehrlich, "Animated Documentaries."

[30] Ward, "Animated Realities"; Ehrlich, "Animated Documentaries"; Kerner, *Film and the Holocaust*, 12.

[31] Landesman and Bendor, "Animated Recollection," 367.

[32] Tobias Ebbrecht, "Migrating Images: Iconic Images of the Holocaust and the Representation of War in Popular Film," *Shofar: An Interdisciplinary Journal of Jewish Studies* 28, no. 4 (Summer 2010): 86–103.

[33] See, for example: Gertz, *A Different Choir*, 78–102; Steir-Livny, *Two Faces in the Mirror*, 96–204; Loshitzky, *Identity Politics*, 195–242; Brad Prager, *After the Fact: The Holocaust in Twenty-First Century Documentary Film* (London: Bloomsbury, 2015).

may thus appeal to viewers who would otherwise have avoided this difficult subject.[34] Animated Holocaust documentaries can attract audiences who tend to avoid Holocaust movies. The use of animation, this extra filter of reality, may be one way to present the Holocaust to audiences who would normally recoil from the realities these documentaries portray, while actually drawing them closer and introducing them to stories they otherwise would have preferred to avoid.

Crucially, animated documentary can also visualize what cannot be captured on camera: the depths of human emotions. It provides insights into people's mental states and can represent memories, fantasies, hallucinations, dreams, and nightmares that are not readily visible. Since animation often foregrounds the subjective, it is an excellent vehicle to represent memory. The creativity and imagination that inform memory are often a keystone of animated works. Animation helps draw attention to an individual's subjective response to events, rather than claiming to represent official or purportedly objective accounts. Tess Takahashi noted that animated documentaries often examine life in wartime. Animation enables moviemakers to present the anxieties of unstable times and represent the experiences of individuals whose lives have been upended[35] by reflecting their fears, emotional scars, fantasies, trauma, and emotions. This is also true of the effects of postmemory on the offspring of Holocaust survivors that can only be described in live action movies but not visualized.

In contrast to Nazi propaganda movies, or even Allied newsreels including the liberation of the concentration camps, very few first-hand Jewish documentary sources were made during the Holocaust. Animation is an effective way to visualize what until then could only be written, told, or heard, but not seen. Animated documentary can show the unfilmed past and depict events that were not or could not be visually documented.

Historian Yosef Hayim Yerushalmi warned in his book *Zakhor* that with the decline of traditional "memory channels" (such as ceremonies and traditional liturgy), the Jewish past will cease to be represented and will not be transmitted from one generation to the next.[36] In response, researchers of Jewish culture have countered that as time passes, new memory channels are replacing the old ones and can convey forms of memory to the

---

[34] Jeanne-Marie Viljoen, "*Waltz with Bashir*: Between Representation and Experience," *Critical Arts* 28, no. 1 (2014): 40–50.
[35] Takahashi, "Experiments," 232.
[36] Yosef Haim Yerusalmy, *Zakhor, Jewish History and Jewish Memory* (Seattle & London: University of Washington Press, 1996), 94–95. (Original Tel-Aviv, 1982, 67.)

new generations.[37] In this sense, animated documentary can be seen as a new Holocaust memory channel which will help keep the past alive for future generations. Modes of representation implemented for those who lived through these events might not be the most adequate or might not work the same way for the next generations.[38] Tom Kless, who directed the animated Holocaust documentary *A Trip to the Other Planet* (2014) about the Holocaust survivor and well-known author Yehiel Di-nur (Ka-Tzetnik), makes this clear:[39]

> We live in a complicated period. We have almost reached the last living survivor and in ten years' time, we will find ourselves devoid of firsthand testimonies. I look at my children's generation, who will be learning about the Holocaust from black and white movies of Auschwitz – all of which seem to be from another planet. For this reason, we need to find new ways to present and exhibit the Holocaust, so that everyone can learn and implement its profound lessons in future generations.[40]

Over the years, the literature on ethics and documentary cinema has defined what constitutes directors' personal commitment to themselves, to the individuals documented, and to the audience. This includes the public's right to know, the right to artistic expression, the participants' consent, and their rights to privacy, information, and the safeguarding of their reputation.[41]

The issue of exploiting the protagonists during the filming of documentaries is a very well-known and complex subject that has fueled public debates and research on documentaries in general, and Holocaust documentaries in particular.[42] For example, Claude Lanzmann's *Shoah* (1985) is considered to be a milestone in Holocaust documentaries. This nine-hour movie took twelve years to produce, during which 350 hours of footage were filmed in fourteen countries. Unlike previous documentaries that often used Nazi

---

[37] Carol Kidron, "Anthropology of Memory: Researchers Discourse," *Dapim leheker hashoah* 23 (2010): 287–291. See 287.

[38] Lior Zylberman and Vicente Sánchez-Biosca, "Reflections on the Significance of Images in Genocide Studies: Some Methodological Considerations," *Genocide Studies and Prevention: An International Journal* 12, no. 2 (2018): 1–17.

[39] See Part II.

[40] *A Trip to the Other Planet*, official website https://bit.ly/3A8WZmP

[41] Garnet Butchart, "Al etica v'kolnoa t'udi: al emet mamashit v'ma'asit" (On Ethics and Documentary Cinema: Practical Truth), *Takriv*, August 2015, https://bit.ly/2XdICis; Brian Winston, "The Tradition of the Victim in Griersonian Documentary," in *New Challenges for Documentary*, ed. Alan Rosenthal (Berkeley: University of California Press, 1988), 269–287; Winston Brian, *Lies, Damn Lies, and Documentaries* (London: British Movie Institute, 2000); Larry Gross, John Stuart Katz, and Jay Ruby, eds., *Image Ethics: The Moral Rights of Subjects in Photographs, Movie, and Television* (New York: Oxford University Press, 2000).

[42] For example: Theodor W. Adorno, *Negative Dialectics*; Saxton, *Haunted Images*, 1–22; Mandel, *Against the Unspeakable*; Godfrey, *Abstraction and the Holocaust*.

visual materials, Lanzmann deliberately refrained from doing so. He argued that he did not want to use scenes filmed from the perpetrators' point of view. He claimed that since there are no Nazi movie reels documenting what happened in the gas chambers, existing Nazi images can provide no more than a dismal, superficial account of what truly took place during the Holocaust. He also did not use the archival footage taken by the Allies that remains the basis for many other Holocaust documentaries. Lanzmann argued that the only way was to focus on testimonies. He thus filmed interviews with survivors, Nazis, collaborators, bystanders, and helpers, who were asked to recall the atrocities.

Some researchers have nevertheless pointed to scenes where in their opinion Lanzmann exploited the survivors' pain and post-trauma. For example, Dominick LaCapra argued that the movie reactivated the survivors' trauma, since Lanzmann got people talking by asking them to think back to their traumatic sites of memory. His use of staging went even further when eliciting the testimony of Abraham Bomba,[43] who was forced to be a barber in Treblinka and to cut the hair of the Jews before they were gassed. Bomba became a hairdresser in his post-Holocaust life but when *Shoah* was filmed, he had already retired. Lanzmann took him to his former barber shop, reopened it and asked him to tell the horrible stories of what it was like being a barber in Treblinka, while cutting somebody's hair during the filming.[44]

Animated documentary masks its protagonists[45] in that the real person is represented through a completely fabricated construction.[46] Animated documentary can thus "conceal and expose" at the same time[47] and shield

---

[43] Janet Walker, *Trauma Cinema: Documenting Incest and the Holocaust* (Berkeley: University of California Press, 2005), 131.

[44] Shlomo Sand, *Hakolnoa kehistoria: ledamyen velevayem et hameah haesrim* (*Movie as History: Imagining and Screening the Twentieth Century*) (Tel-Aviv: Am Oved and Open Univ. Press, 2002), 249–251; Shoshana Felman, "Movie as Witness: Claude Lanzmann's Shoah," in *Holocaust Remembrance: The Shapes of Memory*, ed. Geoffrey Hartman (Oxford: Blackwell, 1994), 90–103; Felman and Laub, *Edut*; Stuart Liebman, ed., *Claude Lanzmann's Shoah: Key Essays* (Oxford: Oxford University Press, 2007); Marianne Hirsch and Leo Spitzer, "Gendered Translations: Claude Lanzmann's Shoah," in Miriam Cooke and Angela Woollacott, *Gendering War Talk* (Princeton: Princeton University Press, 1993); Yosefa Loshitzky, "Holocaust Others: Spielberg's *Schindler's List* versus Lanzman's *Shoah*," in Yosefa Loshitzky ed., *Spielberg's Holocaust: Critical Perspectives on* Schindler's List (Bloomington: Indiana Univ. Press, 1997), 104–118; Ron Rozenbaum, *Hitler: masa el shorshei haro'a* (*Hitler: A Journey to the Roots of Evil*) (Tel-Aviv: Matar, 1999), 247–267.

[45] Landesman and Bendor, "Animated Recollection," 359.

[46] Ward, "Animating with Facts," 297.

[47] Ehrlich, "Animated Documentaries."

the subjects who are documented. It can address shocking, traumatic, or painful personal themes while protecting the people involved and resolving the ethical dilemma of identifying them to viewers.[48]

The esthetics of animated documentaries can also elicit different emotional responses from viewers than other documentary forms. Scott McCloud suggested that because comic book characters and faces in particular tend to be more abstract and symbolic (as opposed to realistic, in the sense of a photograph of a face), greater numbers of people can potentially identify with them. In his view, the stripped back (abstract) images in animated documentary amplify meaning "in a way that realistic art cannot."[49] According to Paul Ward, animated documentary may thus generate responses that come from a deeper wellspring of emotions that respond not only to what things are, but how things *seem*.[50]

Thus overall, animated documentary reminds the viewers that "real life" is much richer, more ambiguous, multifaceted, and complex than can be documented solely through real-live action. Nevertheless, in the last five years, alongside this positive scholarship on animated documentary, scholars, movie critics, and viewers have drawn attention to its problematic qualities and shortcomings.[51]

One critique still questions whether animated documentary can rightfully be called a form of documentary. In the 1990s and more forcefully at the turn of the century there were efforts to categorize animated documentaries into cinema researcher Bill Nichols' classification of the six documentary modes of representation: the expository, observational, poetic, participatory, reflexive, and performative.[52] For example, Sybil Del Gaudio[53] argued that animated documentaries should be considered as an example of the "reflexive mode." Gunnar Strøm[54] classified some animated documentaries

---

[48] Honess-Roe, *Animated Documentary*; Yadin, "But is it Documentary?"; Ehrlich, "Animated Documentaries"; Walden, "Animation and Memory."

[49] Annabelle Honess Roe, "Against Animated Documentary?", 108.

[50] Ward, "Animating with Facts," 303.

[51] Annabelle Honess Roe, "Against Animated Documentary?"; Gunnar Strøm, "Animated Documentary, by Annabelle Honess Roe," *Studies in Documentary Movie* 9, no. 1 (2015): 92–94.

[52] Bill Nichols, *Introduction to Documentary* (Bloomington: Indiana University Press, 2001), 99–138.

[53] Sybil DelGaudio, "If Truth Be Told, can 'Toons Tell It? Documentary and Animation," *Movie History* 9, no. 2, *Non-Fiction Movie* (1997): 189–99, esp. 192.

[54] Gunnar Strøm, "The Animated Documentary," *Animation Journal* 11 (2003): 46–63. See, 52.

as "performative."⁵⁵ However, Jonathan Rozenkrantz⁵⁶ noted that "this tendency to invoke Nichols' typology [...] in the discourse of animated documentary probably rests [...] on the desire of validating such movies as fully-fledged documentaries and on the conviction that this legitimation can be achieved simply by shoehorning them into one of Nichols' categories."⁵⁷

Cristina Formenti argued that animated documentary should not be considered a category of documentary because these movies do not represent an objective record of events. In her view, even if animated documentaries recount events that have occurred, these events are re-enacted for the camera by "fabricated" actors. In animated documentary, figures not only have a different materiality (i.e., they are made of shapes and colors and not flesh and blood), but also frequently do not even resemble their factual counterparts. Animated documentary constitutes a creative (and often imaginative) interpretation of a factual occurrence without a direct relationship to the physical world. These movies re-tell factual occurrences through fictional modes of delivery. She suggests referring to these movies as the sincerest form of docudrama or "docufiction"; in other words, genres that combine documentary content with a fictional form.⁵⁸ Annabelle Honess Roe proposed uniting these differing views through a kind of compromise where animated documentaries are classified as "animated reconstructions of factual events and experiences."⁵⁹

Another critique deals with the question of whether animation is an appropriate vehicle for serious topics. Animated documentaries are sometimes also criticized for their lack of technical prowess or creativity. The argument is that animated documentaries which were produced prior to the new millennium were innovative, original, and experimental in the sense that they pushed new boundaries and explored new ways to combine documentary stories with animated visuals. However, suffering from its own success, the ubiquity of animated animation in the last two decades may be responsible for the shallowness of this sub-genre, because animation can simply bolt on to an existing (documentary) soundtrack and become a visual accompaniment.⁶⁰

Finally, the vast majority of animated Holocaust documentaries are based on testimonies. Scholars have noted that Holocaust projects designed to ensure the preservation of memory through filmed interviews may

---

[55] Cristina Formenti, "The Sincerest Form of Docudrama: Reframing the Animated Documentary," *Studies in Documentary Movie* 8, no. 2 (2014): 103–115.

[56] Jonathan Rozenkrantz, "Colourful Claims: Towards a Theory of Animated Documentary," May 6, 2011, accessed May 10, 2011, https://bit.ly/3ht2fKH

[57] Formenti, "The Sincerest Form of Docudrama," see especially 103–108.

[58] Ibid.

[59] Annabelle Honess Roe, "Against Animated Documentary?"

[60] Ibid.

inadvertently bias the narrative, since it is also dependent on the interaction between interviewer and interviewee.[61] This dual perspective[62] augments the complexity of animated Holocaust documentaries. In other words, what is depicted depends not only on the experiences of the survivors and the way they remember and narrate their past, but also on the lives and worldviews of the moviemakers.[63] Animated documentary scholar Annabele Honess Roe formulated this issue as follows:

> …to think about animated documentaries that confront real experiences of trauma simply as an exchange between the testifier and the viewer is to ignore the significance of both the animators and their imagery. What we see on screen is not simply the testimony unless the animation is also created by the person telling their story—so whose memory is it? The animators are interpreting the interviewees' narratives, thus bringing their own imagining of the past to the representations and drawing attention to their presence as well as that of the person giving testimony.[64]

Bar-On noted that "one generation's story can influence and shape the stories of the next generations,"[65] but in the case of animated documentaries it also works the other way around: the next generation's story shapes the previous generations' narrative. Memory as "the aftertaste of the event"[66] is mixed with what the younger generations can imagine from a distance. The double perspective is always enmeshed with the perception of the viewers, such that the cinematic text derives its meaning through a combination of all three.

This book analyzes Holocaust animated documentaries while addressing these issues. Are animated Holocaust documentaries really documentaries? Do they represent an innovative perspective on the Holocaust or simply a way to tack animation visualization onto the soundtrack? Do they overcome the problem of Holocaust representations as clichés, or do they recreate the same icons in animation? Do they have advantages over live action documentaries that deal with the Holocaust, and if so, what are they? The following chapters will tackle these questions and will be combined with the complex debate over Holocaust survivors' testimonies, truth, and its mediation.

---

[61] For example, Laub and Felman, *Testimony*; Laub, "Bearing Witness," 57–74; Jeffrey Shandler, *Holocaust Memory in the Digital Age: Survivors' Stories and New Media Practices* (Stanford: Stanford University Press, 2017), esp. 43–86.

[62] Victoria Aarons and Alan L. Berger, *Third-Generation Holocaust Representation: Trauma, History, and Memory* (Evanston: Northwestern University Press, 2017), 3–39.

[63] Ilana Rosen, "Personal Historical Narrative Shaping the Past and the Present," *European Journal of Jewish Studies*, (2009): 103–133.

[64] Walden, "*Animation and Memory*."

[65] Aarons and Berger, *Third-Generation*, 3–39.

[66] Ibid.

Part I

"Unimating" the Holocaust

Part I is made up of four chapters that deal with the Nazi period (1933–1945). It explores the techniques employed to deal with the unfilmed past of Holocaust events and ways of visualizing the inner world of the victims. It shows how these documentaries bring the past to life and allow viewers to enter specific sites, as well as experience events and feelings that were not and cannot be captured on camera. The chapters show that the vast majority of movies center on small incidents and fractured positive moments conveying resilience, human kindness, resourcefulness, and redemption. The atrocities are marginalized—the vast majority of movies do not represent mass murder, torture, or starvation. In that sense, the movies "unimate" the Holocaust: instead of animating the horrific events they choose not to discuss them, and create a soft version of Holocaust representations. Only a few exceptions dare deal with the horrific events. Part I analyzes these trends while confronting them with the scholarly debate on this type of narrative.[1] It also draws on research on infamous Holocaust symbols[2] to examine their role in these movies and the relationship between Jewish and universal aspects in these movies.[3]

Historian Yehuda Bauer makes it abundantly clear that "there was nothing positive about the Holocaust." The Holocaust was murder. The attempts at resistance were englobed by murder. There were rescues that mattered at a great deal, but these were part of the overall death and destruction. In Bauer's

---

[1] Lawrence Langer, "Redemptive and Unredemptive Holocaust Memory," in *The Afterdeath of the Holocaust* (London: Palgrave Macmillan, 2021), 37–61. See especially 38–44; Bauer, *Teaching the Holocaust*.

[2] Oren Baruch Stier, *Holocaust Icons: Symbolizing the Shoah in History and Memory* (New Brunswick: Rutgers University Press, 2015), 2–3.

[3] Michman, "Particularist and Universal Interpretations of the Holocaust," 223–243.

words, "If you don't want to talk about the murders, if you want to talk about the positive things—this is a distortion," since the positive events occurred within the framework of a vast orchestration of genocide.[4] Bauer nevertheless stresses that Holocaust distortions are not always the result of ill will:

> For example, a distortion of the Holocaust that comes out of good will and the desire to justify something. We are all aware of the tremendous emphasis on rescue and help to Jews in the Holocaust, partly by Jews but largely by non-Jews. Practically all of them are quite truthful. At the same time, they are of course total distortion because they emphasize a tiny minority.[5]

He insists that educators are also to blame for these distortions, because they feel that these happy ends are needed to depict the Holocaust: "We can't just teach horror and death. We have to provide some kind of an answer and the tiny group of survivors enables us to do so, but by doing so we are distorting the truth because the truth was hell and mass murder. This is a distortion that comes from a positive point of view."[6]

This point of view is also found in Lawrence Langer's works.[7] Langer discusses the differences between what he termed redemptive and unredemptive Holocaust memory: "When was the history of the Holocaust invaded by enthusiasm for redemptive memory—and why? The need for such memory is understandable, for who can bear the burden of an irredeemable evil that consumed so many millions of innocent lives?" Without redemptive memory we leave ourselves exposed "to anguish that is buried beneath the ashes of extermination. No wonder so many members of succeeding generations search for a spark of hope to fare up and assuage their pain." In his view, "redemptive memory" focuses on positive rare moments which help avoid dealing with the incomprehensible horrors of the Holocaust. He sees this representation as a distortion of Holocaust memory.[8] According to Langer, "[when] there is not a single description of specific atrocities […] we never have a clear sense of exactly what is to be remembered or forgotten. The contents of unredemptive memory are absent from texts and the readers are not invited to face the horrors."[9] Although Langer discusses interviews, speeches, and books, his arguments apply equally well to Holocaust animated documentaries.

---

[4] Bauer, *Teaching the Holocaust*.
[5] "Prof. Yehuda Bauer: The Distortion of Holocaust History," 5.5.20, *YouTube*, May 6, 2020, https://bit.ly/3C29Rf8
[6] Ibid.
[7] Langer, "Redemptive and Unredemptive Holocaust Memory," 37–61.
[8] Ibid., 38–44.
[9] Ibid., 57.

Drawing on Bauer's "good will Holocaust distortions" and Langer's "redemptive memory," the chapters in Part I show that when it comes to representing the unfilmed past, the vast majority of directors choose to focus on marginal vignettes that provide a glimmer of hope and carefully skirt around representing the horrors by providing a positive glimmer of bravery, compassion, and resilience. Most directors are aware that they have marginalized the atrocities and explain this as a conscious decision on their part. However, this awareness does not alter the problematic result that most directors take the Holocaust out of the Holocaust[10] and prefer not to deal with starvation, death, massive killings, and brutality. Their focus is on humanity and not inhumanity. There were of course silver linings in these dark times, but when marginalizing the inhumanity, the outcome in most movies is a mellow version of the Holocaust. Nevertheless, several exceptional movies deal with the atrocities and prove that animated documentaries can indeed represent the horrors.

---

[10] This comment is taken from an interview with Fleming, who directed *I Was a Child of Holocaust Survivors*, which is analyzed in Part II. In the interview, the director said "I took the Holocaust out of the Holocaust." See: Wendy Dallian, "I Was a Child of Holocaust Survivors," *Vancouver Observer*, September 17, 2010, accessed September 17, 2010, https://bit.ly/3nqVn4A

CHAPTER 1

Standing up to the Nazis

Female protagonists dominate animated documentaries dealing with the Holocaust. Many of these movies show women and girls who resisted the Nazis, not by combating but through their true grit. Often these girls and women are not ghetto fighters or partisans, but rather have another kind of strength: the ability to stand up to the Nazis verbally, refuse to obey an order, not to fold in the face of evil, hide their identity to survive, demonstrate resourcefulness, and maintain optimism.

Even though women and girls are the protagonists, these movies do not tackle the type of gender issues that have gained popularity in research and the cultural sphere since the 1990s. After years of ignoring and marginalizing gender topics in Holocaust research, persistent calls by women scholars in the 1980s, but especially since the 1990s, have prompted researchers to examine the differences in experiences between men and women in the Holocaust and the fact that Jewish women suffered as Jews, but also specifically as women.[1] By contrast, the stories told in these animated documentaries could have happened to men or boys; there is nothing especially female about them. However, the fact that the protagonists are girls and young women still broadens audiences' realization of the experiences of girls and women in the Holocaust.

Nevertheless, depicting these personal stories of resilience or standing up to the Nazis does not necessarily imply representing the atrocities of the

---

[1] See, for example: Renate Bridenthal, Atina Grossmann, and Marion Kaplan, eds., *When Biology Became Destiny: Women in Weimar and Nazi Germany* (New York: New Feminist Library, 1984); Marlene E. Heinemann, *Gender and Destiny: Women Writers and the Holocaust* (New York: Greenwood Press, 1986); Gizla Bock, "Challenging Dichotomies: Perspectives on Women's History," in *Writing Women's History*, ed. Karen Offen, Ruth Roach Pierson, and Jane Rendall (Bloomington: Indiana Univ. Press, 1991), 1–24; Carol Rittne and John Roth, eds., *Different Voices: Women and the Holocaust* (St. Paul: Paragon House, 1993); Dalia Ofer and Lenore J. Weitzman, *Women in the Holocaust* (New Haven: Yale University Press, 1998); Judy Tydor-Baumel Schwartz, *Double Jeopardy: Gender and the Holocaust* (London: Vallentine Mitchell, 1998); Myrna Goldenberg and Amy H. Shapiro, eds., *Different Horrors, Same Hell: Gender and the Holocaust* (Seattle: University of Washington Press, 2013); Sonja M. Hedgepeth and Rochelle G. Saidel (eds.), *Sexual Violence against Jewish Women during the Holocaust* (Waltham: Brandeis University Press, 2010).

Holocaust. These acts of bravery indeed took place and their representation sheds more light on girls' and young women's behavior under Nazi rule. However, at the same time, these acts dominate the movies and marginalize the atrocities. The movies analyzed in this chapter are *Grandma Mimi* (Shirley Prishkolnik, 2016), *Yehudith* (Daniel Geron, 2015), and *Red Fox—The Story of Zippora Feibelevich* (Daniella Koffler, 2020).

REACTIONS TO KRISTALLNACHT IN *GRANDMA MIMI* (SHIRLEY PERSHKOLNIK, 2016)

Miriam Sagiv (Mimi) was eight years old on *Kristallnacht* (1938, also known as *the November pogrom*)—a series of brutal attacks on Jewish businesses, synagogues, schools, hospitals, and private homes in Germany and Austria on November 9 and 10, 1938. Hundreds of synagogues were destroyed, around 7,500 Jewish businesses were damaged or destroyed, Jewish homes were looted and wrecked, and 30,000 Jewish men were arrested and sent to concentration camps. The movie describes one of these incidents. On Kristallnacht, Sagiv's father was arrested. She and her mother went to look for him, and her mother left her in the hall of an office building and told her to wait. A Nazi officer approached Sagiv and, in a very intimidating fashion, told her to leave. She refused several times and remained there until her mother returned. Sagiv's family immigrated to Israel in 1939.

Pershkolnik turned Sagiv's memory of the situation into an animated documentary. The movie was made as a part of her undergraduate degree at the Holon Institute of Technology, Israel, in collaboration with Yad Vashem. In this project, the students were asked to select testimony or a family story. Pershkolnik felt the need to return to her grandmother's stories. She remembered that Sagiv used to talk about life under the Nazis, and the story about the way she stood up to the Nazi officer was one Sagiv loved to tell and Pershkolnik loved to listen to because she felt it emphasized the courage of a little girl. "It shows that one can find optimism even in such difficult times."[2]

Researchers concur that oral history does not describe the past accurately. Interviewees' testimonies are not pure history but rather selective interpretations. Their view of their experiences depends on many factors other than the events themselves.[3] Recollections are doubly filtered by time and subsequent experience: "Contemporary pressures and sensitivities encourage people to screen their memories in a selective, protective and above all

---

[2] Liat Steir-Livny, "An Interview with Shirley Pershkulnik," November 3, 2019.
[3] Michael Frisch, *A Shared Authority: Essays on the Craft and Meaning of Oral and Public History* (Albany: State University of New York Press), xxiii.

Figure 1.1 Grandma Mimi *(Shirley Prishkolnik, 2016)*

didactic fashion."[4] A memory is not a transcription of the past, but a rebuilding of the past based on how the memory has been coded in the mind and on information obtained after the event occurred.[5]

Pershkolnik illustrated Sagiv as a child and Sagiv's mother from old pictures. She also used archival pictures of the street where Sagiv lived and the synagogue as the basis for her animations.[6] According to Pershkolnik, her grandmother had a visual memory, so she could describe the blazes and bonfires of that night she witnessed in detail, the way the flames burned the Star of David in the synagogue, her walk down the street with her mother, the way the German soldier they encountered looked at them and the way she stood up to the officer. Sagiv's visual descriptions helped Pershkolnik understand the emotions of a little girl who experienced hatred and hostility and how to translate it into animation. However, aside from these details, the space is deliberately depicted in general, nonspecific, and unrealistic ways since the aim of the movie is to tell a story from a child's perspective. This is how someone who experienced this type of trauma as a child might remember the incident. According to Pershkolnik, the historical accuracy ("whether the synagogue's window looked like this or like that") is immaterial because the story is about her grandmother's feelings. It is her sensations that the

---

[4] Alessandro Portelli, "What Makes Oral History Different," in *The Oral History Reader*, ed. Robert Perks and Alistair Thomson (London: Routledge, 1998), 63–74, esp. 67–68.

[5] Marit Slavin, "Bnei adam zochrim gam havayot shelo havu" [People also remember events they did not experience], *Walla*, June 12, 2005, accessed June 13, 2005, https://bit.ly/3zeOepX

[6] "Grandma Mimi," *Facebook*.

viewers need to understand. The drawings were handmade and processed by computer. Pershkolnik chose a very simple Flash animation since in her view, this type of animation fits the childish atmosphere of a story told mostly through a child's perspective. She chose black, white, and gray to emphasize the somber event and touches of color to match Sagiv's stories: the red of the blaze from the synagogue, the blue eyes of the officer.[7]

The Triple Perspective

Sagiv provided recorded testimony, and excerpts are included in the movie's voiceover. Shirley's sister Natalie Pershkolnik narrates the story in the third person and in some scenes as Sagiv in the first person. Pershkolnik used her sister's voice because she did not want to use the voice of the elderly Sagiv. The story is actually told three times: from Sagiv's perspective as a little girl, Sagiv's interpretation of the story as a grownup, and the third generation's postmemory of the event.[8]

In one of the scenes, Sagiv is drawn lying in bed. "On Kristallnacht, they took her father," says the narrator. "He went into her room a moment, in the middle of the night, and said goodbye." The puzzled child opens her eyes and looks around, confused. In the next scene, she is drawn walking down the street with her mother after Kristallnacht heading to Gestapo headquarters. The walls of the gray buildings are covered with hate slogans such as "Achtung Juden" next to the symbol of poison, a swastika, and the word "Juden" to mark shops owned by Jews. Shattered glass from shop windows covers the pavement. The fact that Sagiv, as a little girl, does not understand the enormity of the event is manifested in the fact that she is drawn smiling, walking happily, hand in hand with her mother, whereas her mother's expression is terrified. Still, this event is so awful that even a small child can understand that something is wrong. A children's song in German is heard on the soundtrack (Pershkolnick said in an interview that it was a song repeatedly sung to Sagiv when she was a child).[9] The singing continues along with the sound of flames crackling from inside the remains of the synagogue that is still burning. Sagiv's eyes open with astonishment as she takes in the surroundings. This is the moment when her childhood (as symbolized by the children's song) is swept away by harsh reality.

As Sagiv and her mother are about to enter the gray building, the narration in the third person switches to the first person of the granddaughter, who then

---

[7] Liat Steir-Livny, "An Interview with Shirley Pershkolnik," November 3, 2019.
[8] Ibid.
[9] "Grandama Mimi," *Facebook*.

dubs her grandmother's testimony. This transition symbolizes the enormity of what happened in the building from Pershkolnick's perspective: this is an event she and her sister identify with to such an extent that it is part of their identities. The nature of the voiceover suggests an almost symbiotic relationship. "Mother told me, 'Wait here in the hallway until I return,' so that is what I did." The contradiction between the situation and a child's inability to understand it is illustrated by drawing little Sagiv smiling, standing in the corner of a room decorated with two big Nazi flags. Since the story is told in many scenes from a child's perspective, the animation focuses on the grownups' lower bodies since this is how Sagiv saw them. She sees her mother's legs walking away, then the legs of Nazi officers in uniform and boots. When a Nazi approaches her, the "camera" tilts up as Sagiv lifts her head to look at him. "What are you doing here?" Nathalie's voice imitates the angry intonation of the Nazi. "Waiting for my mom," Sagiv answers. "Wait outside!" he orders, his harsh face in close up. She refuses several times. The animation zooms in on his vicious eyes drawn in red, which amplifies Sagiv's courage. Even when he threatens to hit her, she refuses to leave. Then the unbelievable happens: "He left, and Mommy came back." The scene shows Sagiv clinging to her mother's leg, a big smile on her face, so glad of her small victory that she does not notice her mother's sad, terrified face. As they leave the headquarters, the children's song is heard again. She got her Mommy back, as though she got her childhood back, and cannot understand that this is a minor victory in a fight that the Jews would lose.

Sagiv and her family went through many hardships in Nazi Germany before they escaped. Pershkolnick decided to focus on this little, seemingly insignificant story and not on other Holocaust-related stories she heard, since:

> There is something in the story that seemed different to me. It is a story filled with pain but also with the bravery of a small child, eight years old, who stands her ground, and even though she knows she is supposed to be afraid of the officer standing in front of her, she listens to her mother. Her mother told her to wait there, and that's what she does. At the moment when her family is being wrenched apart, she is the one trying to keep what's left together and to be with her mother when she needs her, and I was very touched by it. I thought about how I would have behaved at the age of eight and wondered if I would have obeyed a Nazi officer who told me to leave. I don't know if I could have behaved so bravely, and it was very important to me to represent my grandma's courage as a child.[10]

She claims she deliberately avoided atrocities, citing Holocaust fatigue (as a third-generation, "sometimes you get fed up" ...), and believes representations of atrocities can alienate viewers instead of drawing them closer to the story:

---

[10] Ibid.

As soon as people see horrors, they close themselves off; they do not want to be touched by it. Life is hard anyway, and in any case, the horror of that time cannot be really grasped by someone who was not there. There can be a horror overdose that makes people indifferent. When you see a lot of atrocities, nothing moves you. When you approach the subject from a small, more optimistic perspective, it is easier for both the movie maker and the audience to deal with. I could have chosen the less positive parts – the Nazis took her dad, and shaved his head, we heard these stories a lot. What we have not heard about is a little girl standing in front of the Nazi officer, a small and insignificant story can reveal another facet about how you do not give up. I have always loved this story and thought more people would love it and be happy to hear it.[11]

THE REFUSAL IN YEHUDIT (DANIEL GIRON, 2015)

Yehudit Arnon (1926–2013), a Czechoslovakian Jew, was sent to Auschwitz when she was a teenager. After the Holocaust, she became a celebrated dancer and the founder and lead dancer of the renowned Kibbutz Dance Company in Kibbutz Ga'aton. In 1998 she won the prestigious Israel Prize for her contribution to Israeli culture.

While in Auschwitz, a Nazi officer noticed her exercising on one of the beams on the ceiling of the barracks and ordered her to dance for him. She refused. As punishment, he forced her to spend the whole night barefoot in the snow. Arnon promised herself that if she survived, she would dedicate her life to dance.[12]

Arnon's story was initially documented in a display devoted to children in the Holocaust in the *Ghetto Fighters Museum*. In 2010, during The Ghetto Fighters Kibbutz's commemoration ceremony on Holocaust Martyrs' and Heroes' Remembrance Day, the moderator Alex Anski told her story. This was followed by *Memorandum*, a choreography by the current director of the Kibbutz Dance Company Rami Be'ir, where the dancer performs on huge wooden beams and never touches the ground.[13]

Arnon's grandson Daniel Giron chose to depict Arnon's vow in his movie *Yehudit*. Out of all his grandmother's stories, he chose to commemorate this story in animation because his grandmother told him she discovered that through dance, she could brighten the lives of the other inmates who

---

[11] Ibid.
[12] "Mahadura Rishona" [First Edition], *Facebook*, May 4, 2016, accessed May 4, 2016, https://bit.ly/398XD82
[13] Anat Bertman Elhalal, *Memorial Ceremonies at Kibbutz Lohamei Haghetaot, 1990–2016*, MA Thesis submitted to The Open University, Ra'anana, 2018, 38.

watched her.[14] *Yehudit* can be categorized into what Honess Roe calls "mimetic" animated documentary, where the animation illustrates something that is impossible to show in conventional live action documentary. Mimetic animation is used to re-enact historical events through reconstruction and reenactment.[15] In *Yehudit*, snippets of Arnon's testimonies are heard in a few scenes of the movie, which primarily uses the soundtrack for music and voices to create the atmosphere. An actor playing the Nazi officer also speaks a few lines.

The movie starts by animating Arnon being crowded onto a cattle car to Auschwitz. Black dominates the frames, and it is hard to see that it is a train. Only the rattle of the wheels on the tracks hint where she is. The light from a crack in the window shines briefly on a young woman's face, as she stands cramped in the middle of the carriage. The Star of David with the word "Jude" written on it appears in transparency as the title of the movie is shown. The sad music completes the exposition of the protagonist, the time and the place. In *Holocaust Icons: Symbolizing the Shoah in History and Memory*, Oren Baruch Stier analyzed several such codified symbols of the Holocaust. He argues that Holocaust icons are

> Certain symbols that have come to represent the Holocaust in encapsulated form – those that summarize complex narratives of the Shoah, simplifying, condensing, and distilling these narratives and producing meanings for cultural consumption [...] it is through the use of iconic symbols that the public meanings and perceptions of the Holocaust are created [...].[16]

He claims these icons are powerful, indispensable devices that enable people to comprehend the Holocaust: "[...] our understandings depend on the distillation of historical events [...] into easily apprehensible symbols that often operate on noncognitive levels [...] [they] cycle and recycle across the postwar landscape, in museums, memorials, art, literature, photography, public and private speech, in our mind [...]." He highlights the strengths and weaknesses of Holocaust icons. On one hand, they can be seen as oversimplifications of complex histories, which lead people to believe they know about the past when they are actually provided with a superficial representation. On the other, however, many people might not know anything about the Holocaust if these icons did not circulate.[17] Stier claims that "the more such icons are repeatedly employed in the service of Holocaust memory and representation, the more [...] people in the present come to feel they know

---

[14] "Mahadura Rishona."
[15] Honess Roe, *Animated Documentary*, 23–24.
[16] Stier, *Holocaust Icons*, 2–3.
[17] Ibid., 184–185.

Figure 1.2 Yehudit *(Daniel Geron, 2015)*

the Holocaust, even if that knowledge is based on a limited number of recycled images."[18] [...] Holocaust icons can thus lead to less awareness of the Holocaust and ultimately to the forgetting of the Shoah."[19] Stier nevertheless argues that Holocaust icons act "as a bulwark against oblivion: their reproduction permits identification and affiliation."

According to Stier, trains are one of the Holocaust icons that are most often used to represent and embody the Holocaust. Trains are an icon of modern, industrialized mass murder that were instrumental in turning human beings into commodities. These railway cars "are among the most powerful and resonant artifacts of the Holocaust [...] they represent a monumental turning point in the destruction of European Jewry: deportation via railway marked a key systemic shift from mobile murders and stationary victims to stationary murderers and mobile victims."[20]

Trains appear in the vast majority of animated Holocaust documentaries and act as a shorthand that enables directors to avoid presenting tragedy directly. They represent the Holocaust "in encapsulated form" not only by "simplifying, condensing, and distilling these narratives" but also by erasing the horrors.[21] The fact that they have become readily identifiable in Western culture allows viewers to enter into the world of the Holocaust painlessly.

---

[18] Ibid., 185.
[19] Ibid., 185, 187, 191.
[20] Ibid., 32–67.
[21] Ibid., 2–3.

By repeating this icon in so many animated Holocaust documentaries as a substitution device, movie directors thus do not broaden the visual limits of Holocaust representations. In this movie, like in many other Holocaust animated documentaries, what stands for the evidence is a patchwork well-known icon: trains, cold, snow, barbed wires and the "Arbeit Macht Frei" sign at the entrance of camps.

Spiritual and Physical Resistance

The movie focuses on an event that happened in Auschwitz and delivers a sense of a concentration camp without showing one. It compresses Auschwitz into several now trivial icons: a number tattooed on an arm, hair being shorn, barracks, snow, Nazis. Grey-blue appears in the first scene and repeats itself three times to designate the place as a human factory. A montage editing shows the intake of a row of prisoners' legs marching, all wearing the same gown, an arm slammed brutally on a wooden table, a tattoo needle being readied, pushed into the arm, the surprised and painful gasp of the inmate, the ink, the mark, the tattooed number, a hand recording the inmate on a list. This repetition suggests that Arnon is one of many. After the third repetition of this scene the camera zooms out to show Arnon the teenager looking sadly at her arm. The sound of dogs barking and people conversing remind the viewer that she is in a busy camp.

This is when evocation takes over and replaces the mimetic representation. The animation enables the viewers to experience the way Arnon's spirituality overcame reality. As she looks at her arm, the numbers fade away and the gray-blue-black colors turn into a warm yellowish hue. Instead of the number, there is a little golden silhouette dancing on her forearm. As she dances, the barking in the soundtrack fades and pleasant classical music is heard. A close-up of Arnon's face shows she is smiling, her face glowing in gold as well. Her imagination makes her forget her dire situation for a few seconds. Suddenly, however, the animation shows the dancer has been shot to death and falls down. The yellowish colors are gone, and the blue-black-gray colors reappear, as does the barking, while Arnon's facial expression changes: her fear has returned.

The emphasis on the importance of spirituality during the Holocaust has been amply researched in Holocaust studies. For example, Victor Frankel, a Holocaust survivor and psychiatrist, included his own story in *Man's Search for Meaning* (1946), where he analyzes the psychological processes the prisoners underwent in the concentration camps. He argued that prisoners could choose one of two paths: maintaining a mental and spiritual perspective that preserved their dignity and the love of humankind, or abandoning self-dignity and a spiritual inner world to become an animal. Frankel believed that the prisoners' choices often determined their fate and their ability to survive. In the difficult life of the camp, a loss of values signified the loss of the "I". Individuals who came to terms with loosening their inner grip on their moral and spiritual "self" fell victim to the degenerate effects of the camp, lost their faith in a better future, and in so doing sealed their fate. Frankel felt that a loss of faith in the future also abolished their spiritual hold on themselves, leading to a deterioration of body and mind. By contrast, even under the terrible conditions in the concentration camps, people who attempted to continue to cultivate the life of the soul and the spirit survived. Inner life allowed these prisoners to "escape" to a life of inner richness and spiritual freedom, thus sheltering them from the emptiness, desolation, and spiritual poverty of camp life.[22]

Holocaust research, especially in the last few decades, has tended to reject Frankel's claims. Many works no longer support the view that mental mechanisms or personal processes determined who would live and who would die. The dominant view today is that survival in the camp was mostly a matter of luck. For example, historian Dina Porat considered that the survivors could not have had common tropes or similar ways of responding. There are countless stories of Holocaust survivors on their way to death whose last-minute exploits or fortuitous instances saved them from their fate, and other stories about many who were executed randomly regardless of their physical, mental, or spiritual life in the camps.[23]

Nevertheless, it is clear that maintaining an inner world helped the inmates in their darkest hours regardless of whether, in the end, they survived or perished. For example, studies have pointed to the importance of black and self-deprecating humor in coping with frightening situations as an important spiritual tool and defense mechanism that helped Jews maintain their humanity in unbearable situations during the Holocaust. Researchers have shown how these types of humor alleviated stress, enabled individuals to cope with negative feelings and harsh situations, mitigated suffering, and dissipated

---

[22] Victor Frankel, *Man's Search for Meaning: An Introduction to Logotherapy* (1946) (Boston: Beacon Press, 1959).

[23] Liat Steir-Livny, "Interview with Prof. Dina Porat," April 10, 2002. Primo Levi wrote about similar incidents during the selection at Auschwitz-Birkenau: "We also know that this systematic sorting to identify those capable of working was not always carried out": when some trains arrived, the Nazis opened "the doors of the carriages on both sides of the tracks, without warning or instructions. To the camps went those who happened to come down from one side. Those who came down from the other side went straight to the gas chambers." Primo Levi, *If This is a Man* (1947) (Tel-Aviv: Am Oved, 1989) [Hebrew translation), 18–19; Primo Levi, *If This is a Man and the Truce* (Little, Brown and Co., 1991).

feelings of anxiety, at least for a certain time.[24] Other studies have dealt with the way prisoners tried to celebrate the religious holidays, and how women found that talking about dishes they used to cook and exchanging recipes as though they were about to go into the kitchen while they were starving helped maintain spiritual resistance.[25] In *Yehudit*, the use of animation to reflect the mind helps understand how the soul influences physical resilience.

Inside the barracks, the soundtrack is composed of silent coughs and crying. The black-gray colors dominate the scene and reinforce the depressing atmosphere. Arnon decides to resist it, as she climbs up to the beam on the ceiling and begins to perform circus-like tumbles. Each time there is a close-up on her face, she breathes deeply. These are not the breaths of someone suffocating, but rather the breaths of someone who has finally begun to breathe peacefully. Within the camp she created freedom for herself and for others. The inmate who was crying is now looking at her with astonishment, wonder, and curiosity, and even smiles. The lightbulb that barely illuminates the room is hung next to the beam and also symbolizes that for Arnon and the other inmates, Arnon's acrobatics are a beacon in the darkness.

A threatening shadow at the door ruptures the calm as a Nazi soldier enters and orders Arnon to step outside with him. She is drawn as though filmed over the shoulder from the Nazi's perspective. He stands with his back to the viewers and is filmed from a high angle so that he appears much taller and broader than she is. He orders her to dance for him. She stands there, little and skinny. A woman versus a man, an inmate versus a perpetrator, a minuscule figure versus a giant. She shakes her head in refusal. He slaps her.

In the next scene, blue dominates the outside scene where she stands alone. Various shades of blue are meant to emphasize the freezing cold of Auschwitz in the snow. The wind whistles. "I was punished and was forced to stand in the snow," her voiceover is heard. She is animated in a circle of light made by the spotlight of the guard tower. She is tiny, fragile, clutching her body to keep warm, with her head bowed down, standing barefoot in the snow that keeps coming down, her shoes next to her. A zoom-in highlights her black eye from being smacked. Arnon is animated in an extreme long shot from a high angle, which makes her look even smaller in the open snowy space. All these components are combined to dramatize her unbelievable

---

[24] Itamar Levin, *Mi'ba'ad la'dmaot: humor Yehudi tahat hashilton hanatsi* [*Through the Tears: Jewish Humor under the Nazi Regime*] (Jerusalem: Yad Vashem, 2004); Haya Ostrower, *L'lo humor hayinu mitabdim* [*Without Humor We Would Have Killed Ourselves*] (Jerusalem: Yad Vashem, 2009).

[25] See, for example: Liat Steir-Livny, "Faith in the Face of Hell," in Irith Knebel (ed.), *A Holocaust Crossroads: Jewish Women and Children in Ravensbrück* (London: Vallentine Mitchell, 2010), 205–220.

survival, by turning the viewers' attention to what helped her survive: her inner world.[26]

The animation evokes her mental escape. The viewers see what she imagined, what helped her maintain her physical resilience: she is in a green meadow with a leafy green tree, the sun is shining, she has a full head of hair and is wearing a bright blue dress. She is animated from a bird's eye view as she floats and dances across the field, barefoot and free. The frame dissolves to live action footage of the elderly Arnon wearing the same dress, her brown hair in the same hairdo as she dances blissfully in her Israeli studio in slow motion. The titles at the end indicate that she survived that night and describe how she dedicated her life to dance.

Yehudit, like other animated Holocaust documentaries, provides one explanation as to how young women survived. These representations contribute to efforts to rebut perceptions in Israel, but also in other countries as to why young women survived. In Israel, for example, rumors about the murders committed in Europe elicited solemn mourning during and especially after World War II within the Jewish community. The shock was mingled with great concern and a desire to help the survivors overcome their suffering. The partisans and ghetto fighters were highly respected, but questions arose as to how Jews who did not resist by force could have survived while six million perished.[27] Alongside the division between rebels and non-rebels, yet another insidious notion suggested that "the best were killed." This notion was fueled by the idea that those who survived had probably been able to "get by," and not always with integrity. It was implied that women survivors used their sexuality or were abused sexually and therefore survived.[28] These beliefs affected attitudes towards Holocaust survivors in Israel in the first decades of the State and only slowly began to disappear in the 1980s for a variety of political-cultural and technological reasons.[29] Highlighting this incident of refusal is thus part of this larger cultural trend in

---

[26] Giron says that before he began the movie, he tried to stand in his shirtsleeves barefoot in the snow in France at 20 degrees below zero, but lasted less than a minute: "It only emphasizes what a great woman she was, stronger than everything."

[27] Anita Shapira, "Hashoah: zikaron prati v'zikaron tziburi" [*The Holocaust: Private Memory and Public Memory*], in *Yehudim Yeshanim, Yehudim Hadashim* [*New Jews, Old Jews*] (Tel-Aviv, Am Oved, 1997), 103–186.

[28] Tom Segev, *Hamillion hashvi'i: haisraelim vehashoah* [*The Seventh Million: The Israelis and the Holocaust*] (Jerusalem: Keter, 1991), (Picador Publishers, 2000), 101–169; Dina Porat, *Café haboker b'reach ha'ashan* [*Smoke-Scented Morning Coffee*] (Jerusalem: Yad Vashem: Am Oved, 2011), 381–415.

[29] Nurith Gertz, *Motion Fiction: Israeli Fiction in Films* (Tel-Aviv: The Open University Press, 1994) [Hebrew], 175–288; Porat, *Smoke-Scented Morning Coffee*, 357–378.

the last four decades to reject shallow negative stereotypes and acknowledge the multiple types of bravery.

THE RUDE REDHEAD IN *RED FOX*—*THE STORY OF ZIPPORA FEIBELEVICH*

This movie is part of a Yad Vashem project entitled *Our Story—Twelve Movies About the Human Spirit in the Holocaust*. Four are animated documentaries, and the others are documentaries that use different cinematic esthetics, including reenactment (*Esther and the Officer*),[30] live action interviews, illustrations and still pictures (*Charm from Grandmother*),[31] archival material documented by the Nazis and the Allies (*A Piece for Dinner*,[32] *A Bird at the End of the World*),[33] or still pictures and drawings from a survivor's album (*Mother's Dream*).[34] This project was designed to honor Holocaust survivors who had not been chosen to light one of the beacons during the annual Holocaust Martyrs' and Heroes' Remembrance Day commemoration ceremony at Yad Vashem.[35] The movies are meant to salute the strength of the human spirit. The abstract for the project states:

> Every year, the number of Holocaust survivors still among us dwindles, and with them the opportunities to hear first-person testimonies. *Our Story* is a Yad Vashem source project that brought together six filmmakers and animators who produced twelve exciting videos that tell the story of Holocaust survivors in different ways. These short videos capture the essence of these striking stories to enable audiences to continue to remember the survivors, their uncompromising Jewish and human spirit, and their heritage.[36]

Some of the movies in the project that are not animated documentaries indeed represent forms of horror. Sometimes this is done verbally through the testimonies of survivors in the soundtrack. For example, in *A Goodluck*

---

[30] "Esther and the Officer: The Story of Esther Miron," *YouTube*, April 16, 2020, https://bit.ly/3zm0PrO

[31] "A Good Luck Charm from Grandma: The Story of Abraham Appelbaum," *YouTube*, April 16, 2020, https://bit.ly/3EpqLq8

[32] "A Piece for Dinner: The Story of Yehudith Ashriel," *YouTube*, April 16, 2020, https://bit.ly/3CgvDfd

[33] "A Bird at the End of the World: The Story of Yehudith Yegermann," *YouTube*, April 16, 2020, https://bit.ly/3EmFzFV

[34] "Mother's Dream: The Story of Miriam Woodislivasky," *YouTube*, April 16, 2020, https://bit.ly/3CjjIgC

[35] Liat Steir-Livny, "An Interview with Daniela Koffler," May 19, 2020.

[36] "Our Story: 12 Short Movies about the Human Spirit in the Holocaust," *YouTube*, April 16, 2020, https://bit.ly/3tKQSmh

Charm from Grandma, Holocaust survivor Avraham Appelbaum tells the tragic story of a woman who was in hiding with him, whose son would not stop crying. Another man who was with them, and feared the boy's crying would reveal their location to the Nazis, forced her to hide the boy in an old cowshed near them. The Nazis and the Poles heard him, and he ran out of the cowshed towards the house, yelling "Mama Mama." "And then all was silent," says Appelbaum, and stops talking. His silence after the story is stronger than words or visual depictions.[37] In *Esther and the Officer*,[38] Miron describes how the Nazis imprisoned her for being a Communist; she was locked in the dark basement of a jail, where she was beaten regularly and interrogated brutally by the officers. In *A Piece for Dinner*,[39] atrocities are not reenacted or shown, but the survivor talks about the chaos, panic, and commotion in Auschwitz-Birkenau. The survivors describe the hunger, cold, and lice, and Auschwitz as a place of death. Their stories are interspersed with Nazi footage and still pictures from the Auschwitz album that capture the atmosphere of death. The horrific conditions in Auschwitz and the agony of the gas chambers are described by the survivor in *A Bird at the End of the World* and backed up with still pictures from the Auschwitz album and footage taken by the Allies when liberating the camps.[40] The obliteration of an entire ghetto and the mass murder of its people by the Nazis and their Ukrainian facilitators is discussed in *Mother's Dream*.[41]

Director Daniella Koffler, who was responsible for the four animated documentaries, says she was instructed by Yad Vashem not to show horrors but to create movies "a family can watch."[42] This directive makes it clear that even today, although attitudes towards animated documentaries have changed and many international tragedies have been documented in animation, for some, animation is still connected with something more juvenile. Thus, the four animated documentaries in the project avoid showing brutality and murder and rather deal with other subjects.

Similar to the narrative essence of *Yehudit* and *Grandma Mimi*, *Red Fox—The Story of Zippora Feibelevich* depicts one woman's courage to stand up to a Nazi officer. Zippora Feibelevich (maiden name Klein) was born in Transylvania. In 1942 her older brothers were sent to forced labor camps, and in 1944 the rest of the family was deported to Auschwitz. Feibelevich and her sister were enslaved in a munitions factory. While there, several women decided to try

---

[37] "A Good Luck Charm."
[38] "Esther and the Officer."
[39] "A Piece for Dinner."
[40] "A Bird at the End of the World."
[41] "Mother's Dream."
[42] "An Interview with Daniella Koffler."

to sabotage the production line and all the women were punished: they were forced to kneel in the snow for the entire night. As a result, Feibelevich fell ill. A Nazi officer decided to help the sick Feibelevich, who yelled at him, though her cheekiness could have led to her death.

Yad Vashem stipulated that all the animated documentaries needed to follow the same narrative structure. This consisted of a short depiction of pre-World War II life, a description of the war and a short ending showing life in Israel after the war. This structure, which transitions from the Holocaust to renewal or from ashes to revival, dominated Israeli movies on Holocaust survivors from the 1940s until the late 1970s. Israeli cinema at the time primarily promoted ideological messages. Movies that promoted Zionist ideals served as an artistic platform for the Zionist establishment to display its political, economic, and national achievements. The vast majority of the documentaries in that era centered on the change from the wretched condition of the survivors to their wholesome lives in Israel.

These narratives slowly adapted in the late 1970s in response to the evolution in Holocaust awareness in Israeli society. Israeli documentaries and fiction movies abandoned the "from Holocaust to revival" narrative. Instead, documentaries focused on personal stories of how the survivors managed to live with their emotional scars and how this affected their families.[43] Thus, the Yad Vashem guidelines constituted a step backwards to the long-abandoned Zionist narrative.

As requested by Yad Vashem, the movie briefly sketches the family's comfortable life in the pre-Holocaust era, a brave act during the Holocaust, and a revival in Israel.[44] However, the narrative is not linear. The movie begins with Feibelevich kneeling in the snow and then switches back and forth combining mimetic animation and evocation as Koffler describes how Feibelevich's visions of a red fox, recalling her red hair, helped her survive. In order to give a sense of real-time, Koffler did not use the voice of the elderly Feibelevich; a young actress reads out quotations from Feibelevich's testimony in the first person in the voiceover.

Feibelevich's childhood is portrayed as pleasant: her mother opens the door with a smile to call her and her sister, both of them giggling, Feibelevich runs free in the woods, her red hair braided, while a small

---

[43] Steir-Livny, *Two Faces in the Mirror*; Gertz, Nurith, *A Different Choir: Holocaust Survivors, Foreigners, and Others in Israeli Cinema and Literature* (Open University of Israel Press, 2004); Moshe Zimmerman, *Do Not Touch my Holocaust* (Haifa: Haifa University Press, 2002) [Hebrew]; Ilan Avisar. "The Holocaust in Israeli Cinema as a Conflict between Survival and Morality," in Miri Talmon and Yaron Peleg (eds.), *Israeli Cinema: Identities in Motion* (Austin: University of Texas Press, 2011), 151–167.

[44] "An Interview with Daniella Koffler," May 19, 2020.

red fox trots behind her against a pleasant musical soundtrack and scenes of idyllic trees and a lake.

Their arrival in Auschwitz shows the selection ramp. The train is behind them, the gate to Auschwitz in the distance. Even though they are drawn in a mimetic way, the animation does not mimic the historical event. They stand alone, as though they are the only ones on the ramp: two parents and three children, no Nazis, no other people, no commotion. "Me and my sister remained alone" she says as her parents and small brother disappear from the gray frame. "We held on to each other with all our strength." Thus, the horrific world of Auschwitz-Birkenau is neutered and only indicated by its icons. Auschwitz is drawn from the sisters' point of view as three brown barracks, a dark sky, black smoke coming out of a chimney and shadows of darkened people walking near the barracks.

Ziva Amishai-Maisels argued that the barbed wire and crematoria chimneys are "primary Holocaust symbols."[45] Similarly, Baruch Stier noted "the most common Holocaust symbols do not directly communicate its brutal violence. This is one of the reasons these particular images and artifacts are so recognizable and so powerful: they are representative without being overwhelming, succinct without being graphic."[46] These repetitive Holocaust icons obliterate the horrors of the Holocaust and replace the unspeakable with the mellow.

Feibelevich and her sister are depicted in a long row of women standing in line. They are the only ones in color. All the others are simply sketched in black and white as though the Nazis had already erased their existence. "The Germans did all they could to deprive us of our humanity," she says as the camera pans left as though to show the end of the process. The sound of scissors cutting hair is followed by the visual of Feibelevich's red braids being thrown to the ground. "But I had no intention to let it happen!" The animation shows that her spirit was not crushed, she stands out from the other women because her short hair is red, and her face is fierce.

The scene of Feibelevich and the other inmates kneeling in the snow appears several times in the movie as a shorthand for her spiritual and physical resistance. "In the hardest and darkest nights, I always had a glimpse of hope which reminded me of home." The barbed wire is shown from her point of view, and behind it, in the wild, there is a red fox. This is her imagination, her image of herself as a free person; its fur is the same color as her hair. She is the red fox that even the Nazis cannot tame or

---

[45] Ziva Amishai-Maisels, *Depiction and Interpretation: The Influence of the Holocaust on the Visual Arts* (Oxford: Pergamon Press, 1993), xxxii.

[46] Stier, *Holocaust Symbols*, 2.

surrender. This image of the fox takes her back in her mind to her home and the animation enables the viewers to travel back in time with her, remembering her free life, and hearing her father's voice again, as the voiceover explains how this defense mechanism helped her survive kneeling in the snow for hours.

The movie suggests that the physical conditions almost killed her. She is animated in what seems to be a hospital bed. She is almost transparent, suggesting that after the night in the snow she is on the verge of death. "A German doctor decided to help me. I don't know why. She kept whispering in my ear 'Don't worry. You'll survive.'" The doctor is animated from Feibelevich's point of view, and her face resembles Feibelevich's mother as once again her imagination helps her to stay alive.

According to the movie, something more than her inner world helped her survive. Similar to *Grandma Mimi* and *Yehudit*, *Red Fox* highlights a young girl's courage to stand up to a Nazi. As an officer enters the hospital barracks, the frame is oblique, which is designed to create an uncomfortable feeling in the audience. He is drawn from a low angle that makes him look threatening. "What are you doing here, red fox?" he says mockingly in German, his sneering face drawn in close-up to demonstrate the way he disparages her. Feibelevich's head is drawn in close-up as she raises her voice. Her face shows her anger: "It is you!! You are to blame!! You did this to us and I won't let you!!" Amused, he says to the doctor: "She is a red fox. She is rude. Give her the shot!" and the needle pricks her arm. In the voiceover, she claims she still does not understand why he helped her.

To comply with Yad Vashem's guidelines, the end of the movie depicts the Zionist happy end and shows her immigration to Israel together with her sister and two brothers who survived as well. Feibelevich as a young woman is animated riding her bicycle together with her small children in

Figure 1.3 Red Fox—The Story of Zippora Feibelevich *(Daniella Koffler, 2020)*

open green fields, her red hair braided again (and her children with red hair as well). "We were young again. We wanted to live life to the fullest and that's what we did." The red fox leaps after them in the meadow looking happily at them.

Koffler, who interviewed Feibelevich for several hours, says Feibelevich told frightening stories in her testimony ("stories I still try to forget"). These stories were not animated. Koffler says she had no intention of animating such stories anyway because they were so graphically horrific.[47] However, animated documentaries have sufficient techniques to represent horrors without turning them into cheap exposures, as shown in the several movies that have done so (see Chapter 4).

As in other animated documentaries, the horror stories in the survivors' testimonies are watered down in the movie and replaced by a narrative that underscores the strength of the human spirit, coupled with familiar Holocaust symbols. The strength of the human spirit is clearly a very important message, but the annulment of the horrors makes it impossible to understand what inmates in the concentration camps experienced.

---

[47] Steir-Livny, "An Interview with Daniella Koffler."

CHAPTER 2

Resourcefulness

In addition to standing up to the Nazis as discussed in the previous chapter, another form of bravery depicted in several movies is the victims' resourcefulness. These movies focus on girls, teenagers, and young women and broaden the visualization of women's responses to the Holocaust. However, as noted, their acts are not defined as gender-related.[1] Once again they focus on incidents that are suggestive of "a ray of light in the darkness" of that era, but marginalize the atrocities in doing so. The movies analyzed in this chapter are *Nyosha* (Liran Kapel and Yael Dekel, 2012),[2] *Bettine Le Beau—A Lucky Girl* (Martin O'Neill and Andrew Griffin, 2015), *The German Nurse* (Daniella Koffler, 2020),[3] *A Thousand Kisses* (Richard Goldgewicht, 2017), and *Overnight Stay* (Übernachtung, Daniela Sherer, 2009).

SURVIVING THE AKTION IN *NYOSHA*

Nyosha is based on the true story of Holocaust survivor Nomi Kapel, the director's grandmother (Nyosha in Polish). When Nyosha was ten years old, her mother took her and fled from the Warsaw ghetto to a small village in Poland called Wengrow. Nyosha was barefoot during their whole escape and suffered injuries to her feet. She became fixated on buying herself a pair of shoes. In the village, little Nyosha worked hard and earned enough money to buy herself one shoe from the shoemaker, who refused to give her the other shoe until she paid separately for it. She was close to fulfilling her dream when the Nazis swept into the village in 1942. She, her mother, the shoemaker, and several other Jews hid in an attic for several days, but were discovered. Nyosha took the shoes, put them near her bed, and hid under the blanket. A Nazi entered the room, saw her, but spared her life and left. She survived, but her mother was murdered along with the other Jews.

---

[1] For another view of gender and the Holocaust see: Kaplan, "Gendering Holocaust Studies."
[2] "Nyosha," *Vimeo*, https://vimeo.com/43928582
[3] "The German Nurse," https://bit.ly/2Z843m5

Liran Kapel, her granddaughter, studied animation at Sapir Academic College, where the movie was her final project. In 2013, six years after Nyosha passed away, Kapel's grandfather emailed her Nyosha's written testimonies. Kapel knew parts of these stories, since her grandmother lectured every year to high school students and soldiers on Holocaust Martyrs and Heroes Remembrance Day. In August 2000 she also travelled back to her hometown and told the story, which was recorded in a home video. However, Kapel says she never really knew all the details. When reading Nyosha's seventy pages of testimony, Kapel began to cry and decided the story must be commemorated beyond the family circle. She decided to "turn the words into a kind of reality" so that the story would not die with her grandmother.[4] The production took two years and primarily implemented Stop Motion Animation and traditional 2D animation.

Animated documentary scholars have argued that animation can attract viewers who would normally shun traumatic topics. In addition, it can be a way for the post-war generations to connect with trauma they did not experience. Victoria Walden used the term "playing through" to describe certain animated documentaries that deal with traumatic events. In her view, although trauma is often considered something that needs to be worked through, some animated Holocaust documentaries (for example stop-motion Lego "brickmovies" about the Holocaust on YouTube)[5] are premised on the notion that the postmemory generations need to "play through" the traumatic past to feel viscerally invested in them. While "working through" necessitates a critical distance and is most appropriate for first-hand witnesses, playing through enables those who did not experience the past to get close to it. The post-war generations' playful engagement with the Holocaust may thus help connect to the past and materialize their imagined memory as they take on the responsibility for remembering what they did not experience first-hand.[6]

The aesthetic choices in *Nyosha* engage the viewers in a toy-like visual. This buffer softens the emotional response to the distressing subject matter and simultaneously creates a kind of playful engagement with the Holocaust.[7] The characters are puppets made of stainless steel, armatures, and sponges. Their heads are made of polymer clay, with dolls' eyes ordered from Korea

---

[4] Ben Porat, "Holocaust Story," "Conference Future of Holocaust Testimonies lll – Nyosha—Animated Movie Based on Holocaust Survivor Testimony," *YouTube*, June 1, 2014, https://bit.ly/2Z2nAEr

[5] See for example: "Hitler e l'Olocausto raccontato con i Lego," *YouTube*, January 22, 2015, https://bit.ly/3kqVPhj

[6] Victoria Walden, "Animation and Memory."

[7] "'Nyosha' by Liran Kapel and Yael Dekel," *animated Documentry.com*, no date, https://bit.ly/3Cs8ExP

pressed into them. The figures' hands and the feet are made from plaster casts filled with latex, a kind of flexible rubber that can be moved gently to simulate animation. To create believable acting, Kapel filmed herself acting in front of the camera as the initial model.[8] Yael Dekel, Kapel's collaborator on this project, also made more than 600 pencil drawings, which were used to create authentic classic animation. Kapel and Dekel photographed 14,000 stills one after the other to create the illusion that the dolls were moving, and then added special visual effects to give the movie its final look.[9]

Voiceover and Perspective

The animation is accompanied by Nomi's voiceover, taken from video testimony she made for Steven Spielberg's Survivors of the Shoah Visual History Foundation.[10] The movie is thus an example of a combination of non-mimetic visualization and documentary voiceover. The outcome is what Ward considered a contradiction, where "the ontological status of the images often contrasts with the indexicality of the sound," because a real interview is the source.[11] Kapel added muffled fictitious voices of the Nazis by recording the voices of German visitors to her kibbutz, whom she asked to play the spoken role of Nazis.[12]

Psychoanalyst Dana Amir suggested that survivors' testimonies and narratives can best be examined through the prism of four modes of witnessing: the Metaphoric (the traumatic events are not only repeated but are also represented from a distance), the Metonymic (the survivor returns to the experience itself, enacts the traumatic experience but is unable to reflect on it because there is no emotional distance), and two psychotic modes of witnessing (the Muselmann[13] and Excessive modes of witnessing). These modes of witnessing reflect different links to the trauma, and the separation between the I and one's memories. These narrative modes are not necessarily hermetic and one narrative testimonial narrative can constitute a combination of modes.[14]

---

[8] Liran Kapel, "Nyosha – Behind the Scenes," *YouTube*, October 23, 2012, https://bit.ly/39mj31K
[9] Porat, "Holocaust Story."
[10] Shamah, "Animated Holocaust Movie."
[11] Paul Ward, "Animating with Facts: The Performative Process of Documentary Animation in *the ten mark* (2010)," *Animation: An Interdisciplinary Journal* 6, no. 3, 296.
[12] Kapel says it was not easy for them to do the Nazis' part. See: "Nyosha – Behind the Scenes."
[13] Slang for starved, exhausted concentration camp inmates, who are between life and death.
[14] Dana Amir, *Bearing Witness to the Witness: A Psychoanalytic Perspective on Four Modes of Traumatic Testimony* (New York: Routledge, 2018).

Nomi tells her story in the metaphoric mode of witnessing. She talks about herself but maintains an emotional distance that enables her to shift from the position of victim to that of witness.[15] Despite the truly horrific nature of the historical narrative, the movie is suffused with naïve optimism by taking the point of view of the child. Events she did not fully understand as a ten-year-old are blended with the testimony of the elderly Nomi. However, in certain scenes the moviemakers rectify both Nomi's and Nyosha's perspective to hint at the nature of events she could not understand as a child, but also does not refer to when an elderly woman. The combination of the testimony of the elderly survivor, the child's perspective, and the third generation's point of view blends the past and the present: young Nyosha, elderly Nomi, and her granddaughter all become part of the same space and time.

The Shoes

Kapel states that she did not want the audience to feel the accuracy of the historical details, but rather have a sense of the protagonist's subjective overview of her past. Nomi believed that the shoes she put by her bed when she hid from the Nazis made the Nazi soldier spare her life. Thus, the shoes are a major leitmotif in the movie.[16]

The importance of the shoes is made clear from the opening scene. The movie begins with a shot of the shoemaker's store. The animation pans over the pictures on the walls, the shoes piled up in a corner, his tools, his hand taking a tool and his silhouette working, hammering a shoe. In the voiceover Nomi introduces herself ("I'm excited. My name is Nomi Kapel. My maiden name is Agrapski or Grapski. I'm not quite sure.") The disconnection between the visuals and the voiceover makes it seem as though the shoemaker's house has a direct biographical connection to her family. This is the moviemaker's way of highlighting the role of the shoes in Nyosha's life.

Nyosha and her mother are only seen for the first time after the shoemaker scenes. They are walking in the woods. Kapel does not use this scene to explain what they are doing in the village, the dangers, or the era. Instead, she sticks with the perspective of the little girl, who does not understand the situation completely: all that matters is the pair of shoes. Thus, in the voiceover, the moviemakers did not insert elderly Nomi's testimony about what happened to them in the Warsaw ghetto, the hunger, the poverty, their escape, but only her comments on the shoes: "I went to the shoemaker and told him I needed a pair of shoes. I bought one shoe, it was shiny, black and

---

[15] Amir, *Bearing Witness*, 10–11.
[16] Ben Porat, "Holocaust Story."

it had a buckle." Young Nyosha's perspective and her inability to grasp the situation are also reflected in the colors of the scene. These hard times could have been depicted in dark colors, but here they are bright and cheerful. Young Nyosha is animated walking hand in hand with her mother in the forest in what seems to be a peaceful afternoon. The sun is shining, the frame is open. There is no visual clue to any hint of danger. The only thing that mildly disturbs the pleasant scene is the close-up of Nyosha's feet, since one is barefoot and the other has a shiny black shoe. The close-up on her feet also reveals her ragged trousers, a hint of their destitution.

When they get to the shoemaker's store, Nyosha glues her face to the dirty window and stares at the other black shoe there, saying "he saved this shoe for me." The shoemaker knew they were poor and selling one shoe to a little girl is cruelly absurd, yet Nyosha fails to grasp the irony. However, the directors subvert her point of view (and misunderstanding) by highlighting the shoemaker's problematic image: after they leave, he gets up and looks out the window, as the marks of Nyosha's little palm appear on the window. He saw them. He could have used this opportunity to give her the other shoe. But he did not. The little palm print intensifies the cruelty Nyosha does not understand and very indirectly broaches a marginalized topic in the Israeli Holocaust narrative: cruelty of Jews towards other Jews during the Holocaust. These misdeeds have primarily been discussed in debates on the roles of Jewish functionaries,[17] but little attention has been paid to the mundane attitudes of ordinary Jews towards one another.

In their small house the walls are cracked, and the shutters are broken. Ignoring her surroundings, Nyosha is only interested in polishing her shoe with a dirty cloth. The sequence is constructed to portray the amount of time that elapsed before she could buy the second shoe. It does not portray her working, but rather the hours of sunlight and darkness. In the bright lighting that portrays daylight, Nyosha gets up, her image dissolves from the frame (as she goes to work), the lighting becomes dark (to symbolize the end of the day) and then bright again (to symbolize dawn) as Nyosha is portrayed getting up again. The coins she is paid pile up in a little box by her bed. These scenes are repeated several times to a pleasant neutral soundtrack, because Nyosha is so obsessed with her shoe that she does not notice other changes. It echoes

---

[17] See for example: Gideon Greif, *We Wept without Tears: Testimonies of the Jewish Sonderkommando from Auschwitz* (New Haven: Yale University Press, 2014); Adam Brown, *Judging "Privileged" Jews: Holocaust Ethics, Representation, and the "Grey Zone"* (New York and Oxford: Berghahn Books, 2013), 134–141; Itamar Levin, *Kapo on Allenby* (Jerusalem: Yad Ben Zvi, 2015) [Hebrew]; Rivka Brut, *In the Gray Zone: The Jewish Kapo on Trial* (Ra'anana: The Open University, 2019) [Hebrew]; Dan Porat, *Bitter Reckoning: Israel Tries Holocaust Survivors as Nazi Collaborators* (New Haven: Harvard University Press, 2019).

testimonies of other survivors who were children during the Holocaust. For example, writer and child Holocaust survivor Alona Frenkel, who survived in hiding, stated that "I don't know how much I understood that life was on the edge." She sat with her notebook and painted pictures. "I was little enough not to understand what was going on."[18]

Kapel and Dekel use Nyosha's coat to show the viewers what she does not see or understand. In one scene the animation focuses on Nyosha's diminutive coat on a chair. In the next scene, it has a yellow badge sewn onto it. They also use the soundtrack to counter the child's perspective: the pleasant music is now undercut by the wail of a siren.

As she heads proudly to buy the other shoe, she discovers it is too late. The store has been ransacked. A bomb explodes in the distance and on the soundtrack Nyosha's mother calls her to come home immediately. Her arms enter the frame and grab Nyosha out of it. The sound of falling coins on the floor captures the end of the dream, suggesting that this is the first time Nyosha has realized something is wrong. The elderly Nomi states: "On Tisha B'av morning we were alerted: They are rounding up the Jews. They are rounding up the Jews." The repetition establishes the child's realization that something bad is happening.

Nyosha's ethnicity is not made explicit and is only indicated indirectly by Jewish and Holocaust symbols such as the Star of David on her coat, or the "Jude" graffiti on the shoemaker's shop, the two candlesticks and the menorah in her home. An audience that is unfamiliar with these symbols may not understand the meaning of these references to Judaism.

Kapel and Dekel use Holocaust icons as a shorthand for the round-ups of the Jews, such as dogs barking, a close-up of Nyosha's coat with the Star of David, loud stamping of marching boots, close-ups of the Nazi uniform of the soldier who enters the house in a robotic goose-step. Their faces are not shown as they scream: "Did you hear it? It is coming from there!" in German. Unlike other scenes in which the directors deviated from Nyosha's perspective to explain what she cannot understand, when filming the round-up they stick with her perspective in the attic and do not animate the arrests, the commotion, or the mass murder. Sounds of gunshots are heard outside, but nothing is shown.

A thin strip of light enters the attic to show there are several people hiding there. The light fades to black and then becomes brighter to mark the passing of time. The Jews in hiding are shot from a high angle, which makes them look small and miserable. The bright colors of the opening scenes are replaced by gray as though the attic is filled with dust. Nyosha is huddled

---

[18] Modi, Anat, "Culture Heroes—A Child," *YouTube*, October 4, 2013, https://bit.ly/3lHgMnj

against her mother; the other Jews are cramped. A clock ticking is reminiscent of a final countdown. Sounds of war outside (bombing and sirens) penetrate the attic. The two-shot of scared Nyosha and her mother holding her and looking into her eyes demonstrates the love Kapel wanted to stress. There are no words between them in the entire movie, just actions and gazes. "We sat there for three days. On the roof, in the attic." Even though the situation is terrible, their connection and their love prompted Kapel and Dekel to use soft rather than dramatic music. These are the last intimate moments between mother and daughter, although neither knew. Elderly Nomi is aware of the significance of this scene, as is her granddaughter, who depicts it as the last days of love.

Then everything falls apart. In the movie the shoemaker emerges as responsible for their discovery. He sits clutching a bucket he brought with him. The other Jews in hiding believe it contains food he refuses to share. This starts a commotion, and he falls from the attic to the floor below, with his bucket, which is revealed to have contained shoes, not food. Nyosha sees everything from the attic. Clinging to her point of view, since her mother covers her eyes, the viewers do not see the Nazis kill him, but only hear their shouting and a gunshot.

When the soundtrack reproduces the sound of the feet of the Jews being herded out, the technique switches to the two-dimension animation made up of Dekel's light, fanciful, spare line drawings. Kapel does not show the Nazis taking Nyosha's mother. Instead, she "escapes" to two-dimensional animation that evokes the event metaphorically. The sad, dramatic soundtrack incorporates soldiers shouting orders in German. Nomi says she does not remember how she got out of the attic and her grandchild chooses a fairytale-style explanation. She accepts her grandmother's "blank" and animates Nyosha's emotional response rather than what really happened. The drawing shows Nyosha in white against a sepia background, shivering, small, and lonely in the frame, covering her ears. Like in a fairytale, a rope winds down to her from high above, her frightened face is represented in a close-up as her hands reach out for it and use it to swing to the floor. The rope turns into a shoelace attached to a shoe, the famous shoe which for her was everything.

As she touches the ground the animation returns to the three-dimensional puppet animation, as though now it is safe to go back to this representation. Only after this horrible event can she fulfill her dream. She picks up the second shoe as the frame widens to show the shoemaker's dead body next to the shoes. In tears, she sees her mother out in the snow: "I'm not saying a word and I'm looking at Mom and I'm shaking my head and she shakes her head back at me and that was all." The Germans are screaming and blowing their whistles as Nyosha's mother disappears from view. A gunshot is heard.

Nomi believes the shoes saved her life, and Kapel animates her conviction. At this crucial moment, the movie turns again to two-dimensional animation. The Nazi's boots are heard on the squeaking floor. "He approaches the bed, but he doesn't lift up the blanket. He touches the blanket on both sides. He touches me on both sides. Like this. He touches me and I'm breathing, breathing heavily, when he touched me, I had no air. I was under the blanket." The drawings evoke what she felt like under the blanket: a frightened little girl walking on a thin tightrope, a shoelace leading to a big shoe, trying to balance, almost falling.

Then the scene returns to the puppet animation and focuses on the shoes near the bed: "He touched my waist. I felt his hands." He says nothing. His foot lines up one shoe against the other and then his footsteps fade away. Nyosha is filmed from above. She is completely covered by the white blanket, as though she were dead. She pulls the blanket off. "I got out of bed, put on my shoes, and I didn't take a coat. I did not take a thing. I had on my dress and my shoes." Not taking the coat with the yellow star helped her survive since when she fled, she concealed her Jewish identity.

The movie does not depict what happened to her after she escaped into the forest, and states the aftermath in the subtitles. She went into the forest and knocked on villagers' doors offering to work. One Polish family took her in. She used a fake Polish name, never letting them know she was Jewish. After the war she was found by Youth Aliyah representatives, who took her

Figure 2.1 Nyosha *(Liran Kapel and Yael Dekel, 2012)*

to Israel, where she rebuilt her life.[19] The subtitles also inform the audience that she passed away in 2006 at the age of 73, surrounded by a large loving family. These subtitles mark another victory, beyond her survival.

Although the deliberate elimination of horrors can be explained narratively and aesthetically by the decision to maintain the child's perspective, the directors sometimes chose to depart from this point of view and thus could have done so to depict events unfolding around Nyosha in all their atrocity. Even though the animation is used to show a past unfilmed, the directors replace it with amorphic symbols and sounds, or watered-down Holocaust icons.

THE GERMAN NURSE—THE STORY OF ELKA BORNSTEIN

Elka Bornstein was born in 1930 in Transylvania, Romania. Her parents died before the war, leaving her and her four siblings orphaned. The five children were separated and raised by relatives, and at the outbreak of World War II were deported separately to Auschwitz. After multiple hardships in the camp, Bornstein was transferred to a smaller labor camp in Germany, and in 1944 was ordered on a death march, from which she managed to escape. After weeks of wandering alone, she reached a refugee camp for German citizens in the town of Hermesdorf in Silesia. She pretended she was a German who had lost her parents in the bombing of Dresden. In this camp, a German nurse named Hildegard Neuingebauer decided to adopt her. Bornstein spent the last year of the war in Neuingebauer's home, hiding her true identity. After World War II ended, she left, looked for her siblings, found her sister, and immigrated with her to Israel.

The German Nurse is part of the Yad Vashem cinematic series entitled *Our Story*, in which directors were asked to create Holocaust animated documentaries "for the entire family." To do so, Bornstein's tragic story is entirely minimized. It is narrated by a young actress, as though Bornstein were telling her story soon after the Liberation. It starts when she was sent to Auschwitz and ordered to a work camp. Her previous life is summarized in several sentences: "A lot of things happened to me during the war. I was already an orphan when I arrived in Auschwitz. I worked in hard labor in a concentration camp named Hochweiler, I walked in the death marches, I survived because in every place, even the worst, people were good to me." While she is speaking,

---

[19] David Shamah, "Animated Holocaust Movie uses Spielberg Online Witness Archive," *The Times of Israel*, April 18, 2012, accessed April 19, 2012, https://bit.ly/3nPsf7i; Shahar Ben Porat, "Holocaust Story Became an Animation Movie," *Mako*, April 18, 2012, accessed April 19, 2012 [Hebrew], https://bit.ly/3lFMTUz

the camera pans from abstract visualizations loaded with symbols of World War II in blue or in yellow including swastikas, soldiers with guns marching in formation, buildings on fire, planes swooping across the sky, a watchtower in a camp, tanks. The images indicate war, but her words center on the good within the bad. The genocide of the Jews is not mentioned at all. These are war images, not Holocaust images.

Neuingebauer is drawn as an attractive young woman who rescues her without knowing her true identity ("I immediately invented a new name for myself. I told her my name was Eli Karl. I lost my parents when the Allies bombed Dresden."). The train ride to Neuingebauer's hometown is animated from an extreme long shot, thus showing the surroundings. Nazi flags are fluttering in the wind, but the countryside is tranquil, showing picture-postcard German scenery with woods, a lake, and German farm villages. The music is pleasant and relaxed. If not for the Nazi flags, it would have looked like a tourist spot.

The Nazi grandparents (the grandfather welcomes them with a Nazi salute) are represented as attractive, lovely people who accept Bornstein as their granddaughter right away. "They told me to call them Oma and Opa [granny and grandpa in German])," she says in a scene encapsulating the complex position that people can be kind but enthusiastic Nazis at the same time. Their house is comfortable. As soft classical music is played on the soundtrack, Bornstein is drawn sitting at a table with beautiful cutlery while Oma serves her a slice of cream cake ("It was unbelievable. I slept in a bed with clean perfumed sheets, I ate cake with Oma.").

The past does not disappear but is made distant and poignant. For example, during their train ride to the village, scenes of the war (not of the Holocaust) appear again for several seconds to mirror Bornstein's thoughts.

Figure 2.2 The German Nurse—The Story of Elka Bornstein *(Daniella Koffler, 2020)*

They seep into the beautiful scenery, and she begins to cry. As Bornstein eats her cake, in the teaspoon she suddenly sees the reflection of war, and the teaspoon in her mind bursts into flame. The frame becomes dark, and she sees her former identity in the spoon. In another scene when she takes a walk with Oma and Opa in the beautiful village, they come across a deserted building, a former synagogue. Bornstein is animated from the back looking in, as the animation evokes a lively synagogue, packed with people in her mind.

Bornstein's story enables the viewers to understand how life continued in small Nazi hamlets. "Outside were mothers with babies in strollers. Alive." She stands near Oma and Opa, looking astounded at mothers who are pushing their babies in strollers as though there is no war or genocide. However, this choice underscores the absence of Holocaust, which is not mentioned or visualized, and the audience is left mainly with its complex portrait of Nazis. They are drawn as nice-looking people, they act politely, they make Bornstein a member of their family, but they are sworn antisemites. As Bornstein looks in the mirror, thinking about her secret and her torn identity, the voiceover states: "Opa hated Jews." Her statement is striking since she uses the term "grandfather," which describes how close they were, while acknowledging his beliefs regarding her people. "He said they are evil animals, smelly pigs, he would have strangled me if he knew." Her image in the mirror changes to black, as the image of the Jews in Opa's mind bursts out in the form of a monster, a pig, a stereotypical devilish image of an ugly Jew as though taken from Nazi propaganda.

The animation zooms in on the Nazi flag floating over one of the buildings in the village as it morphs into the USSR flag to mark the passing of time and the Allied victory. Now the table has turned: the soldiers are looking for Nazis. "Telling them [the Nazi family] who I really was, was the hardest thing I had to do. But Opa said: 'Eli, we rescued you. Now you rescue us.'" This time his and Oma's faces are shown as he goes down on his knees to hug Bornstein and probably ask for her help.

The complex identities of Jewish children after the war, which have been discussed in numerous studies,[20] are manifested in Bornstein's attitude towards her savior. She wants to look for her family but saying goodbye to her adoptive mother, who wanted her to stay, was very hard.

---

[20] For example: Boaz Cohen, "The Children's Voice: Postwar Collection of Testimonies from Child Survivors of the Holocaust," *Holocaust and Genocide Studies* 21, no. 1 (Spring 200): 73–95, https://bit.ly/3kqfiOQ; Sharon Kangisser Cohen and Dalia Ofer (eds.), *Starting Anew: The Rehabilitation of Child Survivors of the Holocaust in the Early Postwar Years* (Jerusalem: Yad Vashem Publications, 2019); Rebecca Clifford, *Survivors: Children's Lives After the Holocaust* (New Haven & London: Yale University Press, 2020).

Bornstein admits that she left even though she wanted to stay. The movie ends with the classic Zionist rescue through titles saying that Bornstein found her sister Malka, immigrated to Palestine in 1947, got married, and had three children. In 1980 a German journalist located Neuingebauer, and they met again. The movie ends with a still picture of them both. After this Zionist happy end, there is apparently no problem in showing their reunion.

"A Rough Patch": *Bettine Le Beau—A Lucky Girl*

Bettine Le Beau was eight years old when the Nazis invaded Belgium. Her father was at a conference in London at the time and advised her mother to travel to Paris to apply for a British visa, but the Nazis invaded France before she could secure one. The family moved to Bordeaux but then was deported to the Gurs concentration camp. An undercover agent of the Oeuvre de Secours aux Enfants (OSE) arrived, bribed the guard, and managed to take several children with her out of the camp to an OSE home in central France. The OSE managed to move the Jewish children from the house to safety before the children's home was raided on SS orders. Le Beau was hidden by a French family nearby. After World War II, in 1945, she immigrated to England and began a successful career as a model, actress, broadcaster, cabaret artist, lecturer, portrait painter, sculptor, graphologist, and author. She founded a cosmetic business and a charity called "The Feminine Touch." She also became a public speaker who lectured about her experiences as a child in the Holocaust. She died in September 2015. Up to her death, she remained in touch with the family that took her in and saved her.[21]

Collage artist Martin O'Neill and animator Andrew Griffin met Le Beau in her north London home, as part of the HMD 2015 *Memory Makers* project, and created a hybrid video art/animation that uses Le Beau's testimony in the voiceover while representing images as streams of consciousness.[22] The movie's title is emblematic of its main topic: luck. This is a key part of Le Beau's optimistic perspective on life, which makes her paint her story as a child under Nazism in rosy hues by highlighting funny events, avoiding

---

[21] Holocaust Educational Trust, "Bettine Le Beau, 1932–2015," https://bit.ly/3ztcDs6; Louette Harding, "Real Lives: Bettine Le Beau 'I Kidded Myself that there was an Angel Looking After Me'", *Mail Online*, January 28, 2013, https://bit.ly/3zzWvFv; Holocaust Memorial Day Trust, "Bettine Le Beau," https://bit.ly/3lJzVoT

[22] Holocaust Memorial Day Trust, "Bettine Le Beau."

Figure 2.3 Bettine Le Beau—A Lucky Girl *(Martin O'Neill and Andrew Griffin, 2015)*

mentions of the atrocities and maintaining her strong morale even when discussing difficult issues. In the first frame, as an animated star opens like a flower, she states, "I have very positive attitude, because I remember my mother said when I was little 'you are a lucky child.'"

In the movie, the time allotted to the Nazis' invasion and the Gurs camp is short, and no horrible stories are seen or heard. In other interviews, much more detailed stories of her memories of the panic and anxiety and awful situations are mentioned: she remembers her mother collecting their savings in gold coins from the bank, the panicking crowds at the Gare du Midi, her brother Harry being pushed off the seats on the train to Paris. She remembers the throngs of desperate people, suitcases abandoned on the road. In Paris, they stayed with friends while applying for a visa from the British consul. The two sons of this family were murdered in a death camp. In this interview, the interviewer talks about the emotional outpouring as Le Beau tells her story, struggling to find words. She makes the horrors explicit: "in the detention camp on the way to Gurs surrounded by barbed wire, I saw men crying for the first time. Now, it started. I knew it was dangerous. The men collapsed. Some were ill: they had diarrhea, they lost their memory. It was the women who were the strongest." In Gurs she only saw her mother through the barbed wire fence between the children's and the women's barracks. There was hunger, lice, fleas, and rats, and it was filthy. All they had to eat was a small portion of bread in the morning and soup for lunch. By the winter of 1940, children were falling sick with dysentery and typhus. "They took to their palliasses, gave up hope and cried all day. We saw a lot die."²³ The episodes from her life in the camp are depicted through illustrations. For example, when she states that in the camp she slept on rags stuffed with straw whereas at home she had a clean bed, the visual moves from a black and white still picture of rags and straw to a black and white still picture of a bed in a small room reminiscent of the 1940s, nothing more.

When describing the new children's home, Le Beau only mentions that she wet the bed at first and was very embarrassed. She says that she had lice, so nobody wanted to play with her. She did not like the place and wanted to go back to the concentration camp. A girl is depicted from behind sitting alone. Later she is shown shutting her eyes tight as though she were crying or upset, but the atmosphere is not gloomy.

She was sent to Switzerland under a false identity. Her name was changed to Betty Frickier ("your father is a prisoner of war; your mother is dead"). Marthe and Abel Marre, a middle-aged childless couple who owned a secluded farm, agreed to take in Le Beau and another girl named Henriette after being approached by their priest. On Christmas Eve 1942, a truck dropped the two ten-year-olds by the side of the main road. "Did this seem like make-believe? Was it fun in any way? 'Fun? No, never fun. But I said to myself, "I can do this,"'"²⁴ she says in the voiceover. However, the movie makes it look like an adventure. The still picture of girls smiling shows their bright dresses and flowers, as she says she was told never to tell anyone she was Jewish. She talks very fondly about the family who took her in and says that she had to stop shouting and telling dirty jokes, since "they were so polite." The collage shows her life: a girl out in the field, a family table set for dinner.

A still of her brother is shown and then a picture of them together, as the background turns into something between a map and veins symbolizing their blood connection, as she says that their saviors housed him elsewhere, where he became a shepherd. He spent most of his time far from her, became very rude, and when the war ended appeared at her house, demanding she go with him, without even a thank you. She did not want to go at first but eventually agreed. An illustration of a chicken and big eggs appears as she says the family was so kind that they told her to take her chicken with her. These scenes refrain from telling the difficult but frequent story of children saved by gentile families who were unwilling to leave at the end of the war. Often these children developed a love for their adoptive parents, drifted apart from their relatives and Jewish identities, and did not want to leave when the

---

²³ Louette Harding, "Real Lives: Bettine Le Beau 'I Kidded Myself that there was an Angel Looking After Me,'" *Mail Online*, January 28, 2013, https://bit.ly/3AqD9Uo
²⁴ Ibid.

war ended.[25] However, the movie represents her departure from the family that saved her life without any emotional wrenching.

Another sad story that the movie neglects to tell is what happened after the children were reunited with their parents. In another interview Le Beau made this clear. During the war her parents separated, and her father started a relationship with another woman, with whom he had a child. Her mother agreed to get back together with him until Le Beau grew up. "So yes, the war destroyed my family. My mother became bitter. She was never interested in my showbusiness career." She adds that she never contacted her half-sister: "What if I liked her? It would be disloyal to my mother."[26] In the movie, however, their reunion is presented as a redemptive ending. "And then the war ended, and then we got reunited with my father and that's it," she says. The text appears in the middle of the frame. A still picture appears of Le Beau's mother holding her as a little girl, followed by a picture of her mother, filled with flowers. The camera moves over these images, as though probing them, as Le Beau says her mother never told her what happened to her and did not ask about the family that adopted her during the war. "I said maybe she suffered so much she doesn't want to let me know, but why doesn't she want to know about the family that wanted to adopt me?" Le Beau thinks that this may have caused her mother to feel jealous. As though to shield her mother, the directors refrain from exploring this relationship or representing the feelings that developed between Le Beau and the adoptive family. The calm colors and drawings of fields, the chicken, and a warm house hint at this wordlessly.

In the movie, none of the physical and emotional hardships are visualized or discussed. Le Beau is not shown, but her voice is constantly heard in the soundtrack as she tells her story in a very positive way, and often bursts out laughing while sharing incidents, even when they were part of what were clearly traumatic episodes. Many other survivors have been able to create an emotional barrier between themselves and their traumatic past and discuss incidents at an emotional distance, sometimes even giggling,[27] but Le Beau's testimony, which is commemorated in a movie that is also visually horror-free, takes this to the next level. If the viewers had not known it was a story about a child in the Holocaust, it would seem like some kind of fairytale. Le Beau's voiceover explains her philosophy of life: sometimes in life there

---

[25] See footnote 32.
[26] Harding, "Real Lives."
[27] See for example, the testimony of Izhak in the movie *Choice and Destiny* (Tzipi Reibenbach, 1993); Michal Friedman, "Witnessing for the Witness: *Choice and Destiny* by Tsipi Reibenbach," *Shofar: An Interdisciplinary Journal of Jewish Studies* 24, no. 1 (Fall 2005): 81–93, Steir-Livny, *Remaking Holocaust Memory*, 154–158.

is a "rough patch," but when one looks back "you realize it is the best thing that happened to you." As still pictures of Le Beau from her days as a model and an actress appear in the middle of a colorful frame, she says that because she had to pretend to be someone she was not in her childhood, it helped her to become an actress. A still picture of two hands holding each other in the middle of a colorful frame that looks somehow divided is immersed in a collage of flowers, a rainbow, stars, and fireworks while she talks about her feeling that she had a guardian angel.

The statements in the movie are indeed Le Beau's testimony and nothing is invented. However, all the traumatic parts mentioned in interviews (and perhaps with the directors themselves) are omitted. The Holocaust is reduced to a "rough patch," such that all the hard times are sugar-coated and visualized as contributing to her career. The terrible situations she witnessed are downplayed into the caricature of a girl who encountered "some" hardships.

LOVE STORY AND THE RIGHTEOUS AMONG THE NATIONS

Lawrence Langer strongly criticized people who focus on "positive" Holocaust-related events, such as love stories during the Holocaust or stories of the Righteous Among the Nations, by pointing out that "The Holocaust is not a story of love. It's a story of hate."[28] He discusses the problematic aspects of what he calls "redemptive Holocaust Memory"; i.e., texts that "tend to honor those rare moments when Jews were not victims of their doom but agents of their fate, restoring to Holocaust vocabulary sentiments like 'tragic dignity' and 'the triumph of the human spirit' and to Holocaust memory a workable mental formula for avoiding an encounter with the unfathomable." The result is a shallow representation of the Holocaust.[29] He rejects this stance: "If we ever hope to absorb the full unsettling complexity of the Holocaust, we need to give unredemptive memory a chance too."[30] Animated documentaries often focus on the topics he rejects by highlighting the ray of light in the darkness while marginalizing the atrocities. The next section analyzes two movies that deal with topics Langer found so inappropriate: love stories and the Righteous among the Nations.

---

[28] "Virtual Book Launch: The Afterdeath of the Holocaust," *YouTube*, March 19, 2021, https://bit.ly/3EbYfIs
[29] Langer, "Redemptive and Unredemptive Holocaust Memory," 38–44.
[30] Ibid., 37–61.

A Love Story Under the Swastika—*A Thousand Kisses*

This movie tells the story of a young Jewish couple in 1933 Berlin, Natalia (Nettie) Haber and Moses Waldmann (whom Nettie nicknamed Martin). She was a German Jew, and he was a Polish Jew. In 1933 Waldmann's older sister Lola asked him to immigrate to Brazil. She had moved there with her husband, Simon, a few years earlier.[31] Haber refused to leave. They made casual plans to reunite on the safe tropical shores of Brazil. As the situation deteriorated in Germany, he was able to arrange entry papers to Brazil for Haber and she joined him.[32]

Richard Goldgewicht, the director, has directed movies in various documentary genres (animation and live action).[33] Eitan Rosenthal, Haber and Waldmann's grandson, is an animation producer. He discovered Waldmann's letters eighty years later in São Paulo.[34] Rosenthal and Goldgewicht decided to adapt them into an animated documentary. Alan Dunne, the illustrator and art director of the movie, noted that the production was an international endeavor. "I was illustrating in Dublin, the animation team was based in Montevideo in Uruguay, the voice actors are German, the director and writer were LA-based, and the producer was in Sao Paolo."[35]

A Thousand Kisses is a combination of animated documentary and fiction animation, a hybrid form that destabilizes dichotomous definitions and represents the range of possibilities for creation in the documentary realm. The segments representing Waldmann's letters are read by a young actor and are direct quotations from his actual letters. Haber's letters were not found. Rosenthal and Goldgewicht knew she worked at the Tietz Department Store, but her side of the love story was unknown, so they invented her part.

According to Goldgewicht, the context of the movie is the Holocaust, but he was primarily interested in a complex love story on what brings people together. He wanted to address the Nazi period from a new angle, as opposed to retelling the same story over and over again. "The way to keep the memory alive is to tell it differently."[36] This comment evokes the problem of "Holocaust fatigue" with respect to well-established canonic Holocaust representations.[37] Live action documentarists have also commented on the need

---

[31] Liat Steir-Livny, "An Interview with Eitan Rozenthal," April 9, 2020.
[32] The movie has been presented at many festivals and won several awards. See: "A Thousand Kisses," https://bit.ly/3CfT8Fr
[33] "Richard Goldgewicht," *A Thousand Kisses*, https://bit.ly/3zY1IXJ
[34] "A Thousand Kisses."
[35] Alan Dunne, "A Thousand Kisses," *Behance*, https://bit.ly/3zaOPt0
[36] Liat Steir-Livny, "An Interview with Richard Goldgewicht," October 7, 2019.
[37] Figley, "Compassion Fatigue," 1–20.

Figure 2.4 A Thousand Kisses *(Richard Goldgewicht, 2017)*

to approach the subject differently, and not make yet "another Holocaust movie."[38] Focusing on this type of story through animation is indeed a different perspective on the era, but the result, as in many other animated Holocaust documentaries, is the minimization of the atrocities.

The movie's aesthetics are far from creating a melancholic, depressing atmosphere. The drawings are bright and multicolored, and there are many scenes in open spaces. At the beginning of the movie, sweet romantic music is heard, accompanied by the sound of a pen squeaking on paper as postcards and letters appear. They are drawn but are mixed with real still pictures and authentic postcards from the 1930s. Dunne says that he designed them with careful attention to accurate detail.[39] As these visuals are represented, a female narrator proclaims that "this is a true story of love and the moment every woman faces when she must decide if she has found the one." The narrator continues to recount their farewell while a still passport picture of Waldmann is shown next to his animated one. The worried face of a young woman standing at the harbor looking at the ship is animated. "She gave no explanation. She just chose to stay." This opening (and the movie itself) reflects what appears in many other animated documentaries—a mixture of the persecution of the Jews and universal themes. This is a love story with a secret, unfolding against the backdrop of Nazism, not vice-versa.

---

[38] Liat Steir-Livny, *Remaking Holocaust Memory: Documentary Cinema by Third-Generation Survivors in Israel* (Syracuse: Syracuse University Press, 2019).

[39] Dunne, "A Thousand Kisses."

Two Worlds: Reality and Fantasy

Waldmann's world is drawn in warm colors. His long journey from Germany to Brazil, according to the movie, does not seem to have been difficult. Rio de Janeiro is depicted as picturesque and welcoming. He is a door-to-door salesman peddling clothing, purses and other items. He swims in the ocean, dines with friends in small, beautiful cafés, under the pine trees, and enjoys beautiful sunsets. Latin music plays in the background to the relaxed, pleasant scenery. According to the movie, even though he loves Haber and is concerned about her, he is incapable of fully understanding the situation in Berlin and the rapid deterioration of the status of the Jews.

The animation of Haber's scenes reflects the deterioration in the Jews' situation in Berlin in the 1930s. It is represented by a double perspective. There are scenes in which Waldmann envisions what she is doing in his absence (while the quotations from his letters appear in the soundtrack) and the animation "follows" his thoughts and imagination.[40] In other scenes the creators insert what they think really happened—which Waldmann did not know and could not understand. A deliberate dissonance is created in these scenes between his words and the animation to highlight what (the creators believe) eluded him.

Berlin of the 1930s is represented as glamorous and enchanting, with its wide streets, elegant department stores, and parks full of greenery. Parts of Waldmann's letters are heard in the soundtrack as he imagines what his beloved girlfriend is doing: "Now you are going to the shop, now you are having lunch and now you have finished work." The visuals show Haber working as a saleswoman in the department store, sitting on a park bench at noon eating lunch, her image going home at night from the big department store. Opposed to this aesthetic in which the animation reflects the soundtrack, in many other scenes, Goldgewicht and Rozenthal use the animation to highlight the disparity between his words and what Haber is going through.[41] For example, in one scene, Moses reacts in a letter to a toothache Haber told him about. "His" voice is heard saying he was sorry to hear about her toothache and angry at the dentist, who had only made it worse. He continues that he is happy she went to a dentist in Berlin because the dentists in Rio de Janeiro are very expensive. To highlight his complete misunderstanding of the deterioration in Berlin, the creators do not show her at a regular dentist. They animate the dentist as Hitler, holding two wrenches

---

[40] Steir-Livny, "An Interview with Richard Goldgewicht"; Steir-Livny, "An Interview with Eitan Rozenthal."
[41] Steir-Livny, "An Interview with Eitan Rozenthal."

with spinning swastikas at their ends, coming towards her frightened face trying to yank out her teeth. This symbolizes the situation she is immersed in, and her inner fears that her lover, who is far away, cannot understand.

His inability to understand her situation is reflected in the things he complains about and the mundane things and trivialities he imagines that have nothing to do with what the animation shows Haber is experiencing. He complains about the herring he ate on the ship to Brazil, the sardines in Vigo in Spain, where the ship stopped on the way ("not as tasty as we used to share"), says he is sorry he is writing in pencil. Later, when she receives the papers and prepares for immigration, he sends her a "wish list," asking her to buy him socks, pajamas, their favorite herring, and so on, as though everything is normal. The items from his wish list appear on the walls of Haber's home as her face twitches angrily. According to Goldgewicht, she sulks because up to then, the letters were a romantic fantasy. There was nothing "earthly" about them, and suddenly when things turn serious, real-life enters—he needs socks. This is not poetry. This is reality.[42] However, it may have a deeper meaning. The contradictions between his writing about the pesky little details of life and the representation of what is really happening in Berlin emphasize that the distance between them is not only geographic. The deterioration was so rapid that even Jews, who were aware of the danger, could not anticipate or understand from afar what was happening. Another example is the scene in which Waldmann writes that he is sure she went canoeing in a park on her birthday. The animation shows the canoe scene, but accompanies it with what actually happened that night when Haber witnessed the burning of books in Bebelplatz, as Moses' voice is heard sending her a thousand kisses and telling her how sad he is because he has not heard from her; she is seen hiding behind a building watching the flames and the saluting Nazis all around them, as Nazi shouts are heard on the soundtrack.

In *Reflections of Nazism: An Essay on Kitsch and Death*, Saul Friedlander analyzed the Nazi images that appeared in the West from the end of World War II until the 1980s. He argued that these images are frightening but at the same time attractive and erotic. Nazism in Western culture from the 1960s onwards is represented by a set of iconic images: red flags with swastikas, carefully pressed SS uniforms, shaven heads, black leather belts and boots, leather jackets, etc. These images could very well be the way the Nazis would like to see themselves: perfect, effective, and a force to be reckoned with.[43]

---

[42] Steir-Livny, "An Interview with Richard Goldgewicht."
[43] Saul Friedlander, *Reflections of Nazism: An Essay on Kitsch and Death* (Jerusalem: Keter Press, 1985) [Hebrew], 21–125; Jean-Pierre Geuens, "Pornography and the Holocaust: The Last Transgression", *Film Criticism* (1995): 114–130.

Dunne designed the Nazi soldiers as silhouettes with graphic textures composed of excerpts from books that were banned and burned, such as *Death in the Afternoon* by Ernst Hemingway, *La Condition humaine* by Andre Malraux, and others.[44] The images of the Nazis drawn in this movie are not attractive, but the animation is spectacular. They look satanic but so powerful, fueled with the red and black of the flag. In their careful design, they echo the problem Friedlander addressed: they are the villains, but the viewers cannot take their eyes off them.

According to the directors, Waldmann did not understand that Haber's world had changed for personal reasons as well. In one scene, a dramatic-looking woman with dark hair, green eyes, and a sweeping gaze enters the department store. She buys a man's hat and leaves an advertisement for a "counter cabaret" on the counter. After the book-burning scene, Haber decides to go there, wandering down streets covered in red—symbolizing Nazism and the blood that will soon flow, and enters a theater through a dark alley. In the cabaret she sees the woman from the department store who plays Hitler on stage, mocking him as she rips a fake mustache off her face. They get closer. In Goldgewicht and Rozenthal's interpretation, from the outset, Haber was probably opposed to leaving with Waldmann because she had a lover—the woman from the cabaret. It is not made explicit in the movie or represented, but there is a hint the connection that develops between them is more than friendship. This impression begins with Haber's shocked reaction when she first sees her in the department store and continues with the intimate way they sit together.[45]

Half a world away, Waldmann is seen running happily to the post office and mailing an envelope. His voiceover announces the wonderful news that her entry papers have been approved. But he is unaware of what is happening. Haber is seen walking to the department store, passing Nazis at the door, their brown uniforms made of pages from books they previously burned. Their alien-like slanted eyes look at her viciously. Another Nazi is pulling on the store's sign (the Tietz department store was owned by Jews), preparing to remove it. Haber enters to find her department filled with Nazi women, their eyes ablaze like flames. The background shows the hate slogans sprayed on the store.

She leaves the department store holding her dismissal note, while the hate slogans fill the store. The scene contradicts Waldmann's words that are heard in the soundtrack, "About your dismissal, don't worry, my darling. It is better for you to relax and get everything in order so we can start building a new life together." She does not look as cheerful as he sounds, wandering as the

---

[44] Dunne, "A Thousand Kisses."
[45] Steir-Livny, "An Interview with Richard Goldgewicht."

streets of the city turn into pages from the books the Nazis burned—now it is not just people—it is all over, she is surrounded by it. While walking to the cabaret, she stops in fear as she sees two Nazis handcuffing her girlfriend and taking her away. The only thing left is the cabaret hat, abandoned on the pavement. Now she has nothing but Moses' letters. They are animated as part of the walls and door of her apartment in which she secludes herself.

At the end of the movie, Haber is seen standing with her baggage at the dock next to a ship. The woman narrator says: "On October 20 I arrived in beautiful Rio and soon we got married and built a life together in Brazil." She adds she never told him why she did not leave with him. Still pictures of the real couple and their family appear in the frame as though confirming this was a wise decision. The viewers are simply left with a little story about resourcefulness and love.

Overnight Stay

Sherer is an indie animator and illustrator and a 2009 graduate of the University of Southern California School of Cinematic Arts. *Overnight Stay* was her senior project. In 2013 she graduated from the Royal College of Art in London with a Master's in Animation.[46] Sherer's grandmother, Irene Steinberg (1923–2014), was originally from Soslovich near Krakow, Poland. After World War II, she moved to Munich. Sherer's mother, Rachela, was born there and immigrated to Israel when she married in her twenties. Sherer's mother spoke German with her, and every year they went back to visit Steinberg.

The movie is based on an interview Sherer conducted in German with Steinberg, who was then eighty-three, during one of these visits. She, her mother, and two sisters were in hiding in the Aryan side of Krakow and were trying to collect the money her father had stashed in different places in the city. One night Steinberg was returning to their hideout, but stopped when she saw suspicious people lurking outside. Steinberg turned around and instead sought shelter in the apartment of a Polish woman who was a black marketer and was known to take in people overnight. The Pole let her in, and in the middle of the cold night, she covered her with a warm blanket.

Steinberg's testimony to Sherer was long and included many grim incidents. Sherer didn't represent them. According to her, something about this little story reflects her approach to humanity: "There is something positive about this that can be expressed briefly, transferred in a few minutes. It

---

[46] "About," *Daniela Sherer*, https://bit.ly/2Z42PrY; Liat Steir-Livny, "An Interview with Daniela Sherer," June 20, 2019.

implicitly conveys the mood of a persecuted individual whose mind has completely changed as a young person about her place in the world. People are hiding, insecure, and in the midst of this, the question is whether one can still trust someone, because he or she is also a person." Sherer said she was interested in a universal message. She looked for insights that could be derived from the tragedy. The belief in goodness helped her to understand how Holocaust survivors could decide to go back to live in Germany after the Holocaust. "It is not just a Holocaust movie. It's a movie about the human condition."[47] These universal aspects may have prompted her to leave all the protagonists nameless in the movie, including herself and her grandmother.

Sherer claims that "as a student of the animation department, I was exposed to many sub-genres of this art form, including the animated documentary, which I found to be a fascinating way of interpreting reality through storytelling."[48] In *Overnight Stay* she used digital and classic animation hand-painted on pages and processed on a computer. She thought something about this manual work would give it a period feel that would be more authentic, better suited to the pre-digital era.

"Do you think that people by nature are good or bad?" Sherer asks Steinberg in a voiceover as the frame opens from black to a grey room with minimalistic artifacts: a bed, a dresser, a window, three pictures on the wall. A white-haired woman in a blue shirt and grey trousers that blend in with the colors of the room stands with her back to the viewers. She opens the window to look at the blue sky outside. Her face is seen in profile. She moves away from the window in silence; only her footsteps are heard. Opening the window to the outside hints at opening the window to her soul and to her past to answer this tough question. Memories stream from the domestic space. Steinberg is seen taking out a light blue blanket from a closet and spreading it on the bed. It is shown from various angles, to imply the importance of this item for her.

Dan Michman noted that there are two different starting points for dealing with the Holocaust: a Jewish approach that advocates the uniqueness of the Holocaust, and a universalist approach that examines it as a prism for general human attitudes and behaviors, psychological motivations, and social behavior. These two approaches have fueled debates in the Western world from the aftermath of World War II onwards. However, the relationship between these approaches is often complex and not binary.[49] Holocaust animated documentaries tend to marginalize the Jewishness of the victims. They depict

---

[47] Steir-Livny, "An Interview with Daniela Sherer."
[48] Dekel, "Overnight Stay."
[49] Michman, "Particularist and Universal Interpretations of the Holocaust," 223–243.

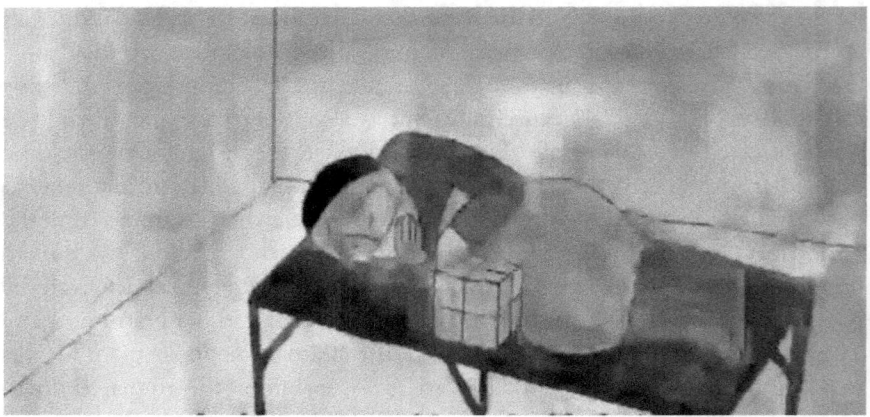

Figure 2.5 Overnight Stay *(Übernachtung, Daniela Sherer, 2009)*

stories of the Holocaust in which universal morality tales of Good, Evil, and what is in between are more prominent than the Jewish identity of the victims and survivors. Certainly, Israeli viewers recognize without being told explicitly that the victims are Jews. However, for viewers who are not Jews and are less familiar with the topic, the identity of the victims is vague. These movies focus more on universal themes such as the human spirit, cruelty, kindness, and survival.

In this movie, the word "Jew" is never uttered, and Steinberg's identity is represented through Jewish artifacts such as a match that lights the Sabbath candles. Nothing else in the animation or testimony explains the hunt for the Jews. She is drawn in black and white, as are all the other people, as she collects a parcel (the money her father hid all over the city), but as she narrates the core of her story that constitutes a ray of light within the darkness, the frame turns colorful. Steinberg is dressed in a long blue coat, her blond hair under a hat, walking down the empty streets of the city at night under curfew. The two people loitering outside her building are shown through her perspective to be a man and a woman, stylishly dressed, leaning on the wall, waiting. She knows they must not see a stranger entering the building ("I would have given away my mother and two sisters"). She realizes they are Polish snitchers.[50] The man and woman have no facial features to convey that they represent a wider phenomenon.

---

[50] See, for example Jan Grabovski, *Rescue for Money: Paid Helpers in Poland, 1939–1945* (Jerusalem: Yad Vashem, 2008); Jan Grabovski, *Hunt for the Jews: Betrayal and Murder in German-Occupied Poland* (Bloomington: Indiana University Press, 2013); Barbara Engelking, *Such a Beautiful Sunny Day: Jews Seeking Refuge in the Polish Countryside, 1942–1945* (Jerusalem: Yad Vashem, 2016).

Informers, or in Yiddish "Shmaltzuvnikim," constituted a threat to all the Jews in hiding on the "Aryan" side and to the Poles who hid them. They included members of the Polish police, extremist antisemitic organizations, Gestapo and Polish agents, the Kripo [Kriminalpolizei, the criminal investigation department], smugglers, criminals, members of Polish antisemitic fascist organizations, and ordinary people who wanted to be rewarded for their tipoffs. They informed the Nazi authorities about Jews in hiding. They often extorted Jews who were hiding, taking everything that they owned, thus causing these Jews to flee, and sometimes return to the ghettos where they met their death. Other times the snitchers turned in the Jews even after receiving exorbitant bribes.

The Żegota, a Polish underground organization composed of Jews and non-Jews which helped to save thousands of Jews, frequently appealed to Polish government representatives in exile to combat blackmailers and snitchers (for example, by threatening to call for the death penalty). These pamphlets were officially published several times in the underground press. In addition, the Żegota itself issued leaflets denouncing extortion and robbery and calling on the public to reach out to help Jews. Out of the several thousand death sentences demanded by the Polish underground against Nazi collaborators, only a few were handed down against blackmailers and informers.[51]

The complex relationship between Jews and Poles is represented in the movie through the contradiction between the snitchers, the Pole who hid Steinberg's family, and the Polish woman who sheltered Steinberg overnight. Even though research indicates that numerous Poles were indifferent, involved in their own problems, or actively helped to hunt down the Jews, extradite them or murder them,[52] the movie centers much more on the "good" Poles who helped the Jews.

When Steinberg gets to the Polish woman's building, her climb up the stairs is portrayed from Steinberg's perspective until she reaches the door, to highlight her fear. The viewers climb slowly with her, approaching the unknown. The animation focuses on Steinberg's young face in close-up and extreme close-up of her sad eyes as she tells the woman her cover story "of course I said I was Polish ... and I told her that my family is ... gone ... they

---

[51] Havi Dreifuss (Ben-Sasson), *Relations Between Jews and Poles during the Holocaust: The Jewish Perspective* (Jerusalem: Yad Vashem, 2017); Joseph Kremish, "Actions by the Council to Aid the Jews (Zagota Council) in Occupied Poland," *Yad Vashem*, https://bit.ly/3AsF0bb

[52] See, for example: Jan Tomasz Gross, *Neighbors: The Destruction of the Jewish Community in Jedwabne* (Princeton: Princeton University Press, 2001); Jan Tomasz Gross and Irena Grudzińska-Gross, *Golden Harvest* (New York: Oxford University Press, 2012); Grabowski, *Hunt for the Jews*; Engelking, *Such a Beautiful Sunny Day*.

were taken away to work in Germany and said I wanted to go to work in Germany too …." An extreme close-up on the woman's face expresses her suspicion: "I told her I didn't have any money and she said that if I cleaned her kitchen then I wouldn't have to pay her."

Steinberg describes the Pole's dirty house ("It was unbelievably dirty because the woman was dealing with chickens … they left their 'stuff' around—they didn't use the toilet"); the animation shows her cleaning up the incredible mess and getting a bed as promised. Throughout the scenes the woman's name remains unknown and her face and body are not seen in full. It is cut, and fragmented: sometimes only the upper part is seen; at others, only her mouth talking or her hand moving as she points towards the bed are depicted. This gives her a harsh profile. There is nothing sensitive or soft about her. She is very laconic, technical, and yet a savior. Steinberg is animated curled up on a bed in a fetal position in the middle of a gray cold empty room, her parcel near her, as she tries to keep herself warm in the unbearably cold Polish winter.

An Act of Kindness

The long cold night is made more poignant by animation showing the girl shivering, trying to fall asleep, holding her parcel tight, from several angles interspersed with fades to gray, to mark the passing of time. The door opens, and the black silhouette of the woman is shown. It is animated at first as a frightening shadow to explain how Steinberg felt when she heard the door opening, but the woman comes in to cover her with a fur blanket.

Sherer stated that when she made the movie, she knew the animation had to go beyond what the protagonist says,[53] especially in the scene when the Pole enters the room. The "camera," as it spins around exploring the space, unrealistically scans the fur blanket, enters it, and fills the frame with it, showing its seams, as though the camera is wrapped in it. Sherer wanted to highlight her grandmother's inner world, her feelings. The fur was cozy and warm, but it was more than that; it was a kind human act in an inhumane period.[54] The image of the teenager crying with gratitude morphs into the elderly grandmother telling the story and saying "that was so nice of her."

In a fast-forward to the present and the homely atmosphere of her grandmother's bedroom, the initial scene showing her light blue blanket now makes more sense. The blanket is kindness, humanity, warmth, and belief in

---

[53] Steir-Livny, "An Interview with Daniela Sherer."
[54] Ibid.

people, it is much more than a bedspread. When returning to the present, the "camera" goes out the window as the director tries to understand more about the world from this individual story. It shows silhouettes of people on the black and white street; some are white, some are black. "Do you think that people, by nature, are good or bad?" Sherer's initial question is heard again. "Every person can be good or bad. There are naturally good and bad people," says Steinberg, "from the wartime I can only remember the people who helped me, those were naturally the good things." This attitude dominates the movie. The snitchers are briefly mentioned, but the act of kindness is the center.

Lawrence Langer condemns people who focus on Holocaust-related "positive aspects" such as love stories during the Holocaust. He calls it "hopescape", suggesting that this is why there is a problem with Righteous Among the Nations stories. People cling to them.

> It's a comfortable subject to study [...] They deserve all the acclaim they receive [...] but if you focus on that you overlook the fact that on each righteous gentile, there were 10,000 unrighteous gentiles in occupied Europe who didn't help Jews, who betrayed Jews, who looted Jewish property etc. If you put the focus on the notion that there is a redemptive meaning to the Holocaust you dissect yourself from what actually happened. It creates a lot of mischief. It enables people to convince themselves that things were not so bad because there were people helping each other [...] you lose the reprehension of what really happened [...] everything you read about the Holocaust must be upsetting.[55]

Sherer says she grew up in a culture of intense Holocaust indoctrination in the educational system, which scared and frightened her. Unlike many high school students in Israel, she did not go on the official trip to the former concentration camps in Poland. It was too difficult for her. "It is a personal experience that I did not want to share with the people I studied with." In her eyes, the Holocaust experience was far more ambivalent and nuanced than what is described in the Israeli educational system. The Polish woman in the movie made a humanitarian gesture that points to more complex features than can be found in state narratives in Israel.[56] But since this focus on small acts of kindness constitutes the bulk of the representation, the Holocaust itself is marginalized.

---

[55] "The Afterdeath of the Holocaust."
[56] Steir-Livny, "An Interview with Daniela Sherer."

CHAPTER 3

Ghettos and Camps

This chapter explores movies that depict ghettos, concentration camps, labor camps, and extermination camps. It shows that the vast majority of directors refrain from representing horror even though they can capitalize on the ability of animation to represent the unfilmed past from the victims' point of view. Rather they make sure nothing is made too alarming or shocking. In so doing, they deprive viewers who do not have a background on the topic of a chance to really understand the true nature of these spaces. The movies analyzed in this chapter are *Silence, My Good Fortune in Auschwitz* (Reber Dosky, 2012), *The Dress* (Hadar Huber, 2013), *Nana* (Ali Kellner, Canada, 2017), *Another Planet* (Amir Yatziv, 2017), *Facing the Sea—The Story of Saul Oren (Horenfeld)* (Daniella Koffler, 2020); *Luck: The Story of Israel Kleinmann* (Anat Kosty, 2020). Comparative examples from the hybrid documentaries *Dear Fredy* (Rubi Gat, 2016) and *Kishon* (Eliav Lilty, 2017) will also be examined.

THERESIENSTADT IN *SILENCE* AND *DEAR FREDY*

Tanna Ross was born in Berlin in 1940. She was separated from her mother (who was sent to Auschwitz and murdered there) in 1942 and sent to Theresienstadt, where she was united with her grandmother. Thanks to her grandmother's resourcefulness and determination Ross was not designated for death. She and her grandmother were liberated from Theresienstadt when Ross was five years old, and were taken to Sweden where her great aunt and uncle lived. There she grew up, and was forbidden to ask questions about her mother's fate or talk about her own experiences. When she was twenty, she immigrated to the USA and only then began to seek out information about her past.[1]

In 1995, one of Ross's friends was involved in curating an exhibition which incorporated a number of paintings by children in the Theresienstadt ghetto. Seeing the pictures prompted Ross to break her long-held silence. She wrote a poem entitled *Through the Silence: a Concerto for Cello and Survivor*. Her friend Noa Ain composed music for the cello along with a recitation of the poem

---

[1] "Silence," *Yadin Productions*, https://bit.ly/3B1g8rr

by Ross. They performed the piece in New York and were invited to perform it in other venues, but Ross did not want to do so more than once. She then asked her friend, the director Orly Yadin, to produce a movie.[2] Yadin initially said no, considering that in an era of multiple Holocaust documentaries, she did not have the proper medium to portray Ross' story in a unique light:

> I was not interested in yet another interview with a survivor talking about events she experienced at a much younger age. So, I kept on saying no to the idea of making a movie. Tana, however, was persistent. She was determined to end her silence but didn't want to face an audience herself.[3]

The solution came from the choice of medium. When Art Spiegelman, the author of the graphic novel *Maus*, was asked why he chose comics, his answer was: "[I]t's the language I feel like I can speak best. Drawing or writing is like second languages […] Comics are the way I actually think. Even though it's a lot of work to get it expressed that way, I feel like I'm sort of coming from closer to my center." For him, as a comic artist, this was the most natural way to represent his subject manner.[4] Like him, Yadin noted that one day she realized she could approach Ross' story from a different angle, as the owner of an animated production company.

> At the time I had a production company called Halo Productions that specialized in animation movies. For more than 10 years I had produced a variety of animation movies, almost all based on true stories or topical subjects. I am not sure, therefore, why it took so long for the penny to drop. Eventually, it was a conversation I had with Sylvie Bringas, my partner at Halo, that led to a flash of inspiration and to a realization that if we could animate Tana's childhood experiences and enter the realm of imagination that way, the movie could work for us.[5]

Silence, the first ever Holocaust animated documentary, was written and produced in collaboration with Ross. It has won twenty-five international awards, was on the 2000's Oscars shortlist, was bought by the *Save the Children* organization, high schools in Stockholm screen it as part of their curriculum, and it appears in the permanent collection of the *MoMA*.[6]

In the movie, Ross discusses what she remembers about the Holocaust and her life in the aftermath of World War II in Sweden on the soundtrack. Yadin says:

---

[2] Ross, 1998 in Copley, "Modes of Representing the Holocaust."
[3] Yadin, "But Is It Documentary?"
[4] Copley, "Modes of Representing the Holocaust."
[5] Yadin, "But Is It Documentary?"
[6] Noa Ain, "Biography," https://bit.ly/39WMXd8; "The 2000 Oscar Shortlist," https://bit.ly/3irDDm7

> Tana came to me with a poem-like piece about her childhood [...] This text needed to be adapted to the medium of movies. It was beautiful in itself, but very long, wordy, and sentimental as a soundtrack. Animation can condense a remarkable amount of material with utmost fluidity and the movie had to be precisely 11 minutes long (a Channel 4 commission). Gradually Sylvie and I deconstructed the poem and stripped it from sentiment and from words that could be better expressed through images. One possibility was to interview Tana and then edit the interview to length, but we decided that with such a short movie and so much to say, the voiceover had to be scripted as tightly as the visuals were storyboarded.[7]

Ross's only visual documentation of her childhood was several letters and photographs that are integrated into *Silence*. Short scenes of live footage of Nazi Berlin are also included for historical contextualization. Still, otherwise, animation is used to portray Ross' subjective perspective and the way she remembers her past. Since Ross worked closely with Yadin, the process of creating the images became a way of working through the trauma for Ross and allowed her to engage in the representation of her own experiences. Yadin combined Ross' voiceover with cut-out and cel animation.[8]

Movies like *Silence* involve recalling traumatic experiences, both forgotten or repressed. Animation becomes a way to revisit the trauma.[9] *Silence* is one of the movies defined by Honess Roe as "evocative." This category of movie conveys subjective experiences, lends itself to the exploration of mental health issues, and deals with experiences that do not have visual manifestations and would be impossible to show in live action.[10] These movies let viewers discover what it is like to experience the world from the protagonists' perspective and empathize with them. Many scenes are non-mimetic; in other words, there is no visual link with reality or the illusion of a filmed image. Rather they are constructed to demonstrate that animation as a medium can express meaning through its aesthetics. In *Silence*, animation provides a creative solution to the absence of filmed material but draws viewers deep into Ross's mind.[11]

The first three minutes of the 11-minute movie deal with the Holocaust.[12] Ross' personal story is contextualized at the beginning of the movie with black and white footage of Nazi Germany. A photograph of a mother and

---

[7] Yadin, "But Is It a Documentary?".
[8] Skoller, "Introduction," 211; Walden, "Animation: Textural Difference."
[9] Skoller, "Introduction," 211.
[10] Honess Roe, *Animated Documentary*, 2.
[11] Honess Roe, *Animated Documentary*, 15, 23–27.
[12] The movie represents the Holocaust and attempts to deal with the trauma after World War II. The parts that deal with her life after 1945 were analyzed in Part II.

a baby is shown as Ross says that one day her mother disappeared, and she never saw her again, and "soon everyone else was gone."

The role of fictional elements in animated documentary has generated a number of debates. Formenti, for example, suggested that at least parts of these movies have recourse to the grammar and aesthetics of fiction moviemaking, but also adhere to animation's 'anarchi' possibilities where the laws of gravity can be defied, or an image can morph into another.[13] For instance, in *Silence*, the baby in the photo turns into an animated infant and then a skinny little child who is sucked into a black hole above the rooftops of Berlin. Then little Ross turns into a train carriage and from there the child's body continues to swirl and falls. She has no face, no clear identity. This image reflects her mental state, as a small child alone in the world with no one to cling to. The memories of her family are a blur.

Walden noted that in animation, sequences where the characters are highly detailed are considered to exhibit extreme fullness and density (in terms of their materiality). By contrast, sequences where characters have no facial features, or are merely an outline against a background with little detail, are considered to lack fullness, and thus have little density. Along with the concept of density, Walden introduced the notion of sketchedness, which refers to the type of line used in animation. A sequence using rough sketched outlines (suggesting a hand-drawn quality) of objects and characters is considered to exhibit sketchedness, whereas one with firm outlines (perhaps suggesting a nod towards more realistic styles of moviemaking) has less sketchedness. A lack of density and extreme sketchedness can suggest incompleteness in the image to the viewer because this contrasts starkly with the physiological role of vision in perceiving reality.[14]

Walden suggests that the black and white outline of Ross as a young girl who floats over the archival footage in the opening sequence signals detachment from the real. Ross' free-floating figure thus invites the viewers to detach themselves from objective notions of the past, as signified by the photographs on which she is superimposed and to focus on the process of memory instead. The animation deliberately lacks the depth or fullness that viewers associate with the natural world. This prompts the viewers to enter into the specific way Ross remembers that world and her interiority.[15]

There is a longstanding debate on the representation/distortion of archival Nazi scenes, and in particular the use of Nazi footage in Holocaust representations. Claude Lanzmann, in his seminal nine-hour movie *Shoah* (1985),

---

[13] Formenti, "The Sincerest Form of Docudrama," 107, 112.
[14] Walden, "Animation: Textural Difference."
[15] Walden, "Animation: Textural Difference."

Figure 3.1 Silence *(Silvie Bringas and Orly Yadin, 1998)*

refused to use archival images on the grounds that it was unethical. Lanzmann himself violated this rule in *The Last of the Unjust* (2014) and used several scenes from the Nazi propaganda 1944 movie *Theresienstadt: Ein Dokumentarmovie aus dem jüdischen Siedlungsgebiet (Terezin: A Documentary Movie from the Jewish Settlement Area)*, which was designed to deceive the Red Cross and the world and depict the "decent and tranquil life" of Jews in the ghetto. Lanzmann was also against the production of fiction movies about the Holocaust because in his view they trivialize it. He also disapproved of montages of archival images with voiceover commentary in documentary movies, arguing that they take the sources out of context and impose a certain interpretation on the spectator. Lanzmann believed that the solution was to collect present-day testimonies, although this record is also incomplete.[16] Historian Lucy Dawidowicz made it clear that Nazi footage is never "objective historical evidence." Since Nazi footage replicates the Nazi ideology and propaganda,[17] using it positions

---

[16] Schweitzer claims that paradoxically, since *Shoah* was filmed more than thirty years ago, and many of the interviewers are dead, the movie itself is archival material. See Ariel Schweitzer, "Archiv, bidyon, ta'amule: America bemilhama" [Archive, Fiction, Propaganda: America in War]. *Takriv*, n.d. https://bit.ly/2ZQ6GJJ

[17] For more on this infamous Nazi propaganda movie that provided a sugar-coated version of Theresienstadt, see for example: "The Three Screenings of a Secret Documentary: Theresienstadt Revised," *Ghetto Films and their Afterlife* (ed. Natascha Drubek); Special Double Issue of *Apparatus. Film, Media and Digital Cultures in Central and Eastern Europe* 2–3, https://bit.ly/39V87bo. There are numerous books and articles about Theresienstadt. See for example, A. G. Adler, *Theresienstadt 1941–1945: The Face of a Coerced Community* (Cambridge:

the spectator as a victimizer, which can potentially elicit a voyeuristic or sadistic response.[18] This stance was adopted by some and rejected by others. For example, Jean-Luc Godard argued that the representation of Nazi footage can be used if the cinema highlights its moviemaking methods and produces a type of cynical, deconstructive outlook on the material.[19]

Silence also takes a critical position towards archival footage. Yadin uses Nazi archival material but distorts it to create montages of archival images with voiceover commentary. The scenes of Nazi Berlin at the beginning of the movie create the context, but when representing Theresienstadt, she avoids using scenes from *Theresienstadt: Ein Dokumentarmovie aus dem jüdischen Siedlungsgebiet*. In addition, the Berlin scenes are very clearly digitally processed, thus undermining their "objectivity," and are also deliberately interrupted by sounds, noise, and music.[20]

The Memories of a Child

Over the years, research has dealt with the importance of oral history in general and the importance of Holocaust survivors' testimonies, but has also dwelled on its shortcomings. Research has examined issues of false memories and the ways the human memory alters reality, and in particular the many "intrusions" of personal memories, although witnesses are certain that what they remember and describe is what actually occurred. This issue becomes even more acute when dealing with testimonies of trauma survivors, and in particular individuals who underwent traumatic experiences when they were children.[21]

Silence could easily have been faced with these problematic aspects of memory, since it deals with the memories of a child who was five years old when she was liberated. Yadin avoids this hurdle, since she did not aim to document "what really happened" but rather Ross' subjective memory. In this cinematographic reality, what matters is what Ross remembers and how she looks back upon her past. Yadin explained this as follows:

Cambridge University Press, 2017); Eva Noack-Mosse, *Last Days of Theresienstadt* (Madison: University of Wisconsin Press, 2018); Anna Hájková, *The Last Ghetto: An Everyday History of Theresienstadt* (New York: Oxford University Press, 2020).

[18] Jessica Copley, "Modes of Representing the Holocaust: A Discussion of the Use of Animation in Art Spiegekman's *Maus* and Orly Yadin and Sylvie Bringas's *Silence*," *Opticon1826*, no. 9 (Autumn 2010): 9, https://bit.ly/2Y9dBN3

[19] Libby Saxton, "Shneihem sonim et Spielberg" [*They Both Hate Spielberg*], *Mita'am*, December 2007, 106–124.

[20] Jessica Copley, "Modes of Representing," 9.

[21] See a summary of the issues involved in the debate over the use and interpretation of oral history in Steir-Livny, *Remaking Holocaust Memory*, pp. 152–187.

> When wanting to represent a child's experience in the Holocaust as remembered 50 years later, how should it be conveyed? Through archival footage of children found by the Allies at the end of the war? Through symbolic effects of dark and light? By an interview with a 60-year-old woman and trying to imagine her as a little girl? Or ... by creating a child's world through animated images? ... As producers of animated movies, our hope was that telling the story through animation would enable us to recreate the little girl's point of view and help the audience to identify with the central character.[22]

According to cinema researcher Aaron Kerner, the victims' point of view can be created very accurately even in movies that are completely abstract. He mentions a short animation made by Amy Kravitz in 1998 entitled *The Trap*. This five-minute black lithographic crayon-on-paper animation movie is based on one sentence from Elie Wiesel's book *Souls on Fire*: "I try to imagine my grandfather in the train that carried him away." What Wiesel tried to imagine, Kravitz decided to animate using complete abstractions made up of shifting shades, shapes, and tones, an absence of realistic figures, and transitions from darkness to light, combined with train sounds. Kerner considered that this abstract rendering remained more faithful to the event than any documentary or narrative movie on the deportation by showing what deportation must have felt like from the victims' point of view. Thus, the spectators themselves are trapped in this world of shades and sounds, struggling to figure out what they are seeing and where they are going.[23]

Silence, however, does more than represent a child's perspective. The movie is narrated by the adult Ross, who talks about her past. The fact that it is the survivor herself who narrates the movie, and that the music was not chosen for aesthetic or cathartic purposes but was composed to a text Ross wrote, allows the point of view of the victim-survivor to dominate the representation.[24] This provides a triple perspective on subjective memory: the world is interpreted by a child (who is visualized), a grown-up (who is heard in the voiceover), and the director, who did not experience the Holocaust.

The cinematic techniques used to depict Theresienstadt suggest indirectly that a child's traumatic past cannot be remembered and visualized in a straightforward way.[25] "They sent me to Theresienstadt," Ross says as the child disappears and an old woman with a Star of David on her dress appears, "there I found my grandmother." In these scenes, one character fades into

---

[22] "Silence," Yadin Poductions; Aaron Kerner, *Film and the Holocaust* (London: Bloomsbury, 2001), 248.
[23] Ibid., 249.
[24] Copley, "Modes of Representing."
[25] Walden, "Animation: Textural Difference."

another and one scene into the next in a type of stream of consciousness: the grandmother holding a bowl of soup is replaced by a sad skinny cello player, who soon turns into a long line of skeletal figures painted at a distance in what resembles a tunnel. "My grandmother says that we must never be sent East because the East is death, Auschwitz and Birkenau," Ross's voiceover is heard as the animated figures are hurled onto a train, disappear into thin air, and are replaced by white smoke that fills the frame.

The Nazis are also represented in blurred animation. Two Nazi officers are animated lighting a cigarette. Their faces are not shown, and they are cued through the now conventionalized symbols of their uniform and the barking of dogs in the background. Tammy Bar Yosef showed how dogs and barking have become Holocaust icons, noting that historically, during the Eichmann trial (1961), whose sessions were filmed and broadcast worldwide on TV, the testimonies and the prosecution revealed how dogs were used to attack Jews during the Holocaust. Numerous Holocaust representations in various cultural fields in Western culture since then have included dogs (and especially German Shepherds). They epitomize a world of torture, humiliation, abuse, and murder.[26] In this case, the barking symbolizes the horrors but also replaces them.

Ross states what she knows about the way her grandmother saved her. A very dark classroom is shown. The skinny teacher is more of a silhouette than a person. The grandmother enters, bribes the teacher with potatoes, and runs away with Ross as the two Nazi officers approach the classroom. Her grandmother puts her in a laundry basket and covers her with a blanket. As Ross' voice recites numbers in German, the animation shows an *Akzia* (action) where the Nazi officers take children from the classroom and shove them into cattle carts waiting on the tracks. Her voice counting numbers is also visualized by a game of hopscotch, which has a double meaning since it also counts the children who board the train to their deaths one by one. Ross is not one of these numbers.

As the doors slam shut, the train metamorphoses into cockroaches swept away by a giant broom. This is the elderly Ross' and Yadin's interpretation of the dehumanization of the Jews by the Nazis and the way the Jews were perceived and represented as vermin that must be exterminated. The cockroaches turn into tiny black, skinny human figures scurrying desperately to escape. The movie avoids any other representations of Theresienstadt as it condenses the time frame. The little child hides under her grandmother's

---

[26] Tammy Bar-Yosef, "Nazis, Dogs and Collective Memory: The Impact of the Holocaust on a Negative Attitude Towards Dogs in Jewish Society in Israel," *Yalkut Moreshet* 99, no. 16, December (2018): 187–215.

dress: "I'm three, I'm four, I'm almost five years old," Ross says as her image in black is outlined next to a large suitcase, larger than the one she hid in. The next scenes already present the aftermath of the Holocaust (see Chapter 5).

Ruth Lingford, the animator, stated that they decided from the outset not to use frightening images and she had to evoke the pathos of Ross' situation without scenes of obvious horror.[27] Theresienstadt is not really shown. It is alluded to through a collection of symbols typical of other animated Holocaust documentaries about ghettos and concentration camps (barbed wire, dogs barking, black and white images, trains, smoke, Nazi figures). The symbols create a kind of shorthand for the atmosphere of a ghetto or a camp, which in fact is amorphous. If Ross had not mentioned it by name in her voiceover, it would not have been clear where she was.[28]

Dear Fredy

The hybrid *Dear Fredy* also presents a problematic depiction of Theresienstadt. The vast majority of Holocaust animated documentaries are short movies. In the last few decades, however, feature-length hybrid documentaries dealing with specific figures and events during the Holocaust combine live action interviews and scenes, still pictures, archival material, and animation to tell a story.

Fredy Hirsch (1916–1944) was a German-Jewish athlete and educator who worked with children and teens. After the Nazis invaded Czechoslovakia in March 1939, Jews were not allowed to go to school and were banned from public places. In Prague, they were only allowed to go to one playing field. Hirsch was hired to be the athletics director by the Jewish community in Prague and he turned it into a venue for athletics, singing, and activities which attracted children and their parents from all over the city. When Jews were deported to Theresienstadt they started a mutual aid society and made Hirsch its head. He was put in charge of the child and adolescent department, which supervised around 4,000 children. He organized and headed children's homes and gave children a place where they could learn, play, and be fed. Later, he and many other inmates were sent to Auschwitz (see Chapter 4). In an interview, director Gat explained why he chose to direct a movie about Hirsch:

> In 2011, I was working as a video editor and content editor on a movie called *The Terezin League*, which came out in 2012 about the soccer league in Theresienstadt ghetto. As part of my research for the movie, I visited various museums. One of them had a picture on the wall of a neatly combed guy

---

[27] Kerner, *Film and the Holocaust*.
[28] See Part II.

and the guide said it was Fredy Hirsch who was in charge of young people in Theresienstadt and added that he was gay. Since I am gay, his comment caught my attention [...] Slowly I discovered his story. I did not sleep much that night. I did not understand why even though his story is reminiscent of Janusz Korczak almost no one has heard of him. I suspected homophobia. I had the phone number of Peter Arben who was interviewed in the movie about the Terezin League. I interviewed him and after seeing the love and warmth, the sparkle in his eyes when he spoke about Fredy Hirsch, I realized I wanted to make a movie about him.[29]

Dear Fredy associates live action interviews with historians, people who knew Hirsch, or were his protégés over the years, still pictures, texts Hirsch wrote, scenes from the Nazi propaganda movie about Theresienstadt, and animation of the still pictures and animation. Gat explains that he was looking for a way to make a movie that would adhere to the stories but also chart new directions in Holocaust commemoration and would appeal to new audiences. His view was that most of the archival material about the Holocaust depicts the big picture of the war, the invasion, and the camps "whereas I tell a private, personal story. There are no filmed scenes of Fredy Hirsch and I wanted to try to connect the viewers emotionally to his personal life, to his intimate surroundings ... and also to his physical being."[30] The movie's main animator is Yael Ozsini (*Mind the Gap* Studio) and the animated scenes constitute a homage to two genres. The first is the graphic novel, where each frame tells a whole story on its own. The second is German Expressionism[31] (which was appropriate in terms of drama, melancholy, and period).

In the part of the movie that deals with Theresienstadt there are only a few animated scenes. For example, a woman survivor's voiceover describes how Hirsch's friends arranged for him to meet two of "the most beautiful and sexy" young women in Theresienstadt. As romantic languid music plays on the soundtrack, Hirsch is drawn from the back being taken by the hand of a beautiful young woman with a seductive look, in a slinky dress. A boy and two men sitting on a nearside bench observe the unfolding events. They look skinny and have a yellow badge on their coats. They do not seem depressed and are amused at the situation. There is no sense of claustrophobia. Apart from the "date" scene, there are only a few animated scenes of Fredy showing him sad in his office, optimistic and smiling in front of the children, or flirting with a young man in one of the cabarets.

---

[29] Liat Steir-Livny, "An Interview with Rubi Gat," January 20, 2020.
[30] Ibid.
[31] Experimental, multifaceted movement in late nineteenth and early twentieth century Germany whose credo was that art should express emotion, and challenge the era's social conservatism.

Most of the depiction of Theresienstadt is based on the Nazi propaganda movie and interviews with Hirsch's former students, who talk about how he impacted their lives. This combination creates a very positive representation of the ghetto. The movie relates the visit of representatives of the Red Cross to Theresienstadt in 1944 and how they were tricked into believing that it was a charming village from which Jews would not be deported. The historian Margalit Shlein then tells the viewers that prior to the visit, the elderly, the orphans and all those who did not correspond to the image the Nazis wanted to convey were deported from Theresienstadt: in total 17,503 people were sent to Birkenau. The deportation is illustrated by using Nazi footage of trains and Nazis on platforms with lists. However, this remains a very clean atrocity-free representation of a horrific event. Viewers who are unaware of the gas chambers at Birkenau may assume that these Jews were simply sent to another camp.

Cultural activity was widespread in Theresienstadt. People made enormous efforts to live, people fell in love, children went to school and engaged in athletics. Nevertheless, describing Theresienstadt mainly through a Nazi propaganda movie is a damaging choice, especially since there are no other scenes that depict hunger, despair, lack of hygiene, or death. This is exactly where animation could have filled the gap by representing the unfilmed. "Nothing good came out of the Holocaust, it was a genocide," says Historian Anna Hajkova, who has written about Theresienstadt.[32] The Theresienstadt in *Dear Fredy* looks like the place the Nazis wanted the world to believe it was: a nice place to be. Only later, when the movie tells the story of Auschwitz, does the atmosphere change (see Chapter 4).

BUDAPEST AND JOLSVA LABOR CAMP IN SLOVAKIA IN *KISHON*

Ephraim Kishon was one of the great satirists who shaped Israeli humor over the course of his fifty years of publications. Kishon wrote countless satirical columns, books, plays, and movies. His works have been translated into numerous languages and sold millions of copies all over the world. He was nominated twice for an Oscar for best director and won two Golden Globe Awards. Towards the age of seventy he invited journalist and writer friend Yaron London to his home in the Swiss town of Apenzel. For a week, London interviewed Kishon, and their conversations were published as Kishon's biography. Twelve years after his death, these interviews were used as the basis for a hybrid documentary entitled *Kishon*, which combines live

---

[32] Anna Hajkova – Theresienstadt, "A conversation on Anna Hajkova's 'The Last Ghetto: An Everyday History of Theresienstadt,'" UMass Amherst March 9, 2021.

action and animation. It was also broadcast as a three-part hybrid documentary series entitled *A. Kishon: His Name Goes Before Him.*

The producer Eric Bernstein and director Eliav Lilti filmed actor Shmuel Vilozny talking with London. Second-generation Vilozny mimics Kishon's heavy Hungarian accent in Hebrew. Then, a team of animators drew over the footage in a technique known as Rotoscoping, a type of mimetic animation in which the characters look very human, where the aim is to make the body movements and facial expressions as close to the pictured reality as possible. It visualizes the unfilmed past, namely his talks with London. The animation also inserts them into 1940s footage of Budapest, where they comment on Kishon's life during World War II. His whereabouts in the Jolsva labor camp are visualized by animating Kishon's paintings. The movie incorporates the animated scenes with live action interviews with his children, Nazi footage, still pictures, family photos, and 8mm movies from Kishon's private archive, Kishon's drawings, and non-mimetic animation when dealing with his imprisonment in the labor camp and his escape.

In *Kishon*, sixteen minutes out of the eighty-six-minute movie are devoted to his whereabouts during the Holocaust. In some scenes Kishon and London's animated images sit in an animated room talking, or they are shown talking in an animated train, while through the windows, black and white footage of World War II streams past. This technique emphasizes communing with the past in the present and the process of remembering.

The Nazis invaded Budapest in March 1944. During the months they occupied the country (until January 1945), Jews were persecuted, humiliated, and many were shot in cold blood and thrown into the Danube by the Nazis and the Hungarian gendarmes. These episodes are not shown. The only acts of humiliation Kishon discusses, as his and London's animated images are inserted into 1940s Budapest footage, are those in which Jews are herded along Rakoczi Street, their hands raised up in the air as dogs bark in the background against the hustle and bustle of the city.

The hybrid animation highlights the humiliation of all those who all of a sudden were marked as less than human. For example, journalist Yaron London, whose animated image interviews the animated Kishon, asks him: "When did you first sense that the Jews were no longer good Hungarians?" The movie moves to a video of 1940s Budapest with pleasant classical music in the background, and the voices of the city. Kishon describes a young woman he saw every day when he crossed the bridge over the Danube. "If these were normal times perhaps the smiles would have become a date in the park, but meanwhile the Germans had occupied Hungary." The images from the bridge change to footage of Nazi tanks entering Budapest and the crowd along the sides cheering. "The first thing they did was mark the Jews with an 8cm yellow Star of David." As Kishon continues to tell his story, their animated characters appear against the background of the video from the bridge. They are drawn in black and white, as though they are an integral part of the 1940s bridge. "So the next morning I walked over the bridge and the girl walked towards me. We smiled at one another. And then her smile froze and turned into profound loathing. I'll never forget it." Kishon's voice begins trembling. "She saw the yellow star and I …"—a yellow star appears on Kishon's overcoat, standing out in the black and white scenery—"I was no longer a young lad, but rather a miserable flea."

In other scenes, Kishon talks about his experiences in the Jolsva labor camp in Slovakia. Against the backdrop of a still picture of inmates being marched outside the city, Kishon comments that by the end of 1944 the Nazis took all the graduates of the Jewish high school of Budapest and "marched us to Slovakia." He says that they had to walk dozens of miles a day for two or three weeks, sleep on the pavement, and drink from puddles, which gave him typhus. These images are not animated and are only narrated against the stills of the inmates marching. Even when he says the officer decided that each tenth person would be executed and these people were taken over a hill and shot, this is not illustrated in any way (amorphic or otherwise) in animation. Rather, the frame trembles to the sound of the gunshots as though from the detonations.

Although in the camp Kishon must have seen horrible things, the animation does not portray them. Even though he calls it a "slaughterhouse" no slaughter is shown. The animation in the camp scenes is not mimetic as in Kishon and London's talks, as though the creators preferred to avoid any visualization that would be too close to reality. Instead, the creators used Kishon's own drawings, which were found in his daughter Renana's personal archive. In an interview, Lilti, the director, said that they did not know whether Kishon intended to draw episodes from the Nazi period (since not all the illustrations show direct connections to Nazism), but decided to use this material to tell his story through his own drawings. They then animated these drawings by inserting movement.[33] Lilti comments that in one of Kishon's war stories, he talked about the fact that his house was cut in half by a bomb and he was saved because he was sitting in a corner. Lilty said that in his mind the description evoked a cartoon: a bomb drops, cuts a house in two "and Bugs Bunny is saved," which is reflected in the cartoon-like way Lilty shows the camp and Kishon's escape story.[34]

---

[33] Liat Steir-Livny, "An Interview with Eliav Lilty," April 14, 2020.
[34] Ibid.

Lilty uses Kishon's drawings to evoke his fears. Kishon says that "In the labor camp they even let us rest on the Sabbath. Do you understand the absurdity of it? Like turning off the ovens in hell so as not to violate a work hours code." As he comments, the frame depicts dozens of small figures drawn in black against a yellowish background. They have no distinguishing physical features: just silhouettes strapped to large heavy weights. All of the weights have faces, and they look at the inmates who are forced to carry them with shifty sadistic looks as though pleased that they can cause suffering. "The camera" pans as the inmates struggle to walk forward, to show a giant monster laughing cruelly while lifting its foot to crush the inmates in their striped uniforms who are sleeping on a three-tiered bunk. However, the cartoonish way in which the drawings turn to animation gives the camp description a more entertaining feel, comparable to watching the bad guys stomp the good guys in cartoons. It is not frightening nor truly intimidating.

The animated scenes in the sequence that deals with the labor camp are intertwined with live action interviews with Kishon's children. In one of them, his daughter Renana says that when she tried to ask her father what happened in the labor camp, he always replied cynically with statements such as "so, the soda pop was flat [...] he'd make fun of me for asking until I stopped asking. He was too sarcastic. How much sarcasm can a kid take?" What Kishon did not say, the moviemakers could have easily retrieved by conducting historical research, but they chose not to, and left the camp life unexplained and unexplored to focus on his escape story.

"One Sabbath we were playing chess and I heard a whisper behind me, 'That's the wrong move.'" The scene depicts one of the skeletal figures tied to the round weights staggering across the chess board, dragging itself forward as an ugly brutal monster with the Nazi armband appears from behind. "I turned around and there was God himself: the regional military commander." They gaze at each other: the image of the inmate looks frightened as Kishon describes the conversation between them: "with a trembling voice I said: 'the move is based on Geza Maroczy's opening theory (he was the Hungarian champ at that time).'" As he talks, his image shrinks as the vicious commander snarls "'Wrong. According to his book you should move like this and this.'" An imaginary boxing ring appears behind them to make it clear that this is not a conversation but a mortal combat, which will determine the inmate's fate. "I said 'Sir, you may recall that at the end of his book there is a list of typos, and it says that the right move is bishop to B5." As he talks a skull appears, seemingly talking, seemingly shaking, symbolizing the thin hungry inmate who responds fearfully to the commander. The camera cuts to an interview with Kishon's son, who says that the commander immediately sent a boy to get the book, looked at it, realized

Kishon was right and took him to his office to become his assistant and his chess teacher.

His new position also meant more food. "I would eat whatever I could, and then hide the leftovers to take to Lisi and Laci (his friends)." The soundtrack is filled with chewing sounds and the figure of an inmate with a long nose, whose hair has grown again, who is gulping down the food in front of him as fast as possible. He is far different from the frail *Muselmann* he was before. He resembles antisemitic stereotypes that depict an ugly, big-nosed Jew, perhaps to symbolize the way the commander saw him, or perhaps because Kishon felt guilty of being privileged while others were starving.

In the office he overhears a conversation between officers saying that everyone in the camp is going to be exterminated. Using Kishon's illustrations, numerous Stars of David are drawn next to one another in coffin-like boxes. While the animation zooms out to reveal more and more of them, the soundtrack is composed of gunshots and dogs barking, evoking Kishon's fear of the future.

The escape story is also represented in a cartoonish way that neutralizes the terrifying atmosphere of the time. The head of a nice-looking young man pops out of a black hall, half smiling, rolling his eyes in an attempt at burlesque as Kishon describes a Slovak worker who was imprisoned in the camp and was part of the underground. Kishon gave him money to buy two train tickets for him and for his friend. The Slovak is animated looking pleased as bags with the dollar sign fall from the sky, accompanied by the clinking of coins.

Kishon commented that he looked at his past in the Holocaust as though it were a movie and indeed talks about it in the metaphoric mode of witnessing.[35] Lilty extends this notion to that of a graphic novel: an animated book from which Kishon seemingly reads out loud as the cartoon-like story unfolds to show paintings of figures blinking their eyes, a train, and funny-looking figures are animated as Kishon's voiceover tells how they stole the clothes, shoes, and IDs of Slovak workers, left the camp, and got on a train. He says that they were sure they would get caught when two Slovak workers who knew him from the camp boarded the train as well, and sat across from them but said nothing. Several times he says they were sure this was the end, but nothing in the visualization supports it, and adheres to the typical suspense of escape scenes in children's cartoons.

Lilty stated in an interview that there were several reasons why he chose not to show the horror of the Holocaust. The prime reason was that Kishon himself did not describe the horrors and did not draw them. Lilty in general

---

[35] Amir, *Bearing Witness*, 10–11.

does not believe in portraying graphic violence and has tried to avoid it in other projects as well, because he considers that the Holocaust cannot be represented. "To illustrate the un-illustratable is impossible. It is destined to fail. I cannot watch fiction movies about the Holocaust. It cheapens the trauma. I cannot believe anything I see. I would not have been able to visualize what happened there and others cannot either."[36] However, the result is that the representation of the camp is banalized, and even the scariest moments in the escape story are reduced to a cartoon plot.

KRAKOW GHETTO, PLASZOW, MAUTHAUSEN, AND MELK IN *LUCK: THE STORY OF ISRAEL KLEINMANN*

Israel Kleinman was born in Kielce, Poland. In 1942, he was separated from his family. During the next three years, he was moved to different ghettos and camps, from one hellish zone to another including the Krakow ghetto, the Plaszow concentration camp, Mauthausen, and Melk. His entire family perished in the Holocaust. At the end of the war, Israel took a boat to Argentina, where his aunt, his only surviving relative, was living. In 2012, Israel and his wife immigrated to Israel.

Luck: The Story of Israel Kleinmann is also part of the Yad Vashem series *Our Story*. Koffler, who oversaw the project, interviewed Kleinmann. She says he talked for hours and told horrific stories. None are included in the movie, since, as noted, Yad Vashem stipulated that the movie had to meet their criterion to be suitable for all ages.

The first scene of *Luck: The Story of Israel Kleinmann* shows Kleinmann as a prisoner in a striped uniform: this is the only clue to the fact that he is imprisoned in a camp, since the camp is not animated. Kleinmann is drawn alone against the background of an empty frame. There is nothing but him and his shadow. The extreme long shot that makes him small against the emptiness gives a feeling of profound loneliness, and that he is alone in the world. An actor's voice in the soundtrack quotes sentences from his testimony as though it were Kleinmann talking in the first person: "I'm standing here trying to understand how I reached this point," he says as barbed wire appears, one strand after the other, imprisoning him. He is drawn in medium shot; his face is serious and sad. Gazing unfocused at a blank spot in front of him as though he is in deep thought, he says he cannot believe he survived "all that. It is like a nightmare turned into reality and I lived in a horror movie." Similar to *Kishon*, Kleinmann's defense mechanism takes the form of an emotional dissociation from his biography, where he looks at the past

---

[36] Steir-Livny, "An Interview with Eliav Lilty."

Figure 3.2 Luck: The Story of Israel Kleinmann *(Anat Kosty, 2020)*

as though it happened to somebody else. The animation reflects this attitude as the "camera" zooms into the frame, sinks down, and turns into a movie projector—he asks: "Who cast me in this role? Who is the perverse screenwriter who wrote my life story up to now?"

Drawings that symbolize war (tanks, airplanes) appear alongside symbols of a ghetto (a brick wall) and sounds that indicate war (a siren) as he tells bits and pieces of his story. The animation is not mimetic, in that it chooses symbols over reality. The purple tint of the whole movie contributes to its lack of realism. The family decided to move to his grandfather's house in rural Poland and thus "bought" themselves a year of freedom. From a bird's eye view, train tracks enter the frame as the images of people, their backs bent, lay the trestles: "We were forced into hard labor, but we felt like free people." The sound of birds in the soundtrack reinforces this feeling. The frame keeps panning to mark the unfolding of time and stops when a group of people are drawn from the back. "At the end of the year the Germans decided to concentrate all the Jews in a remote place." They stand there, near the trees, and the frame funnels into a circle like at the end of silent movies. This is not the end of this movie but the end of an era, which Kleinmann recalls nostalgically despite the working conditions, because he and his family were together. From then on things would change. This change is signaled first of all by the animation.

As the frame opens again, the father and his children are drawn differently, like papercuts, in white. The camera focuses on the frightened faces of the children: "Father gave us a hug and told us 'Do your best to keep yourselves safe. You are still young. Maybe you will be lucky.'" A coin with the word "mazal" (luck in Hebrew) flips in the air and spins again and again. "Luck? Can you say I was lucky? I lived this tale of horror for four years. Each time in a different role."

But the horror is never shown. The names of the camps and ghettos where Kleinmann was sent are listed in the upper left-hand corner of the screen as he briefly states what he did there. The sentences are short, reveal almost nothing and the animation contributes to a neutral, horror-free atmosphere: "In Porokocim I was cast to shine the boots of Nazi officers without getting any food," he says as a white boot appears, a shoe brush shines the shoe, and then turns into an empty plate that falls down. As it morphs, a glow typical of fairy tales suffuses the screen. The drawings of several barracks appear with the words "Plaszow Camp, Poland" as he states that in Plaszow he was saved from certain death. "I became 'Israel Gutman' instead of 'Kleinmann' so they wouldn't realize the mistake." The word "Kleinmann" is written on the roof of the barracks and then the word "Gutman" replaces it. This information generates more questions than it answers, such as what certain death, what happened, and why he changed his name. The fact that the movie does not explain or elaborate and the "grocery list"-like narration prevents the viewers from understanding what he went through.

This representation continues as he mentions Mauthausen and Melk and then returns to the initial shots of the Liberation. After the war he looks for his family, but does not find anyone. Now he looks older, his hair has grown back, he has gained some weight, but the image is drawn as it was in the camp: he stands alone in the frame, shown from an extreme long shot, the colors are the same, no context, only loneliness. "I'm the only one who survived the war." The coin with the word "luck" reappears and fills the frame, giving the word a very questionable meaning. "I don't know if one can call it luck, but this is all I had."

YELLOW STAR HOUSES, HARD LABOR, AND A CAMP IN AUSTRIA IN *NANA*

In *Nana*, Ali Kellner tells the story of her grandmother, Holocaust survivor Vera Reiner. In 1944 Reiner was fifteen years old. In March 1944, when the Nazis entered Hungary, she was betrayed by a former boyfriend. He denounced her to the Nazis, and she was deported to a camp in Austria. She and the other women were liberated by the Red Army on January 13, 1945. Reiner returned to Budapest and was reunited with her family.

Kellner was born and raised in Montreal, Quebec. She enrolled in the movie animation program at Concordia University and later graduated from Sheridan College's Bachelor of Animation program. *Nana* was her thesis movie. It has been showcased internationally and officially selected in more than thirty festivals worldwide. *Nana* also received the bronze award at the

DOC LA movie festival and is screened on Air Canada international flights.[37] Kellner describes the background to the movie as follows:

> I grew up living only ten minutes away from my grandparents. I was and still am very close to my grandmother. Despite the fact that I moved to Toronto and left my family in Montreal, I would call my grandmother every week and talk to her while walking home from school. She is a huge part of my life and I also consider her a close friend [...] Growing up, I had known about my grandmother's story, but only pieces of it. She would tell me here and there different things about the war, but she would never really give the whole story. Not even her own son and daughter knew how she survived the Holocaust. I decided one day I would record her story, just to have it on tape. I felt it was important and hearing it in my grandmother's own voice would be special. Once we finished recording, I had twenty minutes worth of audio, and I knew right away I had to make this movie.[38]

Kellner feels that animation enables the director and viewers to "go anywhere your imagination goes."[39] The movie was made in 2D digital animation. She drew all the backgrounds in ink, scanned them into the computer, and then painted them digitally. She animated everything traditionally and on the computer, using Toon Boom Animation software and Wacom Cintiq.[40]

Kellner decided to make the movie in black and white for several reasons. Black and white was used as a homage to the many movies about the Holocaust. "The movie *Schindler's List*, of course, came to mind when I started this movie, and the fact that it is a black and white movie played a part in my development process," says Kellner. Black and white also suited the atmosphere ("everything in their world was dark and grey"). She added yellow to represent the yellow Jewish star Jews were forced to wear.[41]

In *Nana*, Kellner embraces rather than undermines her grandmother's words and perspectives. The representation follows the story. Reiner's voiceover is heard throughout the movie and is accompanied by Kellner's postmemory, i.e., the way she interprets and envisions her grandmother's stories.

Reiner describes everything from a distance. She does not break down or cry. She uses the same detached tone, and sometimes even giggles. Kellner comments that:

> My grandmother is very funny when she talks about her past in the war. She does not necessarily skip the hard parts, but she tells them in a way that is so

---

[37] Ali Kellner, "Nana."
[38] Liat Steir-Livny, "An Interview with Ali Kellner," October 15, 2019.
[39] Ibid.
[40] Ibid.
[41] Ibid.

distinctive. For instance, the camp she was in was liberated by the Russians. My grandmother said the Russians "weren't very nice" and they wanted to sexually assault the girls at the camp. My grandmother said that they did not choose her because she was "skinny and ugly", but really it was only because she had typhus fever. She even laughed when she said that. I think that my grandmother has a very dark but very good sense of humor.[42]

Budapest first appears from a bird's eye view as an impressive but grey and depressing city. Their house in Budapest "that was especially for Jews" has a yellow star on the lintel.[43] The animation does not show the inside of the house, so that the family's poverty and squalor are not shown. Reiner as a fifteen-year-old is drawn in gray against gray surroundings wearing a yellow Star of David on her chest. She says that the Nazis ordered the deportation of all women aged sixteen to forty-two. She was denounced by a jilted former boyfriend. The way Reiner and Kellner feel about him is manifested symbolically in the frames: Reiner is animated in the foreground standing proud and pretty. The boy's silhouette is small, thin, and dark in the background. Later when he approaches the Nazis, he is drawn as half their size, in a frame that attempts to ridicule him.

The animation of the Nazis is not realistic but intentionally ludicrous, in that Reiner chose to draw the Nazis with small heads:

> [...] because I didn't want to give them any more attention than I needed for their scenes. If I had to give them a real head, then I would have had to add features, and I did not want to humanize them. To me they were just all the same, distorted figures, with no real human features on their face. Some of it was aesthetics too, but I wanted to make them forgettable. They were not the stars of the movie.[44]

All the women were sent to a soccer field in Budapest prior to deportation. Reiner looks very small from behind the barbed wire. Much taller women standing next to her highlight how young Reiner was. The disparity is also used to evoke the fear of a teenager jettisoned into the unknown. Even though the movie is about Reiner when she was an adolescent, in the animation she is sometimes drawn as a teenager and at others as a little girl. Kellner explains:

> when she looks like a little girl, I wanted her to show her as innocent as possible. She was taken at the age of fifteen, which was one year younger

---

[42] Ibid.

[43] After the Nazis invaded Hungary, "yellow-star houses," around 1,950 buildings in Budapest, were requisitioned to house 220,000 Jews (from June 1944 until late November 1944). Their residents were obligated to wear the yellow star. See: Tim Cole, *Holocaust City: The Making of a Jewish Ghetto* (London and New York: Routledge, 2003).

[44] Liat Steir-Livny, "An Interview with Ali Kellner."

than the women who were deported. The fact that my grandmother was taken at age fifteen was unfair because she was underage. She was the youngest out of all of them, and she must have felt so small, like a little girl. I think switching from a young girl to a teenager throughout the movie makes you remember that a girl who is 15–16 years old is not that old, she was still a child and still had to find her way on her own without her mother.[45]

Reiner says that the Nazis forced the women to march 300 kilometers on foot. The long route is illustrated by a globe that highlights their path. A shovel digs soil from the globe as Reiner describes the forced labor: "to dig trenches against the Russian tanks." Her sense of humor and her optimistic view of the world are manifested as she giggles "luckily I had good shoes." The animation focuses on her dark shoes and then tilts up, imitating her point of view looking at the other women working, and the big trenches they are digging. There are no whips, shouts, or torture. On the contrary, Reiner and her friends are even drawn resting from time to time.

According to Reiner, when the Nazis learned that the Red Army was approaching, they took them to a train station and from there to a camp in Austria. She says that in the camp they had nothing and just sat there, waiting for the unknown. This horrible experience of hunger, cold, uncertainty is not pursued in either the narrative or the visuals. The camp is drawn in gray, as a large building, with a gate and a fence. The women are seen sitting, depressed, their heads bowed. Two Nazi guards are watching them but there is no physical or verbal contact between them. Reiner herself does not elaborate but simply makes short statements, and Kellner adheres to her narrative. Reiner mentions the physical state of the survivors: 90 per cent had typhoid fever. Of the 1,200 women sent to the camp originally, 300 came out alive, a short, dry statistic that is not backed by stories or images, thus becoming lost in the movie.

The minimization of atrocities is also manifested in a scene in which Reiner talks about how she and her girlfriend were saved from being raped, since the Nazis had already fled before the Russians showed up.[46] A tank enters the frame behind the sitting women. Reiner is seen climbing a hill with her friend and saying that she herself was skinny and ugly, but her friend was beautiful: "The Russians wanted to rape her." The shadow of a tank approaching spreads over their faces and then controls the frame as they lie curled up on the edge of the road. Reiner says she and her friend fled to the hills: "They [the Russians] didn't [didn't rape her]." This is the end of this

---

[45] Ibid.
[46] Ibid.

Figure 3.3 Nana *(Ali Kellner, Canada, 2017)*

story, which only alludes indirectly to the broader topic of sexual abuse of Jewish women during the Holocaust and in its aftermath.[47]

The following scenes describe Reiner's life after the Liberation and adhere to a redemptive memory mode. Reiner chuckles as she says she returned home wearing the same dress she wore when she was deported, and that it hung loose on her because she had lost so much weight. The train is drawn as though stopping in front of "the Jewish house." A woman comes out of the alley behind the house, Reiner looks at her with a tiny smile. It is her mother smiling at her: "All my family was OK. Unbelievable." They hug, and the movie ends.

AUSCHWITZ IN *THE DRESS, MY GOOD FORTUNE IN AUSCHWITZ, FACING THE SEA—THE STORY OF SAUL OREN (HORENFELD),* AND *ANOTHER PLANET*

Today, Auschwitz is a universally recognized symbol, and for many *the* symbol of World War II and the Holocaust. Over the years it has taken on a variety of meanings in the Western world including a symbol of Nazi brutality, a symbol of suffering and death of people from various countries and various nationalities, a symbol of human suffering, mass murder, genocide and crimes against humanity, a symbol of universal evil (especially for the Jews), and the main symbol of the Holocaust. Alongside representations of Auschwitz by its survivors,

---

[47] On this topic in research and its representation in one animated documentary, see Chapter 4.

numerous secondary witnesses to World War II have dealt with Auschwitz in a variety of cultural fields and artistic forms.[48] In 2005, the General Assembly of the United Nations designated January 27—the day Auschwitz-Birkenau was liberated—as "an annual International Day of Commemoration in memory of the victims of the Holocaust." Since the new millennium, animated documentaries about the Holocaust have also dealt with Auschwitz. The examples below highlight the difference between dealing with and representing.

The Dress was Hadar Huber's final project at the Department of Visual Communication of the WIZO academy of design in Haifa, Israel. Hadar says:

> In 1996, my grandmother Haya Huber (rest her soul) recorded her Holocaust testimony at Yad Vashem, but some pages were missing and that left me with some unanswered questions about that period in her life. The movie reflects this uncertainty after her death. Listening to her testimony revealed whole new sides of this woman, her family and her past. A whole heritage, which is also my past.[49]

Hadar only took a few vignettes from her grandmother's lengthy testimony, which were chosen because she could imagine them, unlike the other stories, which "remained flat." She deliberately left them partial and fragmented so viewers can imagine the rest but still be unsure, just as she was after listening to her grandmother's testimony.[50]

The Dress begins with the sound of the woman interviewer who provides the vital statistics: date (August 26, 1996), place (Haifa), interviewee (Haya Huber), her year of birth (1923), place of birth (Zelich, Czechoslovakia). As Haya's voice is heard over the black screen, the movie's title *The Dress* (*Simla* in Hebrew) appears. Hadar decided to add her grandmother's voice at the start of the movie to show that the movie is based on actual testimony.[51] The dissonance between the interviewer's emotionless enumeration of facts and the unexplained title draws attention and intrigues.

The movie does not aim to mimic reality. It starts with what appears to be papercuts or scenery for a puppet show. A young girl sits in an extreme long shot next to a tree. The weather changes, the sky turns blue, and birds appear

---

[48] See, for example: Marek Haltof, *Screening Auschwitz: Wanda Jakubowska's The Last Stage and the Politics of Commemoration* (Evanston: Northwestern University Press, 2018); Sue Vice, "British Representations of the Camps," *Holocaust Studies* 22, no. 2–3 (2016): 303–17; Marek Kucia, "The Meanings of Auschwitz in Poland, 1945 to the Present," *Holocaust Studies* 25, no. 3 (2019): 220–247; Anna Ouza, *In Search of Memory: The Legacy of Auschwitz in Photography and Art*, MA in Sustainable Heritage Management, Aarhus University. https://bit.ly/3iol4PY
[49] Huber, "The Dress."
[50] Liat Steir-Livny, "An Interview with Hadar Huber," September 26, 2019.
[51] Ibid.

Figure 3.4 The Dress *(Hadar Huber, 2013)*

in the sky as a silhouette of another girl on a swing appears. Haya states: "On Shavuot eve we were the last transport to Auschwitz." The streetlamp in the frame goes up in flames as a way to foreshadow the future, along with the crunch of footsteps on the gravel as Haya says they were ordered to walk to the train station far away.

According to Hadar, since her grandmother does not break down and cry but rather tells her story at an emotional distance, she decided to add drama and emotions through the visuals and sounds that create the atmosphere. For example, the frame focuses on the clock in the clock tower as its hands click forward. The clock manifests how mundane artifacts became a part of the tragedy: "The clock is something simple and trivial in day-to-day life but has a strong meaning in the Holocaust. Time signified the minutes, hours, days, years that had passed […]."[52]

Another cinematic technique she used to heighten drama and emotions was to insert words and sentences Hadar considered crucial from her grandmother's testimony into the frame.[53] For example, in a scene that represents a papercut of a train station, silhouettes of people walking are seen combined with isolated fragments from Haya's testimony such as "father said," "hold on and remember."

The transport is briefly represented in a non-mimetic way within the cattle car, from the victims' perspective. It is dark, the papercuts of trees are seen

---

[52] Ibid.
[53] Ibid.

slipping by as though through the window. "We traveled for two days and two nights." Auschwitz, as they first see it, is represented by a large, crooked gate. Hadar says she decided to make the gate unrealistic on purpose to avoid the infamous "Arbeit Macht Frei" inscription. Instead, it appears in wrought iron, which in her opinion gave it a culturally European look that highlights the contrast between the beauty of Europe on the outside and the horrific acts of its non-Jewish peoples. According to Hadar, the unrealistic gate is her response to the never-ending debate on how the Holocaust can be represented:

> In my opinion, we will never understand what was there so let me get wild with my imagination the way I want. The movie is a mix of the adult me and the child me. My grandmother passed away when I was fourteen years old. I did not ask her back then about her life. If I could be fourteen again and ask her, this is what I would have imagined. That is why the animation has something innocent and childish—a combination of the adult director and the girl I was.[54]

An extreme long shot of a woman's silhouette is seen behind a barbed wire. The electrified barbed wire fence shoots sparks as Haya's voice states "We stood outside naked, skinny" as the text "We stood outside naked" is seen above the barbed wire. This is Huber's attempt to convey that the laconic description is in fact an incomprehensible event, which in the end fails to make its point since Auschwitz is not represented. It is summarized through an unrealistic gate and the words "naked and skinny" which appear on the screen.

Hadar felt the need to produce a story with an encouraging message at the end, with something positive, since this is how Haya saw life. "Maybe if I did not have such a close emotional connection to the story, I could have dealt with the horrors. Because this story is so close to me, I preferred to focus on the positive, on the cheerier details."[55] The movie ends in what seems to be a forest, probably during a death march (not clarified at all in the movie). The silhouettes of Haya and her two sisters (Feigi and Rivka) are shown as Haya says that the only thing the Nazis threw at them was a dress. The movie ends with the word "dress" in the frame and the picture of a dress. Hadar chose this as the title because her grandmother's hobby was drawing fashion sketches. "For her, it was something positive. Therefore, the texture (in the movie) is positive, an iron with flowers and trees, and the word 'dress' that meant so much to her, written in big letters on a beautiful texture, form an optimistic ending."[56]

---

[54] Ibid.
[55] Ibid.
[56] Ibid.

This combination of the redemptive meaning of the ending and the decision to produce an incoherent narrative result in a fragmented, confusing movie where Auschwitz is not really represented. Researchers have argued that it is impossible to describe the events of the Holocaust as a coherent story with an orderly beginning, middle, and end since there will always be parts that are unclear and elusive, thus suggesting narratives that try to fully understand these historical events or give them meaning are bound to fail. Such stories bypass what cannot be represented, since the traumatic experience leaves lacunae that cannot be expressed.[57] Hadar's work confirms this claim but also deliberately disregards key aspects of the truth by focusing on personal symbolism and optimism.

My Good Fortune in Auschwitz

My Good Fortune in Auschwitz by Reber Dosky[58] is a hybrid documentary that combines live action interviews with comic book 3-D graphics to relate how Hajo Meyer (87) survived Auschwitz thanks to his good fortune, friendship, and solidarity. Meyer is interviewed in live-action scenes which are accompanied by blender animation that depicts several stories from his testimony. This twelve-minute movie was part of a project for the Dutch Movie Academy. Dosky drew more than 1,200 frames.

Historian Yehuda Bauer noted that Holocaust distortions are not always deliberately misleading. Cynically he notes:

> Auschwitz is an excellent example. There are many testimonies, all of which are quite reliable, about help that was offered in Auschwitz to individuals who survived and could tell the story. When you read all that, you think "what a wonderful place Auschwitz was to be in. Everyone was helping everyone else. There were wonderful people there and yes there were terrible Nazis, but they are really unimportant. What is important is the help." This is a total distortion. Auschwitz was hell. These truthful cases are a tiny minority in hell.[59]

---

[57] Dominic LaCapra, *Writing History, Writing Trauma* (Baltimore: Johns Hopkins University Press, 2000), 37–74; Saul Friedländer, "Trauma, Memory, and Transference," in Holocaust Remembrance: The Shapes of Memory, ed. Geoffrey Hartman (Oxford: Basil Blackwell, 1994), 252–264; Henry Greenspan, "Lives as Text: Symptoms as Modes of Recounting in the Life Histories of Holocaust Survivors," in Storied Lives: The Cultural Politics of Self-Understanding, ed. George C. Rosenwald and Richard L. Ochberg (New Haven: Yale University Press, 1992), 14–65; Milton E. Jucovy, "Telling the Holocaust Story: A Link between the Generations," Psychoanalytic Inquiry 5 (1985): 31–50.

[58] "My Good Fortune in Auschwitz," https://vimeo.com/142921363

[59] "Prof. Yehuda Bauer: The Distortion of Holocaust History," 5.5.20, *YouTube*, May 6, 2020, https://bit.ly/3mmAHZo

Figure 3.5   My Good Fortune in Auschwitz *(Reber Dosky, 2012)*

The title *My Good Fortune in Auschwitz* suggests that like the vast majority of Holocaust animated documentaries, it also focuses on redemptive narrative and on the "brighter sides" of the Holocaust. In the movie, the animated scenes in Auschwitz do not include the ineffable. The animation is in black and white, and Auschwitz is epitomized in the representation of the two friends Hajo and Jos, with their shaved heads and their striped uniforms with the Star of David, looking sad. The animation depicts scenes of them helping one another, leaning on each other physically and mentally as Meyer talks about specific incidents and the importance of friendship that helped them stay alive. The two friends are illustrated sharing food, walking together, pulling up a blanket in bed together, working together, finding something to sell for a piece of bread together, and looking into each other's eyes to give comfort without words. The message of the movie is that this togetherness is what kept them alive.

Auschwitz is depicted through fragmented Holocaust icons that are animated such as an arm being tattooed (and the sound of the electric needle), barbed wire (they walk past it with their heads bent), the infamous train track to the gate, the striped uniforms, a long shot of barracks, the sounds of dogs barking, and gunshots.

In other live-action scenes, Meyer is shown as he plays a sad melody on his violin, loading the scenes with a dark atmosphere. The combination of the music and the well-known Holocaust icons creates the feeling of watching a Holocaust movie, but in fact, nothing is seen: not the huge camp, nor the atrocities. When asked in the live action scenes about stealing food or goods in the camp, Meyer says that people stole from him but that he and Joe never stole, and this complex topic, which appears in many testimonies, ends there. The only time the lower body of an SS soldier is shown, it relates to "the good Nazi." He is drawn approaching Meyer, who sits powerless on the ground, his rifle dominating in the frame. Meyer says he was sure the Nazi was going to kill him, but he handed him bread instead. In the live interviews, Meyer talks about people whom he describes as the brainwashed group of Nazis who chose not to descend into dehumanization. As opposed to "the good Nazi" the movie also mentions "a bad Nazi" as Meir tells the story of a commander who wanted to order his dog to hunt the inmates, but the dog refused. As he tells the story, the animation zooms into an empty barrack from a dog's perspective. Barking and the sound of scrambling paws are heard in the soundtrack. The inmates, the dog, and the commander are not shown. The camera returns to Meyer looking preoccupied, shaking his head in disbelief at the commander, who could be so inhumane, and the animal that was more humane than he was. The viewers are left with a depiction of a world in which there are two types of Nazis: the good and the bad. It suggests that there was an equal number of both.

This obfuscated representation of Auschwitz is also true of *Yehudit*, which was analyzed in Chapter 1, where animation, as in all the other animated documentaries, could have been an opportunity to represent what was not filmed. It depicts one incident of despair and the abuse suffered by the women in the barracks, but adheres to a redemptive narrative and does not represent the unbelievable hardships of everyday life in Auschwitz at all. The camp is symbolized in the animation in the form of a single barracks set in snowy surroundings with a guard tower. The extreme long shots represent the barracks as isolated in a wide expanse of nothingness. Auschwitz is reduced to the notions of cold, despair, barbed wire, watch towers, and a cruel Nazi. Yehudit's bravery and resistance are astonishing, but the movie narrows down the atrocities of Auschwitz to an 'easy to digest' story.

Facing the Sea

Auschwitz and Sachsenhausen are also dealt with in *Facing the Sea* by Daniella Koffler. It tells the story of Saul Oren (Hornfeld), who was deported to Auschwitz with his younger brother in 1943, where they were imprisoned for several months. Oren was sure a horrific fate awaited them and convinced a German officer to take his brother's name off the transport list to Sachsenhausen. Oren and the rest of the group were sent to Sachsenhausen, where they became guinea pigs for Dr. Dohmen's medical experiments. He deliberately infected them with jaundice as part of his experiments on a

Figure 3.6 Facing the Sea—The Story of Saul Oren (Horenfeld) *(Daniella Koffler, 2020)*

vaccine for hepatitis. Despite undergoing these experiments, their conditions were better than those in Auschwitz, and Oren agonized over the decision to leave his brother there. He was sure he would never see him again, but after the war they were reunited in Israel.

Facing the Sea is another movie in the Yad Vashem series *Our Story*, which is aimed at producing Holocaust movies "for viewers of all ages."[60] Koffler states that when Yad Vashem approached her to direct an animated documentary of Oren's story, they asked her to conduct an in-depth interview with him:

> Choosing one story from a long interview is not straightforward. Many stories had to be left on the floor of the splicing room […] We asked him about 'The Group of 19' he was a part of a group selected in Auschwitz by a German officer and transferred to Sachsenhausen to be guinea pigs for Dr. Dohmen's medical experiments. Saul told many stories about his life before the Holocaust, the Holocaust, the Liberation and how he went to Paris and started over again, became an engineer and met his wife. At this point, after hours of interviewing, his wife, a charming woman intervened, saying "He was only ready to get married and start a family after he found his brother Moses.'" The documentary instinct in me was kindled. "I asked his wife what she meant. 'Ask him about Moses, ask,' his wife advised me. So, I asked."[61]

This is the story Koffler decided to focus on. Auschwitz is represented as snow, darkness, smoke, and flames. Two children, one a bit older, hanging onto a barbed wire fence look at the "camera." A train crosses the snowy

---

[60] Daniella Koffler, "The Holocaust Animation Journey—Part I: "Facing the Sea—The Story of Saul Oren," *Moonfash*, April 19, 2020, https://bit.ly/3D34Gfl

[61] Koffler, "The Holocaust Animation Journey."

landscape of the frame as Oren says he and his brother were sent from "the ghetto" to Auschwitz. The frame of the train is cold and dark, the ground is covered with snow, the trees are black and there are plumes of smoke coming out of the Auschwitz crematoria that dominate the upper third of the frame.

A group of children in dark colors is animated standing around a Nazi officer who is in yellow and orange as though he is the fire that is about to burn them. Oren explains how they were selected as a group. Behind him are amorphous red flames symbolizing their temporary reprieve from death. Oren talks about the hunger that eludes description, as a child is drawn on the Nazi's hand and then becomes paper-thin and disappears. "Seven weeks we were in Auschwitz, and we still didn't know why they took us from the group we came with." The animation zooms in on the crematoria with the smoke coming out. Parts are drawn like clouds and resemble the inmates' striped uniforms. "I was sure they were going to send us to the gas chambers."

Oren's time in Sachsenhausen is also discussed, but the camp is not really represented. At their arrival, Sachsenhausen is animated from his perspective from the cattle car's slats, showing parts of a gate with "Arbeit Macht Frei" on it. Stier noted that the infamous sign "Arbeit Macht Frei" is an iconization of the camp system, the threshold or crossing point into Hell. For many it "summarizes the perverted logic of Nazism's assault on European Jewry [...] it appears frequently in Western culture as the symbol par excellence of the Holocaust."[62] However, this icon and others are incomplete: "Railway cars recall deportations but do not engage roundups and mass shootings [...]; 'Arbeit Macht Frei' represents incarceration and irony but says nothing about starvation [...]."[63]

The partial representation continues as the camp is animated as big and almost empty, with a tree in the large open area and a large barracks isolated in its midst. Oren says they were sent to the camp hospital for experiments. He and the animation summarize it briefly without going into detail. Oren's voice is heard: "the doctor came—injections, blood tests, injections, blood tests" and the animation shows the image of a child's upper body, in a striped uniform, a doctor's hand (in a white coat) injecting him, the yellowish frame is then covered in red and then turns darker. "We were in the hospital, block 2, room 51, for two years." The frame fades to black and then returns to mark the passing of time. The war ends, as symbolized by airplanes flying over his head. Later scenes present his search for his brother and his happiness when he found him in Israel.

---

[62] Stier, *Holocaust Icons*, 68–99.
[63] Ibid., 185.

Another Planet

Another Planet is also an animated documentary that deals with Auschwitz, but differs since it is not meant to discuss a past unfilmed, rather to deal with the present and future of Auschwitz commemoration. It is a movie about the digital representations of Auschwitz. Director Yatziv presents five different models of the camp.[64]

Yatziv, a video artist and graduate of the Bezalel Academy of the Arts, says the idea for this movie came to him after he discovered the Auschwitz computer model created for the Stuttgart trial of an elderly Nazi:

> I met the prosecutor and he showed me the interactive simulation on the computer. In less than five minutes we found ourselves sitting like two kids, and he showed me the computer game he invented: how he makes rain in the model, how he changes the lighting, moves trains and changes the characters. This attempt to re-represent the memory of this place, in a very different and contemporary way interested me a lot. Suddenly I realized that it was very interesting to treat Auschwitz, which Google says is the most highly documented site of the 20th century—in a new way [...] There was something very refreshing about this encounter, and I went on to research it more thoroughly over the course of about a year.[65]

Yatziv deals with the representation of Auschwitz-Birkenau as an integral part of institutional Holocaust commemoration, but more broadly as a contemporary commemoration that would interest the younger generations.[66] During the movie, Yatziv both encourages and challenges his interviewees to highlight the complexity of representation in today's technological era. On the one hand, he supports the interviewees who believe in the necessity and the power of their models, and their closeness and resemblance to the real. On the other, he constantly undermines their perceptions through cinematic language such as the angles of animation, contradictions between sounds and voices, and the insertion of parts of interviews that should have been left out.

On September 4, 2003, three Israeli F-15 planes flew over Auschwitz, to symbolize the strength of Israel in the face of death. The pilots were

---

[64] Gila'd Reich, "A Model and an Anti-model in Holocaust Representation," *Takriv*, no date, [Hebrew], https://bit.ly/3F6GOcF

[65] Nirit Anderman, "'Another Planet': A Documentary About the Obsession to Build Auschwitz in 3D," *Haaretz*, February 1, 2017 [Hebrew], https://bit.ly/3utFiwt

[66] See, for example: Adi Perl, "A Virtual Reality Project Suggests Touring the Anne Frank House," *Geektime*, May 5, 2015, [Hebrew] https://bit.ly/3FcI2TA; Nirit Anderman, "Telling the Holocaust in Virtual Reality," *Haaretz*, August 8, 2017, [Hebrew] https://bit.ly/3om8PXO

second-generation Holocaust survivors. The Polish administration of the Auschwitz-Birkenau Museum protested what they considered to be an undue demonstration of power. Parts of the Israeli public were moved, but others expressed criticism. For example, Yehuda Bauer wrote:

> In a cemetery, one does not raise flags … In a cemetery, there are no coordinated shows between a flight and the ceremony on the ground, for there, that is theater. In a cemetery, one walks on tiptoes and cries … The flight over Auschwitz was a childish, extravagant act, quite unnecessary, that indicated only the shallowness of those who think that it helps preserve the memory of the Holocaust.[67]

In a certain sense, this flight was a simulation of what would have happened if there had been a Jewish state during the Holocaust and implied that the Israeli air force would have saved them. Thus, by focusing on a simulation of this flight, which is represented in animation, Yatziv deals with what Jean Baudrillard referred to as a simulacrum; namely, an imitation of an imitation that distances itself one step further from the real historical event. It is a representation that has no source because it is composed of a representation of the representation that preceded it. Culture, according to Baudrillard, becomes a series of unrelated imitations of reality, which in themselves do not refer to the historical source, but rather to a collection of images. The difference between the representative and the represented is eliminated and there is no real distinction between representation and its representation. This turns cultural discourse into movements between empty representations that have long forgotten what their source was.[68]

The movie begins with animated scenes of this simulacrum of the flight designed by three Israeli teens and returns to it several times during the movie, thus strengthening the feeling of the ineluctable journey to Auschwitz as the movie unfolds. The pilots are only heard communicating by radio and are not seen. The perspective is from the cockpit, forcing the viewers to see what the young Israelis simulating the flight saw as though they were the pilots. However, when the planes reach Auschwitz, Yatziv changes perspective and animates the planes from above Auschwitz as though the spectators were looking up, not letting the viewers feel they reached their destination. The subtext conveyed by this aesthetic choice is that digital simulation can never convey the truth, the real.

The second commemorative project is a forensic model of Auschwitz. While in Auschwitz, Yatziv's avatar stands facing the German who is in

---

[67] Yehuda Bauer, "The Shallowness of the Flight over Auschwitz," *Haaretz*, October 6, 2013 [Hebrew], https://bit.ly/3B0KvxX
[68] Jean Baudrillard, *Simulacra and Simulation*, Tel-Aviv: Resling, 2007.

charge of the model of the camp, which was built by the forensic department of the Bavarian Police specifically for the trial of a ninety-four-year-old German who was prosecuted for his part in the extermination in Auschwitz.[69] Yatziv's avatar interviews the German modelmaker's avatar within an animation of the model, again creating a simulacrum. "This man [the former Nazi] is a good actor and claims he suffers from loss of memory. We want to show that he actually used his acting skills to blur certain memories," explains the model maker. They wanted the model to reactivate his memory so that the prosecutors could confront him in court with locations in Auschwitz since he could not travel there given his ill health.[70]

The animation shows the former Nazi from behind looking at the barracks as if he is within the model. His face is not shown, he is breathing heavily, and he shrugs his shoulders to indicate he does not remember. His body movements suggest he is fabricating his memory loss so that the model in court is useless. The model maker states that from the guard tower, the guard could see the prisoners disembarking. However, the Auschwitz depicted in animation is contemporary Auschwitz with its tourist buses at the entrance. They are the ones coming in—not the prisoners. Hence the director questions not only the model, but the ability of the Auschwitz reconstruction to show "what really was."

The third commemorative digital project is the computer game *The Sonderkommando Revolt*, which elicited heated debate in 2010. Maxim Genis, an Israeli who was born in Ukraine, designed this game which simulates Auschwitz during the October 7, 1944, Sonderkommando revolt. The Sonderkommando ("the special squad") were prisoners in Auschwitz-Birkenau, most of them Jews, who were forced to work in the killing installations. For a long period, the Sonderkommando and the underground in Auschwitz-Birkenau planned to revolt, hiding gunpowder smuggled out by women prisoners who worked at the Weichsel-Union-Metallwerke munitions factory. On October 7, 1944, the Sonderkommando from crematorium IV managed to disable one crematorium and destroy another crematorium, attack over twenty SS men, and kill some, and several hundred of them managed to escape from the camp. The Nazis found and killed many of them and killed many others in reprisal.[71]

This act of rebellion is well-known, and Jewish organizations were shocked by the use of its memory for what they considered 'entertainment

---

[69] Jordan Adler, "Two TJFF Docs Deserve a Wider Audience," May 17, 2018, *CJN—The Canadian Jewish News*, https://bit.ly/3A2nxoS
[70] Anderman, "Another Planet."
[71] Gideon Grief, *We Wept Without Tears* (New Haven: Yale University Press, 2015).

purposes' in the form of a computer game. The Anti-Defamation League called it "horrific and inappropriate." Its spokesperson made it clear that "this rudimentary video game is an offensive portrayal of the Holocaust [...] With its unnecessarily gruesome and gratuitous graphics, it is a crude effort to depict Jewish resistance during this painful period which should never be trivialized."[72] In response, Genis decided not to release the game.[73]

The Sonderkommando Revolt is not the only computer game that deals with the Holocaust. Researchers have called attention to the role played by these games in strengthening the identity of neo-fascist and neo-Nazi groups. However, some scholars have suggested that computer games could perpetuate rather than undermine Holocaust memory. Studies have called for the need to rethink the rejection of Holocaust computer games by canonical memory institutions.[74] In *Another Planet*, Genis defends the game and its accuracy. "This sign is based on an original image, the same font, same sign," he says as the camera shows a gate with the word "Arbeit" on it. "I realize that many people would not see the difference if I made it with one font or another, but it is putting your soul into the game you create, and the people who play it sense it. It is not that I'm trying to please them, I'm creating the game for myself." Yatziv supports this naïve belief but also ridicules it.

Genis is not mentioned by name. He is not shown, and viewers only hear his voice. During the interview, he explains what motivated him to create the game and its unfortunate consequences for him. Genis in fact believes that in a former life he was a prisoner in Auschwitz, who worked in the gas chambers and then in a crematorium, as an assistant driver, and then a driver. "I said to myself I can create a world, even a real place, the ability to relive my previous life [...] instead of dying, I will escape, I will rebel, so I wanted

---

[72] Goel Beno, "Holocaust Video Game Pulled," *Ynetnews*, December 26, 2010, https://bit.ly/3zV5eCh; Stephen Arbib, "Holocaust Video Game Draws Criticism," *Ynetnews*, December 14, 2010, https://bit.ly/3mjWiBk

[73] Anderman, "Another Planet"; Beno, "Holocaust Video Game Pulled."

[74] For example, Wulf Kansteiner, "Digital Memory with and Beyond the Holocaust," *Playing the Holocaust—Part 1, Digital Holocaust Memory*, November 11, 2020, https://bit.ly/3ip8Hms; Kate Marrison, "Why Call of Duty: WWII Struggled to Show the Horrors of the Holocaust," *Playing the Holocaust—Part 1, Digital Holocaust Memory*, November 11, 2020, https://bit.ly/3ip8Hms; Tabea Widmann, "Responsibility at Play? Memory Cultures and Digital Games," *Playing the Holocaust—Part 1, Digital Holocaust Memory*, https://bit.ly/3ip8Hms; Pieter Van den Heede, "Playing the Holocaust: Online Roundtable Panel Contribution: Towards Productive Moments of Historical Revelation," *Playing the Holocaust—Part 1, Digital Holocaust Memory* https://bit.ly/3ip8Hms; Victoria Grace Walden, "A Potted History of Games," *Playing the Holocaust—Part 1, Digital Holocaust Memory*, November 11, 2020, https://bit.ly/3ip8Hms. Also see Oded Yaron, "Is it Time for Holocaust Games?," *Haaretz*, October 3, 2013 [Hebrew], https://bit.ly/3mdrjqR

to start there and change the past, change the end of my previous life." As he talks, the game is shown and takes over the movie, showing the gas chambers from within, dead bodies, barking dogs, and forced labor. The images are completely pixelized, as in old-fashioned 1980s games, and electronic Pac-Man-like music plays in the background so that it completely neutralizes the horrors. In an interview, Yatziv commented that:

> It's a pixel game, and these huge pixels are the most deconstructed images in the digital age [...] this is why he [Genis] thought that creating images of the Holocaust by using these kinds of visuals could not hurt. But it shows the harshest things, all the horrors—bodies, blood, fire, skeletons—and so it is a tough game, it's a Holocaust pornography.[75]

Presumably, this is why he pixelized it in *Another Planet*.

The computer characters are seen for long seconds running around in the camp, mostly in the direction of the viewers as though attacking them. The soundtrack is an Israeli song which has nothing to do with this theme: "Trains In The Mountains" sung by historian Gideon Grief, who specializes in Auschwitz and is also interviewed in the movie about one of the other models (in his youth he was a singer). The dissonance between this song with its cowboy Western tune and the visuals completely deconstructs any aspect of truth Genis aimed for or thought he was creating in the video game. It deliberately cheapens the Holocaust by eliminating any serious aspect of the game.

When Yatziv interviewed Genis he admitted that "It's just a game, because I've never been to Auschwitz." Yatziv noted that "This sentence captivated me, because the man worked four years making this game, but did not go there at all. The place itself does not interest him. In my opinion, this is the movie's metaphor, that there is an obsession with something that in itself is no longer important."[76]

The fourth project is the Polish 3D Model of Auschwitz. In this part of the movie, the anonymous Polish creator of the Auschwitz 3D model describes how he came across the Google program "Sketch Up," began to sketch, and created various models of Auschwitz-Birkenau and other camps. His avatar is shown wearing 3D glasses standing inside the model, on virtual snow of his own creation. The viewer's perspective blends with his, as the frame imitates what he sees from his headset: the entrance to a concentration camp in the snow. He says he wanted museums to purchase it to let visitors walk in the camp in 3D: "The contrast between now and then is huge and if we add some elements of atmosphere like music, weather and actors it will be believable."

---

[75] Anderman, "Another Planet."
[76] Anderman Nirit, "Another Planet."

Yatziv cuts between the image of his avatar being interviewed and what he sees through the glasses. However, here again, Yatziv undermines the perception that representation can replace the real as it shows the digital gate sinking into the snow, with no camp behind it, as the Pole admits there is a spelling mistake in the sign.

The fifth model was created by historian Gideon Grief and architect Peter Sieber. Their avatars sit next to each other looking at Auschwitz and introducing themselves. Unlike the flight simulators and the German in charge of the forensic model, they have names and titles. Grief talks about his work over the last forty years dealing with Auschwitz as a historian, while Siebers discusses his fifteen-year engagement with the topic: he visited the Auschwitz Museum thirty to forty times to take measurements in order to make an accurate model.

Siebers and Grief's avatars are seen measuring Auschwitz while within the model they built. Grief is thrilled with the model and repeatedly stresses the accuracy of the project ("It is 100% [accurate], everything was measured on-site"). But as he comments, a crew appears and approaches the two. In an interview, Yatziv said that as a director he let himself add elements to the model: "My characters and theirs, and details like flowers, birds and more."[77] These additions undermine Grief's declarations of historical accuracy. Another way for Yatziv to challenge Grief's belief in the accurate reproduction of the real has to do with the use of colors. Grief talks at length about the importance of a model in color: "Auschwitz was not black and white [...] the sky was blue, the soil was brown, the trees were green. There was the color." Yatziv, however, shows all the scenes related to them and their model in black and white.

But Yatziv also accepts parts of Grief's perceptions about Auschwitz. The movie's title is "another planet," a term coined by Auschwitz survivor Yehiel Dinur (K. Tzetnik) and the way he described Auschwitz during his testimony at the Eichmann trial (1961). Even though K. Tzetnik later claimed he was wrong, and Auschwitz was not another planet, but man-made hell on Earth, Greif sticks with the initial idiom: "It was truly another planet like K. Tzetnik said," he comments. "I think he was right. It was indeed on earth being operated by human beings, but it wasn't a normal place by any means ... an orchestra and medical experiments on dwarfs ... like some insane asylum, but also a place with some sense of normality."[78]

By contrasting and simultaneously accepting Grief's perceptions, Yatziv places himself within a cinematic tradition and a theoretical debate on the

---

[77] Ibid.
[78] Reich, "A Model and an Anti-model."

Figure 3.7   Another Planet *(Amir Yatziv, 2017)*

possibilities of representing the Holocaust, what can and cannot be shown, and the eventuality, as the philosopher and art philosopher Georges Didi-Huberman suggested, of working with the image through its limitations.[79] To stress the disparity between representation and truth, Yatziv chooses to end the movie with "a lesson" he teaches Grief that he uses to educate the viewers. Grief's avatar looks nothing like him. It is the creation and the interpretation of the director. At the end of the movie the animated avatar looks at itself in a mirror as Grief's voice is heard: "This is not me, not at all, oh my ... can't you show me the way I look? It's not me. Well ... do what you want, oh no ... it's awful, what does it do artistically or cinematically?" The movie ends with this question. This scene makes the point that representation is an interpretive act and that connections between the image and the real are problematic.[80] Representation is never the reality or a mirror of reality, so imitations of reality call for extra caution. Clearly, an Auschwitz without horrors is far from reality.

Thus, the movies analyzed in this chapter supposedly represent ghettos and camps, but actually drain the "Holocaust" of its atrocities. They leave the viewers with stories that do not even begin to explain what happened. It is understood that these were bad times, families were separated, there was cold, hunger, loneliness, people were afraid of getting killed, and some even died, but nothing more. The movies spare the viewers actual "hard to

---

[79] Ibid.
[80] Ibid.

swallow" details. Apart from the Yad Vashem project, in which the directors were asked to make movies suitable for family viewing, the other directors chose this approach for their own reasons. They all had the best intentions, but the result is a series of redemptive movies which sugar-coat the unspeakable. The few who chose to enter the lion's den and deal with the atrocities are discussed in the next chapter.

CHAPTER 4

The Exceptional—Representing the Horrors

Alongside movies that marginalize the atrocities or create aseptic representations of the Holocaust, a handful of movies have taken advantage of the power of animated documentary to deal with the horrific events without recourse to graphic or pornographic violence. The movies analyzed in this chapter are *Noch Am Leben* (*Still Alive*, Anita Lester, 2017), *7 Minutes in the Warsaw Ghetto*, *Kol Nidrei* (Shira Meishar, 2020) and *Eva Kor: The Holocaust Survivor who Forgave the Nazis* (Anna Humphries and Amelia Chiew, 2020). This chapter also discusses segments of the feature-length hybrid documentaries *Karski and the Lords of Humanity* (Slawomir Grünberg, Poland, 2015) and *Dear Fredy* (Rubi Gat, 2016).

MASS MURDER BY SHOOTING INTO PITS AND RAPE IN *NOCH AM LEBEN*[1]

Lester (born May 5, 1986) is a Melbourne-based multidisciplinary artist who graduated from RMIT in illustration and animation. She has published children's books and did the illustrations for a Holocaust book for preteens.[2] *Noch Am Leben* was awarded multiple prizes and has been screened in over twenty festivals, including Oscar-contending festivals in the US, UK, and EU.[3]

Victoria Aarons and Alan L. Berger argue that for members of the third generation, the Holocaust stories that they overhear and seek out become a magnet for identification, and a complicated projection of their own fears and desires. The excavation of the past also fills a void in the individual, an emptiness that yearns to be satisfied through identification with the other, the object of both desire and longing, but also dread and fear. They suggest that in third generation literature, the memoirist is not only a time traveler

---

[1] A. D. Lester, "Noch Am Leben (Still Alive)," Vimeo, https://vimeo.com/263945041
[2] Liat Steir-Livny, "An Interview with Anita Lester," November 3, 2019.
[3] "Salute Your Shorts 2018—Still Alive/Noch Am Leben," *We Are Moving Stories*, https://bit.ly/3FfbcSk; "Täglich einen Kurzen: Noch Am Leben (Still Alive)," INDAC, January 30, 2019, https://bit.ly/3a0BzNh

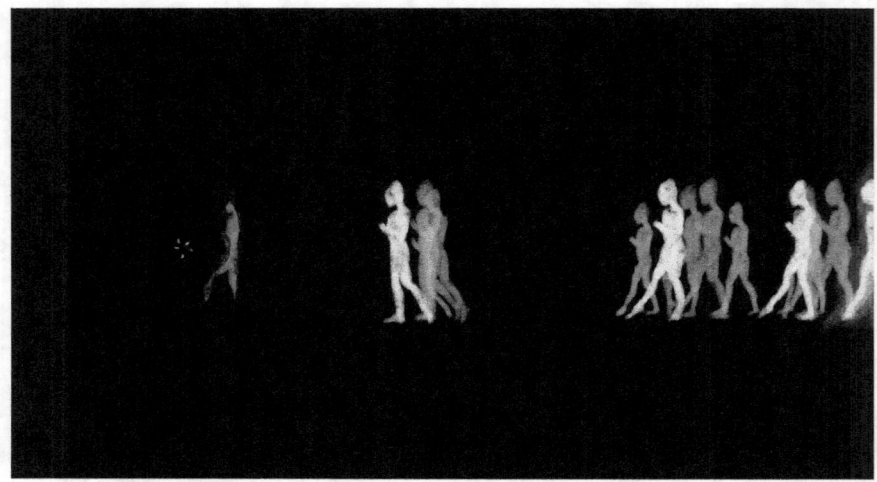

Figure 4.1 Noch Am Leben [Still Alive] *(Anita Lester, 2017)*

but also shares the physical space with the victims in a sharply defined moment.[4]

From its haunting beginning to the very end, *Noch Am Leben* reflects this definition. It tells the story of Lester's recollections of her great aunt Eva Nagler, a Holocaust survivor. Lester knew Nagler her entire life and would meet her three to four times a year. "When I saw her for the last time, she was heavily medicated, became psychotic and finally was committed to an asylum."[5] *Noch Am Leben* deals with Eva's whereabouts during the Holocaust, and with the transmission of the psychological repercussions of the Holocaust from one generation to the next (see Chapter 7).

Unlike the other movies analyzed in this book, this movie is not an animated documentary narrated in the first person by the survivor. Rather, Lester tells Nagler's story from her own perspective and talks a few times in the first person as Nagler. She does not downplay the horrors, but rather faces the atrocities Nagler experienced directly: she was raped multiple times, and watched her sister being shot to death during one of the death marches on the Baltic Sea. Nagler was shot as well, but her sister lay on top of her, thus saving her life. She got out of the pit alive and bore this pain her whole life.

Nagler gave three testimonies, two of which are audio (one for Yad Vashem and the other recorded by an Australian historian) and one video

---

[4] Victoria Aarons and Alan L. Berger, *Third-Generation Holocaust Representation: Trauma, History, and Memory* (Northwestern University Press, 2017), 3–39.

[5] Steir-Livny, "An Interview with Lester Lester."

for the Spielberg project. She also wrote a book entitled *A Massacre on the Baltic*, twenty years before she passed away.[6] Lester based her movie on these testimonies.

Researchers have discussed the importance of oral testimonies[7] and the way they enable a better understanding of the psychological impact of historical events. They cast a different light on historical processes since subjectivity is as much the business of history as are the more visible facts. It is acknowledged today that "erroneous" statements are still psychologically "true."[8]

Aside from these positive qualities of testimonies, and the concomitant acknowledgment of the problematic and nonobjective nature of written documents,[9] studies have also examined the difficult issue of false memories and the ways the human memory alters reality. Works have dealt with the many "intrusions" of personal memories, although witnesses are certain that what was described actually happened.[10] Studies have suggested that memory is better understood as a state of continual becoming, is related to the present more than the past, and should be seen as a creative, networked process rather than as a simple transmission of historical data. Memory refers to people's experience of the past in the present. It is incomplete, inaccurate, messy, and subjective.[11]

Traumatic memory is even more complex. Research has stressed the importance of survivors' testimonies as well as the issues associated with them. The gray zones associated with oral history in general are compounded in Holocaust survivors' testimonies given their complexity, their integration with collective memory (often survivors are affected by what they have read or watched about the Holocaust over the years),[12] personal growth and change, and overlap with imagination and false memories.[13] The memories that lie within people are not carved in stone; not only do they tend to fade as the years go by, but they often change, or can be bolstered by incorporating extraneous features.[14] Survivors' testimony integrates the factual

---

[6] Eva Nagler, *Massacre on the Baltic*, 1995.
[7] Dan Sipe, "The Future of Oral History and Moving Images," in *The Oral History Reader*, 2nd ed., eds. Robert Perks and Alistair Thomson (London: Routledge, 2006), 379–388, esp. 382.
[8] Alessandro Portelli, "What Makes Oral History Different," in *The Oral History Reader*, ed. Robert Perks and Alistair Thomson (London: Routledge, 1998), 63–74, esp. 67–68.
[9] Hayden White, "The Historical Text as Literary Artifact," in *Tropics of Discourse: Essays in Cultural Criticism*, ed. Hayden White (Baltimore: Johns Hopkins University Press, 1978).
[10] "Az'akat emet" [A True Alarm], *Dyukan*, July 14, 2017, 36–40 [Hebrew].
[11] Walden, "Animation and Memory."
[12] Shandler, *Holocaust Memory in the Digital Age*, 43–86.
[13] James E. Young, *Writing and Rewriting the Holocaust: Narrative and the Consequence of Interpretation* (Bloomington: Indiana University Press, 1988), 171.
[14] Primo Levi, *Hashokim vehanitzolim* [*The Drowned and the Saved*] (Tel Aviv: Am Oved, 1991).

truths of the historians' narratives and the contingent truths of the victims' memory.¹⁵ In addition, there are differences between professional narrators and spontaneous narrators: Jeffry Shandler noted that some survivors are in fact telling their story for the first time whereas others have related their life stories repeatedly (thus enabling them to hone their narratives).¹⁶ Yohai Ataria remarked that a story told over and over again becomes automatic and in many ways loses some of its authenticity. It ceases to be connected to the event itself and becomes a kind of recitation. In an era where survivors feel obligated to document their stories, this documentation may distance their memories from the spontaneous story connected to their initial experience.¹⁷ Thus survivors' memory, despite its many virtues, can be misleading.

Lester noted the discrepancies between Eva's four testimonies:

> Eva says she saw her mother being shot but it is not clear. Her mother was probably taken away. I embrace her story even though she may be wrong. She also got the numbers of the women on the death march wrong. We believed there were 50 thousand people in the death march and the numbers went down in each of her testimonies. There were other discrepancies—the moment of the shooting. It is hard to know what is true and what is not. It was mind blowing for me to understand that there are discrepancies in her testimony. It was difficult to think I can write about that particular thing when I had no solid facts. So I took the parts I knew were true and told it from my perspective.¹⁸

Animation has long been interested in depicting things which are impossible to represent in live action, and the embodied, fluid experience of memory is certainly something that a photograph or live-action movie cannot satisfactorily capture. Animation's ability to emphasize subjective reality enables it to explore people's emotional responses to historical events rather than show them photographically. Animation helps draw attention to an individual's subjective response to events, rather than claiming to represent official or purportedly objective accounts of an event.¹⁹

Animation was not Lester's first choice. She was awarded a grant to make a documentary about her great aunt, went to Israel to do the research, and thought it would be a real-life short documentary. She also did research for the documentary in London where she was living, but one incident changed

---

[15] James E. Young, "Toward a Received History of the Holocaust," *History and Theory* 36, no. 4 (1997): 37–39.

[16] Shandler, *Holocaust Memory in the Digital Age*, 43–86.

[17] Yohay Ataria, "Mot haed be'idan haedut" [The Death of the Witness in the Testimony era"], *Ma'arag*, 6, 2015: 177–214; Walden, "Animation and Memory."

[18] Steir-Livny, "An Interview with Anita Lester."

[19] Walden, "Animation and Memory."

her initial intentions: "I woke up one night with the image of women walking in a long line (which finally found its place in the movie). I woke up and animated it for six hours. When I came to in the morning, I wrote a spoken word text and began animating it. I closed my eyes and I tried to feel it."[20] According to Lester "the imagery of the Holocaust is so profound [...] There is a real fatigue with Holocaust imagery, and I wanted to use another iconography [...] The animation is abstract because it is based on feelings that I drew from Eva's historical experiences and testimonies."[21] Thus the movie is not realistic and the animation is not mimetic. There are no "real" figures in the movie; rather, the viewers see vignettes of her perspective that are distorted to deal with and represent muffled memories.

Unlike other animated documentaries that adhere to the metaphoric or the metonymic mode of witnessing, Lester's narration corresponds to what Amir called the psychotic or excessive mode of witnessing. Amir argued that this mode presents articulated and well-developed language, with multiple rhetorical devices, but is traversed by a language that undermines the connections, voids the events and does not allow the subject to undergo transformation. In this mode, the language collapses into rhetoric. The linguistic excessiveness does not create a vital link with the trauma. It fixates the traumatic object in the center while pushing the reflective subject to the margins.[22]

In *Noch Am Leben* the survivor does not tell her story; rather her relative deliberately decided to represent her great aunt's biography through this type of narrative. Lester is what Laub called "a witness to the witness." Her enormous identification with Nagler's pain results in an eloquent epic poem recited by Lester in a dramatic voiceover.

The excessive mode of witnessing is not only conveyed through language but also through the red, black and white color scheme chosen for the movie that echoes the Nazi flag. The fact that these colors are also used to depict the post-war period reflects the post-trauma and her aunt's inability to create a buffer between her present and her past. Lester says

> I didn't intend to use the red initially. I thought about black and white. I decided to use black and white because when we think about the Holocaust we think about black and white. I don't think it was influenced by *Schindler's List*. I saw it as a teenager so maybe unconsciously. But it didn't cross my mind. But I animated the draft with red so I could see some parts more clearly and then I understood what it could do emotionally so I left it.[23]

---

[20] Steir-Livny, "An Interview with Anita Lester."
[21] Ibid.
[22] Amir, *Bearing Witness*, 14–16.
[23] Steir-Livny, "An Interview with Anita Lester."

By contrast to other animated documentaries that represent the peaceful times before the Holocaust, *Noch Am Leben* does not show this era. The image of Nagler as a child drawn in white holding her mother's outstretched hand is depicted against a black background, which hints at an "unhinged destiny" as of her childhood. The black surroundings change into urban scenery where large houses are painted white, and red marks appear between them. A wall separates the houses and the street, signifying the ghetto. The wall is quickly filled with antisemitic slogans and barbed wire. Lester does not say which ghetto Nagler was imprisoned in. She talks about Nagler's older brother and sister who died in the uprising, her younger brother and father who died of disease, her mother and other relatives who were forced onto trains to a death camp. Lester talks about Nagler's desire to return to the period before these events. But the frame, and apparently Nagler's mind, do not enable her to do so. From the ghetto images the frame moves to the darkness in the trains rushing towards the death camps. Tens of pairs of frightened eyes blink in the dark, flashes of images of people for brief seconds. The fact that Lester does not mention a specific town or camp turns this personal story into a broader narrative of victims who lost everything.

Nagler is animated as an abstract figure staring ahead, cradling her head dejectedly in her arms. Lester mentions this image when discussing the limits of presentation: "There is no Hollywood filter that lies atop of death. You can't point a camera at the stench of rotting corpses and smoke blowing out of the Auschwitz chimneys." She does not try: instead, she shows a black figure running aimlessly from place to place, trying to escape, but unable to do so. Is it Nagler trying to escape the Nazis, trying later to escape her memories, or Lester herself trying to escape the memories handed down to her? The girl runs as Lester continues to discuss the inability to represent what Nagler cannot let go of: "There is no soundtrack loud and long enough to muffle the cries of families lost in a breath, or tired feet in ill-fitting shoes, marching for days on end in the snow." Unlike the many directors who have avoided the representations of horrors and have chosen to focus on small, mainly brighter moments in the Holocaust, this perception of the Holocaust as "unrepresentable" does not stop Lester from diving into atrocity. She uses the abstract, the symbolic, and the lyric (the spoken word) to represent the terrible incidents in Eva's life.

Lester says that the focal point of the movie is Sonia, Nagler's older sister, who saved Nagler. After Auschwitz (which is not represented), both were taken on a death march along with 10,000 women near the Baltic Sea. They were shot from the cliff above, and Sonia was wounded. Nagler wanted to scream "I'm still alive" so the soldiers would shoot her too, but Sonia told her to be quiet, and to stay still so the Nazis would not notice she was alive, and died on top of her. "The difference in age between myself and my older sister is the same, so I wondered whether I would do the same for her," says Lester.[24]

Lester indeed represents the horrific mass murder of Nagler's sister and other prisoners who were shot into pits. On the red screen, the image of a small white girl is shown falling down into the red, which eventually turns black as she lies on it. Sonia is a red image as they lie next to each other: a white image and a red image against the black screen. Among the dead and the dying, Lester's commentary turns into the first person as she cries what Nagler cried: "I'm still alive, I'm still alive," and then returns to the third person as she mourns: "Sonia. The human shield. Sonia. The newlywed. Sonia, 24, but somehow a brave and biblical matriarch. Sonia. Taking the bullets for her sister, just as I would for mine. Sonia. Eva's forever shadow." White and gray images of women, looking like ghosts or shadows, walk in a straight line, as she tells it, implying again that this is not the experience of a single woman. Lester talks about a specific event but shows a line of women in the same posture. Girls, women who were protected by other women, who sacrificed their lives for them.

This is not the only atrocity Lester deals with. She talks about Nagler's rape by a German soldier but does not show anything that mimics a sexual assault. She talks bluntly about the German soldier that mounted Nagler and "fucked" her and suggests that she wondered whether staying alive after that was worth it "on tombstone-paved paths." Lester represents this in a scene by a white spotlight that shines in the middle of black scenery, and a dancer-like image of a woman enters the frame and bows. In an interview Lester says that Nagler and a few survivors escaped from the death march. Nagler hid in a potato basket and was saved. She was caught by soldiers who imprisoned her and every single day she was taken and used for sex.

> She didn't hide it. She talked about it and wrote about it in her book. The dance scene is a fantasy she created for herself. Eva wanted to be a performer, a Vaudeville performer. In her good moments she was very outgoing. That was one reason, but the other thing is something that my grandfather said about art being a luxury. Dance is a gift that you are able to do, something you couldn't do at that time.[25]

Dance can also be seen as Nagler's mental way of detaching herself from the rape. This is the place she escapes to in her mind, an evocation enabled by the animated documentary.

---

[24] Steir-Livny, "An Interview with Anita Lester."
[25] Ibid.

After the end of the movie, titles appear and Nagler's real voice is heard against a white screen as she talks about her sister: "I turn my whole attention to my sister. That girl she was 24. She tried so hard not to die," she says in a voice filled with tears. This additional narration by Nagler was taken from the Spielberg Holocaust archives. Lester explains why she chose to add it to the movie: "I listened to her testimonies many times and every time I heard her say that line it made me cry. I feel that her story about her sister is the most honest one. For me that is where the story is. So, I wanted her to come to life at the end."[26] Thus, the movie ends with the broken voice of a survivor who has been through hell and never recovered.

Mass Murder by Shooting in *Kol Nidrei*

This movie presents yet another story of a miraculous escape from death, by the family of Moshe Kaptain. The YouTube text states: "Moses was saved twice, once it was a matter of luck and the other, a divine intervention." The voice of a man narrates the movie in the first person (maybe Kaptain himself). He begins by briefly introducing his observant family, which was imprisoned in the Dombrowitza ghetto in Poland (now Dubrovytsia, Ukraine). The story focuses on incidents that occurred on the Day of Atonement (Yom Kippur) during the Holocaust.

Eastern Poland was occupied at the beginning of World War II by the USSR. Yom Kippur is used to suggest why Moshe's father did not initially understand that the USSR invasion was the lesser of two evils. The colors of the scenes are yellowish-brown and black as Kaptain explains that his father, who was a tailor, later cried because the Russians forced the Jews to work on the Day of Atonement. A sewing machine is seen and the words of the solemn prayer "Kol Nidrei" scroll over it to highlight his father's crisis. The movie does not mention the Nazi invasion in June 1941 of areas previously controlled by the USSR, but rather depicts the change of regime through the symbols of a swastika and a microphone screaming in German. In his voiceover Kaptain explains that the Nazi speaker announced they were taking the Jews to new places of work and that they must get ready to leave the ghetto.

To highlight the Jews' misunderstanding of their destiny, Kaptain describes the joy that erupted in the city (the Jews believed they were going to a place of work and that they would get food), followed by a somber forest animated from a low angle so that the viewers are peering up at the dark sky. Rows of pits appear on a yellowish frame. One after the other, the open pits with soil around them dot the frame like ant hills as Kaptain states that a local hinted

---

[26] Ibid.

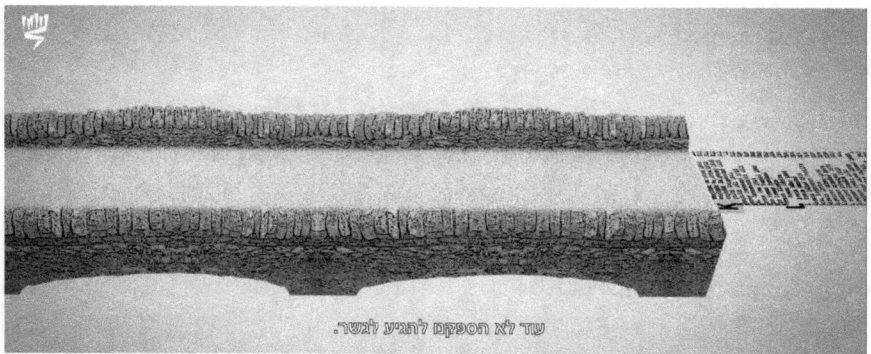

Figure 4.2 Kol Nidrei *(Shira Meishar, 2020)*

to a Jewish friend that he had dug pits himself the day before and that the Jews were going to get killed. The scene is accompanied by the sounds of masses of people. The animation zooms into one pit and sinks into its darkness to symbolize the upcoming mass murder. Kaptain describes how a Jew screamed in Yiddish that they were going to get killed. The words appear in Hebrew on the black screen to focus on the moment. The voices become louder as images of people are animated trying to escape by jumping into the water off a grey bridge drawn on the screen. Instead of showing people walking across the bridge to their deaths, a list of names from A to J inches forward towards the bridge. "The first ones who jumped off the bridge were shot." The list dissolves in the water to symbolize those who were murdered. The camera zooms out to show the remainder of the list lying like a ribbon on the ground. The letter "K" is highlighted in yellow as Kaptain says "We were K, we had not gotten to the bridge yet."

The list from K to Z then detaches from the bridge and slides away into the trees: "Father and mother grabbed us, and we started to run into the woods. At night we ran, in the daytime we hid." It is interesting that this is not the miracle of the movie. In fact, the miracle is yet to come as Kaptain's voiceover describes how on the evening of the Day of Atonement, "Leil Kol Nidrei," his father took him and his brother out of their hiding place to pray and suddenly felt they must escape. Shortly after they ran away, the Nazis found their hiding place and burned it down. The movie, like many others, has a redemptive narrative: Kaptain states he believes it was a divine intervention and the final frame shows the elderly Kaptain in a live action shot, smiling as the titles say that his father and sister were murdered but that the rest of the family survived and immigrated to Israel. Nevertheless, within this redemptive narrative (comparable to many animated documentaries), unvarnished atrocities are discussed.

Auschwitz in *Eva Kor: The Holocaust Survivor who Forgave the Nazis*, *Dear Fredy*, and *Sabotage*

The story of Holocaust survivor Eva Kor (1934–2019) has become world-famous over the last ten years in a series of movies, articles, and interviews. Eva and her twin sister Miriam were sent with their family to Auschwitz, where they were selected for the infamous experiments Mengele conducted on twins.[27] They underwent atrocious experiments but survived. As an elderly woman, after her sister passed away, Kor decided that the way to best help herself would be to forgive the Nazis. She met with several former Nazis who served in Auschwitz and expressed her forgiveness. This unique gesture appeared in the Western press and stirred up considerable controversy and even anger, especially among survivors. To the day of her death, Eva never relinquished her stand.

The movie is a BBC production (made by Studio Panda). It tells her life story, including scenes from Auschwitz and her life after World War II when she decided to forgive. The movie does not depict the experiments graphically but does not whitewash them entirely. It is accompanied by Kor's voiceover (the titles say she died during the production of the movie) who talks about her experiences, thoughts, and decisions in the first person, as the animation visualizes it by using mimetic animation and evocation.

While other movies, mainly by Israelis, tend to narrate a story composed of the pre-Holocaust period followed by post-Holocaust redemption in Israel, the narrative of this movie is focused on the Holocaust (it begins in 1944) and redemption through "the power of forgiveness."

The first scene depicts a Nazi round-up as Kor says that her family was arrested in 1944 "packed into cattle cars with no food or water." The visuals show Nazi officers deporting them, Kor and her twin clutching each other in fear. The cattle cars are filled with black-gray images with her family dominating the scene, since they and the Nazis who deported them are drawn in color. The same goes for the platform in Auschwitz. The drawing focuses on the frightened faces of the little twins clinging to their mother and then being dragged away crying by a Nazi. He is animated from the girls' perspective waist down to emphasize their distress. Their mother is also drawn from a lower angle, from their point of view, screaming and fighting as two Nazi

---

[27] Considerable research has been written about Mengele. See for example: Gerald Posner, *Mengele: The Complete Story* (New York Press: Cooper Square Press, 2000); Anna Revell, *Josef Mengele: Angel of Death: A Biography of Nazi Evil* (Amazon Digital Services LLC, 2017); David Marwell, *Mengele: Unmasking the "Angel of Death"* (New York: W. W. Norton & Company, 2020).

guards hold her back ("I did not know at that time that I would never see her again").

In the scenes relating to the experiments, the titles explain that "10-year-old Eva and her sister were spared because they were twins, but they were subjected to a series of horrific experiments at the hands of the notorious Nazi doctor Josef Mengele." The movie is mostly in color, but when it depicts their first night it turns gray, black, and white. The titles warn the viewers about what they are about to see ("their first night was terrifying"). The "camera" zooms out of a gray room; a weak beam of light enters from a window showing it is a latrine. Kor's voice is heard: "On the filthy floor there were the scattered corpses of three little girls." The animation does not focus on the corpses. "The camera" moves away from them but the gray silhouettes of three little bodies are shown. "Their bodies were naked and their eyes wide open," she says, but the director chooses not to graphically portray the naked bodies, rather focus in extreme close-up on the hand of one of the girls and an eye before turning to a close-up of Kor's terrified face, her eyes wide open in fear, her mouth quivering, her hands covering her eyes as her voiceover says, "It was a horrifying look. I had never seen anybody dead before." She and her sister hug on a bunk bed, where other twins sleep as well; they dominate the frame by being painted in stronger colors. The "camera" that hovers over them makes them look even smaller and a mouse that crosses the frame highlights the horrible conditions they are in: "So that hit me very very hard, and I made a silent pledge that I would do whatever was within my power to make sure that Miriam and I would not end up on that latrine floor and that somehow we would survive and walk out of this camp alive." This choice of representation propels the viewers into the horrific world to which Kor and her sister were exposed. It successfully represents the horrors without turning into a pornographic representation of the experiments.

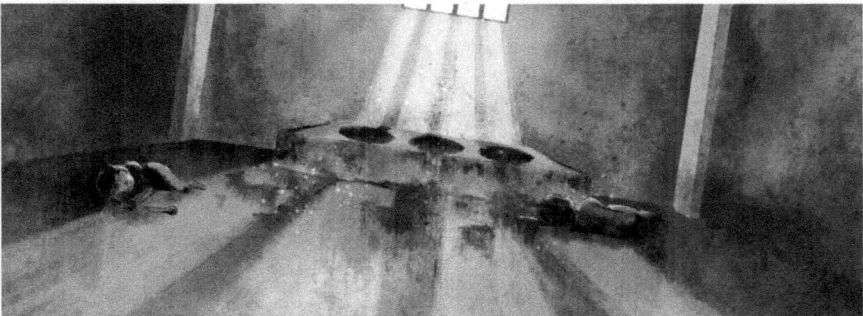

Figure 4.3 Eva Kor: The Holocaust Survivor Who Forgave the Nazis *(Anna Humphries and Amelia Chiew, 2020)*

An example of the experiments is visualized. The twins are drawn naked from their chest up as hands enter the frame with pencils and charts and a tape measure. Kor's voice is heard: "We were naked for hours and every part of our bodies was measured. It was horrible and humiliating." Moving to a gray room the titles declare: "After one injection Eva became very ill," while the frame moves to little Kor surrounded by doctors in white scrubs. Only their lower bodies from her angle of view are seen, as the grown-up Eva recalls that Dr. Mengele said "Too bad, she's so young, she has only two weeks to live." They leave and little Kor bows her sad face, but the voiceover of elderly Kor declares she refused to die: "If I died, Miriam would have been given a lethal injection so he could cut open both of our bodies and compare the autopsies." The animation demonstrates what could have happened by focusing on a tattooed hand being injected, and then moves to two legs of two dead bodies. The animation makes it sufficiently possible to visualize the past unfilmed and to represent Eva's inner world—her thoughts, fears, and imagination—thus strengthening the viewers' understanding of her dire straits.

A close-up of her sick, extenuated face highlights her condition; the frame is dark, and the black rings under her eyes symbolize her illness, she is coughing, walks into the darkness, almost stumbles since she cannot walk straight, and falls down: "For the next two weeks I was between life and death and all I remember, was crawling on the barracks floor because I no longer could walk." The camera dissolves into the latrine, moves as if on her body, towards the window in the grey latrine, showing her hands trying to reach the wall, fading to black and returning to the scene, "And as I was crawling, I would fade in and out of consciousness and I kept telling myself 'I must survive, I must survive.'" The titles reveal that the twins survived, and the remaining four minutes of the movie are dedicated to the way she dealt with her post-trauma (see Chapter 5).

These images bring to mind the ongoing debate over Holocaust representations. As Saul Friedländer put it, "We are dealing with an event which tests our traditional conceptual and representational categories."[28] According to Lior Zylberman and Vicente Sánchez-Biosca, the core issue of an adequate representation of these types of mass violence dates back to ancient times. If indeed a representation is possible, what should characterize it? Since the term "adequate" is polysemic, these questions lead to new ones, such as their adequacy in relation to reality, the experiences of the

---

[28] Bovekerk, *The Representation of Gas Chambers in Holocaust Movies, 1944–2013*, MA Present(ed) History, Radboud University, Supervised by Dr. Remco Ensel, 2013, 16.

victims who suffered the violence, the transmission of memory, and from whose perspective.[29]

Libby Saxton claimed the question of whether the Holocaust "could or should be represented" needs to be replaced with the question of "how it might adequately or responsibly be represented." She has examined how Holocaust moviemakers can encourage responsible as opposed to voyeuristic spectatorship.[30]

The Story of Eva Kor, like the few other animated documentaries that dare to deal with the atrocities, manifests how a director can represent some horrors of Auschwitz without turning them into a graphic or pornographic series of images. This trend is also found indirectly, in the scenes in the hybrid documentary *Dear Fredy*, which tells the story of Fredy Hirsch and the children he attempted to save during their imprisonment in Theresienstadt and Auschwitz. Theresienstadt is represented as a horror-free space (as analyzed in Chapter 3). But when the movie turns to describe Auschwitz, it shows how horror can be addressed without being graphic.

In 1943 Hirsch and thousands of others were deported from Theresienstadt to Auschwitz-Birkenau and were separated from the other inmates and placed in a special family sub-camp. The conditions were horrible, but the families were together. Hirsch founded the children's block (Block 31) and through his relentless work, gave the children hope. The Nazis appointed him Kapo, and he used his connections to ease the lives of the hundreds of children under fourteen who were allowed in his block. They received better food and were provided with care and education. Hirsch learned from the camp underground that their transport would be probably sent to the gas chambers in March 1944, exactly six months after the first transport of families arrived. The underground, which acknowledged him as a leader, suggested they rebel. Hirsch, who still had hope that the families would be saved, thought that in a rebellion all the children would be killed. He asked for time to think and then took poison to commit suicide. On March 7, 1944, the Nazis indeed sent all the people in his transport to the gas chambers. Only the few who were selected for work survived.[31]

---

[29] Lior Zylberman and Vicente Sánchez-Biosca, "Reflections on the Significance of Images in Genocide Studies: Some Methodological Considerations," *Genocide Studies and Prevention: An International Journal* 12, no. 2 (2018): 1–17.

[30] Bovekerk, *The Representation of Gas Chambers*, 9.

[31] Nili Keren, "The Family Camp in Auschwitz-Birkenau," *Yad Vashem* (no date), [Hebrew], https://bit.ly/3D4c0Yj; Ruth Bondi, "Playing in the Shade of the Crematoria: The Children's Home in the Birkenau Family Camp (September 1943–July 1944)," *Yad Vashem* (No Date) [Hebrew], https://bit.ly/3oo2B9U

In the movie, director Gat incorporated animated scenes of specific stories that caught his attention while conducting research. These are mostly inserted in the part of the movie about Auschwitz. Gat explains:

> As the movie follows the timeline, the level of authentic documentation and quality decreases. There are some pictures from Prague, there are Nazi materials from Therezin but there are hardly any materials from Auschwitz. But Auschwitz was the peak of Hirsch's activity and the moment when his character crystallized into who he was, both in terms of his actions (heroism) and in terms of his inner development and coming to terms with his sexuality ... so Auschwitz occupies a significant share of the movie. For the part of the movie that talks about Auschwitz I needed more animation that corresponded to my intention to create a separate world, a bubble. This is how I understood Fredy's children's hut walled off from the Hell outside.[32]

Since this is a hybrid feature length documentary, it shows the time at Auschwitz at length, and combines the animation with live action interviews with survivors. The train ride is represented in animation: only the legs of the deportees are shown in the cattle car. A survivor says there was only one toilet bucket, which was soon full, and everyone had to stand in what overflowed. But since the people's faces are not seen, it makes it hard for viewers to experience the disgust because all that is seen of the people is their legs. Their arrival is symbolized by footage of the sign "Arbeit Macht Frei," dogs barking, and the voice of a survivor who says his mother told him that "We won't get out of here." As the doors of the railway cars open, the Jews' legs are shown again, a red stain appears and grows larger and larger on the floor as a gunshot is heard and part of a hand falls on the ground to indicate the killing of a person from their transport. The live action interviewees describe the tattooing and the family camp.

Hirsch is depicted as being as handsome and lively as ever. The interviewees recall that he became the Lagerkapo who was in charge of the camp, but never misused his power as other Kapos did,[33] and never hurt anyone. He is drawn standing in front of the children with his back to the "camera," but the children's faces show what his presence means to them: they are smiling and do not look frightened at all. This is the confidence he gave them.

Prof. Dov Kolka, who was one of Hirsch's "children," is interviewed in live action as an elderly man but animated as a child as he describes how every morning he went to the last hut, and saw guards taking out corpses through the back door—"And I got around it. I jumped past it"—and went to the children's home, which he refers to as a bubble. Kolka the child is animated

---

[32] Liat Steir-Livny, "An Interview with Rubi Gat," January 20, 2020.
[33] On the complex actions of Jewish Kapos see: Levin, *Kapo on Allenby*.

in a gray frame walking between the barracks and the barbed wire, looking to the side. Nothing is shown. The animation follows the bubble he created for himself.

The "camera" pans to what seems to be a large wall filled with children's fairytale images and famous cartoon figures in bright happy colors, some of which come to life through animation (Mickey Mouse is jumping, the birds around Snow White are fluttering) as a survivor talks about how Hirsch asked her to paint the walls of the children's barracks and managed to get the supplies for it.

To mark the passing of time and the families' approaching deaths, in the following scenes Hirsch is drawn older and looks tired. But when entering the children's block there is no despair. Sounds of children talking and laughing are heard. The "camera" zooms out from the barracks to the rooftops outside in the snow, until it reaches the barbed wire that locks them in, as one of the survivors' voices explains this dichotomy by saying the children were so busy playing, learning, singing, creating that they may not have fully understood what was going on around them. They are animated performing and singing. Some say there was always an atmosphere of death in the air; others say that under Hirsch's supervision there was always hope. The wonderful voices of the children's choir are heard, singing about an era of love, happiness, and forgiveness as one of the survivors describes how their music may have accompanied those being sent to their deaths. The "camera" visualizes this jarring contradiction as it zooms out from the rooftops of the children's block and the family's camp to the flames coming out of the gas chambers. Through animation, director Gat succeeds in making it vivid by simultaneously creating an atmosphere in which death hovers over everything but also serves as a premonition (this is where the children will end up). This disparity in awareness between the animated children and the viewers is shocking and painful.

To depict Hirsch's death, director Gat shifts between live action interviews with survivors stating they do not know whether it was suicide or murder. Still, they raise the possibility that he did not kill himself but was poisoned by camp doctors who were promised they would not be sent to the gas chambers. Historically his death remains unclear, and the animation does not substantiate either version. Two inmates are animated carrying a stretcher with Hirsch's body on it. Gat is aware of the fact that the movie does not visualize atrocities graphically:

> As a child I was shocked by a movie I saw on Holocaust Heroes' and Martyrs' Remembrance Day in school (in Israel). I looked away from the screen. It was clear to me that I would not use graphic materials, not even Muselmann

> for example, because it is a simplistic technique in my opinion to churn up the viewer emotionally and also because if someone in the audience turns away, I lose them. We tried to drape the illustrations in melancholy without creating "shocking" situations, without drawings that would drag the viewer into sadness directly. Because the whole setting of the story is so hard and horrible, I decided to use as few graphic drawings depicting untenable situations as possible.[34]

According to Gat, this aesthetic and thematic choice culminates in the final scene:

> We debated about how to depict the gas chambers. In his book *In the Heart of Hell* Zalman Gradowski, who was in the Sonderkommando, describes the night that Fredy died and everyone who came with him from the Therezin ghetto to Auschwitz in the September transport was murdered. We were tempted to put the viewers in the gas chambers. We considered a final animation of legs in the dark of the gas chambers and people's heads crammed in from the victims' perspective on the inside. In the end I decided to delete this image. I even censored the scene of the bare feet walking towards the gas chambers. At first, the animators showed legs above the knee line, but it scared me terribly ... it seemed to me too much, and we decided to change it to feet.[35]

In the final scenes, as melancholic music is heard on the soundtrack, the "camera" pans from Hirsch's body to a line of bare feet marching. A survivor's voiceover says that the transport was gassed that very night: "The babies, the children—everybody was gone." As the animation continues to pan on the bare feet, another survivor says that a few children survived and some of the older teachers.

These minimalistic scenes suggest that horrors can be represented without graphic images. The image of the bare feet of small children and the testimonies in the soundtrack are enough to convey the enormity of the disaster and create a chilling ending: Hirsch, who was represented as larger than life, is dead, and the children, who were animated in many scenes as singing, dancing, laughing, are being marched to their deaths. The movie ends with the live action scenes of a survivor who talks about her large family today, and a football match on an Israeli kibbutz to commemorate the anniversary of Hirsch's 100th birthday that was organized by one of the former teachers. The LGBTQ flag flies among the others on the field. There is life after the Holocaust, there is partial redemption for a few, but the atrocities are permanent.

---

[34] Steir-Livny, "An Interview with Rubi Gat."
[35] Ibid.

Sabotage

Sabotage (Noa Aharoni, 2022) is the story of the female prisoners who worked in the munitions factory in Auschwitz-Birkenau and risked their lives when they sabotaged the factory's machinery. Each department sabotaged in its way, until the factory management received letters with complaints that the ammunition did not explode when it should or that it exploded in the hands of the Germans. These women were brutally beaten so that they would see and be seen. But instead of ceasing their activity, they assisted in smuggling gunpowder out of the factory, risking their lives, and secretly transferring it to the Sonderkommando—Jews who worked in the gas chambers and the crematorium. With their help the Sonderkommando were able to rebel. On October 7, 1944, the rebellion broke out, the Sonderkommandos blew up crematorium number 4. Four of the women were caught and hanged.

Sabotage is a hybrid movie that combines testimonies recorded in the 1990s by survivors, black and white, almost sepia animation which creates a dark atmosphere, footage from various munitions factories that operated during World War II, footage of the camps filmed by the Allied armies, photos from the Auschwitz album, and narration of translated sections from the diary of Anna Weisblom Heilman, the youngest member of the underground (she was sent to Auschwitz when she was fourteen years old) and the sister of Esther (Estusha) (eighteen years old), who is one of the prisoners who was hanged. Anna talks about her and her sister's faith during the Holocaust from two perspectives: as an elderly woman in the 1990s and the narration from the diary she wrote in Auschwitz. It was burned in the camp and she rewrote everything she remembered six months after the war ended.

Aharoni says that producer and director Levi Zini started making this movie, but then decided to stop. "At some point he realized that a woman should do it and turned to me. When I entered the picture, I changed the concept. I decided to put the women and the testimonies in the foreground without the assistance of memory agents: the children and grandchildren of the survivors [...] I wanted to let the testimonies speak for themselves."[36] She had no budget for reconstruction of Auschwitz, but more importantly

> Some people think that even the dramas made by directors like Spielberg or Polanski are problematic. In addition, the use of animation helps with foreignization. We wanted to move away from realism, so everything is sketched

---

[36] Ruta Kupfer, "'Sabotage': An Extraordinary Film About Jewish Women Prisoners in Auschwitz who Risked Themselves to Destroy the Crematoria," *Calcalist*, 27 April, 2022, https://bit.ly/3SCSlGa

by hand, as much as possible, without a lot of background, clean and clear because the story is so difficult and unbearable."[37]

The result is that nothing too difficult is shown: Auschwitz as a camp is simply suggested. At times there are barracks, snow, barbed wire, and smoke from the crematorium chimneys. There are no Muselmanner, no mass bodies, and the horrific torture the inmates suffered is not shown. However, the fact is that this is a hybrid movie, and the combination of all the aesthetic elements represent the life of the prisoners in Auschwitz-Birkenau in more complexity than the combination of snow and sadness that appears in other animated movies. Without becoming graphic or turning to pornography of violence, this helps depict chilling moments in the lives of the prisoners, the constant fear, and the tragedy of the inmates when the Nazis discovered that gunpower had been smuggled out of the factory.

The movie depicts the exhausting routine, hunger, torture, and death, and succeeds in doing so alongside the presentation of points of light in the great darkness, as for example when Anna describes the hours after work in which the women sat together and talked and even managed to laugh.

The hybridity of the movie and the fact that the animation is combined with scenes filmed by the Allied armies contributes to the stark representation of Auschwitz. For example, the two sisters were sent to Auschwitz in September 1943 from Majdanek. The movie combines testimonies and representations of the humiliation in the nude selection. The animation does not focus on a naked body but on bare backs, the frightened faces of the women, an inmate hiding her breasts while switching between live action testimonies, the narration from the diary of Anna, who wrote about these horrible moments in which they did not know who would survive the selection and who would be sent to her death, live action testimonies, and animation.

The smuggling plan in the factory is represented in a horror-movie-like atmosphere. The animation and testimonies are accompanied by chilling music and the sound of heartbeats that highlight the fear and terrifying atmosphere.

The gunpowder residue leads the Gestapo investigators to the women working in the factory's gunpowder room. The women are subjected to extreme torture (which is not shown) but do not break. "Astusha came back like raw meat," says the elderly Anna, and the narration of the passage from her diary states "Astusha came back more dead than alive. She was black and blue (from the beatings) from head to toes. The skin on her back was lacerated. She couldn't move. She couldn't talk." The animation shows the

---

[37] Kupfer, "Sabotage."

skinny body of a woman, whip marks all over her face, in the arms of her sister. Marta (another inmate) is wiping her face. There is no graphic violence and there is no need for it. The moments of suffering are understood. As the "camera" zooms out, there is a feeling of relief as Esthusha is being taken care of so gently and Anna believes the worst is over.

However, a girl named Klara, who was caught with bread, told Nazis who smuggled the gunpowder out. She gave them Esthusha's name, and she was tortured. The animation shows a woman hanging by her hands on a wall and pulled up as though her arms are being ripped out. It is animated in long-shot, her face is not clear, but the situation is horrible as a vicious dog barks at her hanging body. She gave only three names: Regina, Estusha, and Roza Robota. This led to the hanging.

On January 6, 1945, not long before the camp's liberation by the Red Army, the four young women prisoners were hanged. The commander of the women's camp, Franz Hessler, is represented in animation while making a speech about the women who betrayed him and committed an "act of sabotage." He yells as the gallows are shown, together with the rows of women inmates who were forced to watch the execution.[38] The hanging sequence is very long. Parts of it start the movie and the movie dedicates about seven minutes to it towards the end. The animation, created by Avi A. Katz, represents the unfilmed past and also uses evocation to add poetic elements. These form some of the most touching moments in the movie, including the moment when Anna sees her sister, who is being led to the gallows for the last time. The animation shows them communicating with their eyes for the last time between the lines of inmates. Pink ballet shoes suddenly appear on Estusha's feet. In her last moments and in a place that has erased her identity and dignity, the director restores her humanity by highlighting her hobby, her life, and identity before she was a number in Auschwitz.

The scene is structured like an action movie, with parallel editing between close-ups of the noose and the commander's shouts in German about "sabotage," Anna's heartbeats, her terrified face, her scream "Astusha" that splits the air, the pale and thin Estusha walking to her death, the hands on Anna's mouth that stifle her cry so that she too will not be punished, and the hands of her friends dragging her away so she will not see her sister being hanged.

The animation shows the viewers what Anna didn't see: Skinny Roza Robota is animated, walking towards the gallows, the noose around her neck. When Estusha's turn arrives, the feet moving towards the gallows wear ballet shoes. The animation focuses on Estusha's tormented face as the rope hangs

---

[38] Nadav Menuhin, "This Film Tells About the Heroism of Female Prisoners in Auschwitz, but it is Also Very Brave," Walla, 28 April, 2022, https://bit.ly/3gEsDnu

around her neck. The chair falls and the legs of the ballet shoes dangle in the wind. A survivor is interviewed in live action saying that Estusha did not die immediately. Yaacov the executioner, who could not watch her suffer, pulled on her body, and she died. Pink ballet shoes that stop twitching end the horrible sequence, as the elderly Anna states that she heard a collective scream and knew it was the end. The long minutes dedicated to this event, the parallel editing between live action scenes of the interviewees and animation, the screams in German, and Anna's tormented face create a hard-to-watch sequence even though very little is shown.

THE HORRORS OF THE WARSAW GHETTO IN *7 MINUTES IN THE WARSAW GHETTO* AND *KARSKI AND THE LORDS OF HUMANITY*

7 Minutes in the Warsaw Ghetto differs from other animated documentaries because it is based on one sentence. Richard Raskin, a Danish Jewish professor of film studies, wrote the script. According to Raskin, *7 Minutes in the Warsaw Ghetto* was inspired by an actual event commemorated by one of the Warsaw ghetto inmates: "One day a small Jewish boy was killed on Biala Street as he attempted to pull a carrot lying in the gutter on the Aryan side through a hole in the fence. A German spotted him, inserted his gun in the hole, and killed the boy with one well-aimed shot."[39] The movie does not include text but rather visualizes this incident. It has won seven awards at international movie festivals and has been included in the official selection of more than 120 festivals around the world, from Buenos Aires to Hiroshima.[40]

The script was written in 2003 and was initially titled "Four Minutes in the Warsaw Ghetto."[41] Danish director Johan Oeslinger has Jewish roots: his great-grandfather was an Austrian Jew who fell in love with a Christian. They were stigmatized so they moved to Denmark, and he became a fisherman. His family perished in the Holocaust. As a child, Oeslinger was told the story and was curious about it.[42] Raskin approached him and offered to direct it. It was Oeslinger's first professional movie.[43] Together with Raskin,

---

[39] Richard Raskin, "Art and the Holocaust: Positioning *Seven Minutes in the Warsaw Ghetto*," *Short Movie Studies* 4, no.2 (2014), 223–226. The story is commemorated in: Michal Grynberg (ed.), *Words to Outlive Us: Voices from the Warsaw Ghetto* (New York: Metropolitan Books, 2002), 41–42.

[40] Raskin, "Art and the Holocaust"; Richard Raskin, "Seven Minutes in the Warsaw Ghetto and With Raised Hands—A Movie Ebook" (Arhus: Arhus University Press, 2013), 12–13.

[41] Raskin, "Seven Minutes," 28–30.

[42] Liat Steir-Livny, "An Interview with Johan Oeslinger," June 3, 2020.

[43] Steir-Livny, "An Interview with Johan Oeslinger."

they decided to turn it into a seven-minute movie entitled *7 Minutes in the Warsaw Ghetto*:

> The goal for me was to create a movie in which we experience the ghetto situation as seen through a child's eyes. We added new scenes about being a child, playing, and the child's mind. We also gave the birds more space and meaning to create parallels between the animal's and the child's simple mindset.[44]

The movie is a stop-motion puppet production,[45] in which the creators move inanimate objects in front of the camera (as in *Nyosha*). According to Oeslinger, the animation is perfect for this kind of movie. It can be much more heartfelt than live action because elements that are not needed to tell a specific story can be eliminated:

> For me stop-motion animation is very powerful because it is based on real things and real textures. You can relate to it very quickly as a human because it is a real environment. Even though you know it is fake, these are inanimate objects, puppets, almost toys, you get attached to them quickly. It is something from childhood when we had our toys. Puppets that are moving in a magical way is very powerful in evoking feelings.[46]

The puppets representing the Jews (the child, his mother, his grandmother) look as though they are made of cracked porcelain. Fissures appear on their emaciated faces and bodies to represent their fragile existence. They can break apart at any moment. Video effects are used to simulate smoke, fog, dust, and steam in some of the shots. The eyes and effects were added in post-production with the use of composite software.[47] Raskin claims that the careful composition of human eyes enhances the audience's ability to enter

---

[44] Raskin, "Seven Minutes," 32.

[45] Another puppet animation movie is the stop-motion animation *Body Memory* (Ülo Pikkov, 2011, 9 min., Estonia), whose central concept is that the body remembers the pain of individuals' ancestors in addition to its own experiences. The movie is a classical puppet animation that creates a powerful visualization of subconscious processes and the hidden horror of deportation inspired by historical events; in this case, the Soviet deportations from Estonia in the 1940s. It shows knitted puppets inside a deportation train as they try to cope with their tragic present and future. There is no text, just the squeaking sound of the images on their way to Hell. The movie ends with a scene of a real train crossing the snow that gradually morphs into a giant gray snake, which slithers on the ground. See: "Body Memory," *YouTube*, November 21, 2012, https://bit.ly/3B8k9Ky; *Body Memory* has been screened in many festivals and won numerous awards. See: "Body Memory," *Nukumovie*, https://bit.ly/3Fgszlx

[46] Liat Steir-Livny, "An interview with Johan Oeslinger," June 3, 2020.

[47] Raskin, "Seven Minutes," 33.

into their experience and identify with them.[48] Oeslinger says that the eyes are the window to the soul and express people's deepest feelings. "For that reason, I had the eyes of actors composited onto the puppets' faces. This brings the puppets to life, and it is in the subtlety and loveliness of the eyes, rather than theatrical gestures, that the puppets express their thoughts and feelings."[49]

During the pre-production, Raskin and Oeslinger watched movies about the Warsaw ghetto and consulted pictures and books. Oeslinger says the animation is based on historical pictures but is deliberately distorted. They aimed to visualize the ghetto rather than represent it in a mimetic way:

> I was not interested in making it a copy of the place. I wanted it to reference the place. I was interested in the story of five people and everything else is excluded so that in itself it is not natural because the ghetto was a crowded place. In addition, I wanted to represent the ghetto from the child's point of view and when you are a child you live in your own bubble, you don't see everything. There might be people around you but as a child you are just good at excluding everything. You see things differently. Therefore, everything is stretched in an unnatural way – the buildings, the windows, the courtyard are much bigger than at that time because this is how he sees it.[50]

The puppet world fits this bubble well. The movie is animated in black and white. Oeslinger says he chose these colors to give it a historical feeling. It also underscores the dichotomy between the child and the Nazis. The child is shown in white because he is an innocent being in the midst of this blackness. Oeslinger wanted the viewers to focus on the child and differentiate him from the darkness by being in white.[51]

A crow is an important leitmotif in the movie. In the opening scene, a crow pecks at a dried-up carrot lying on the ground, then flies upward towards a wall, past warning signs in German and Polish, and over the barbed wire covering the top of the ghetto wall. The bird descends into a courtyard inside the ghetto wall. The title, visible as the shot begins, is partially obscured as the bird crosses in front of it. After the bird lands on the ground, the title fades out in waves, just like the family in the movie.[52] According to Oeslinger, the crow takes on contradictory symbolism. On the one hand, it symbolizes freedom; it can fly away. It is a part of the boy's play world, and he is drawn to

---

[48] Raskin, "Art and the Holocaust," 223–226.
[49] Raskin, "Seven Minutes," 31. See: "Making of Eyes," *YouTube*, April 23, 2012, https://bit.ly/3oxros2
[50] Steir-Livny, "An Interview with Johan Oeslinger."
[51] Ibid.
[52] Raskin, "Seven Minutes," 14.

it. Even though he is in this horrible place he still finds nature there. On the other hand, it also mourns the dead. This is the first hint that this movie is not going to end with the triumph of life over death. Raskin states that it "serves both as emblems of death and as allies of the child."[53]

The combination of black and white, the crow, the image of the crumbling ghetto, and the soundtrack composed primarily on a synthesizer, which gives the movie a non-human and indeterminate mood, make all this clear from the beginning: this is a horror movie. According to Oeslinger: "The synthesizer music contrasts sharply with the textured visual style, and the two are combined to create a dreamy atmosphere,"[54] but this is more of a nightmare than a dream.

The audience is then introduced to the family: the child, his mother, and grandmother—none of whom are mentioned by name in the movie. The names are only provided in the script: the boy's name is Samek, his mother's name is Yetta, and the grandmother's name is not mentioned, turning an individual story into a collective story of the Jews in the Warsaw ghetto. Unlike other movies there is no exposition describing their pastoral pre-Nazi life.

As the family members appear, the puppets have almost completely cracked, and when the puppets touch one another there is a sound of porcelain fissuring. They are very fragile, about to shatter any minute. Samek, as an eight-year-old boy, is lying on the floor of a sparsely furnished apartment, drawing a picture. As he draws, his mother and grandmother are animated in the background, preparing food.[55] A close-up on the grandmother's hand shows that what she is trying to cook is a damaged, almost rotten potato. Samek is drawing Hitler, as a black feather lands on his paper. He picks up the feather and tenderly brushes his cheek with it, closing his eyes in enjoyment. Hence without words, the dark world in which they live is represented—a world of hunger, and darkness, between life and death, a world in which a child's game is drawing Hitler, and a feather is an absolute joy.

Few events occur in the house. The occupants do not talk to each other. An atmosphere of despair and indifference hovers over them. Yetta, Samek's mother, approaches him to see what he is drawing, takes it and shows it to her mother, who shrugs and then pushes it into the oven. Samek does not protest. It seems he does not have the strength. Samek's hand reaches into a nearby bowl and pulls out a carrot. He waves the carrot in the air, flying it like a plane, and Yetta snatches it from his hand. The movements are not quick or

---

[53] Raskin, "Art and the Holocaust," 223–226.
[54] Raskin, "Seven Minutes," 31, 33.
[55] Ibid., 14–15, 33.

filled with real rage. It seems her strength is waning fast. Oeslinger claims that in the changes from script to a movie they altered the relationship of one of the women from aunt to grandmother, "to shape two stereotypical forms of love. The mother shows her love for the boy by protecting and scolding him, while the grandmother shows a more accepting and understanding kind of love."[56] Samek buries his face in his grandmother's bosom for comfort. She kisses his face, and he leaves the apartment.[57]

In the courtyard, after carefully making sure he is not being observed, he removes a metal sheet concealing his cache of little treasures[58] made up of a collection of stones, pinecones and other simple objects. He adds the feather he hid in his pocket to his treasures. The movie evokes his feelings and enters his mind as Samek lets go of the feather, and like in a magical scene it floats down to the stones and to the other objects in the box, making them spin and glow; one stone even flies in the air, highlighting the importance of maintaining an inner world as a way to survive. The movie strengthens the perspective that maintaining an inner world helped people to survive.

Lying on his stomach, he begins to peer through a small hole in the ghetto wall. When he sees a rotten carrot on the other side, he takes a small wire out of his treasure box and tries to hook the carrot. What the viewers see, and he does not, is that besides the carrot there are two Nazi guards. Their names are mentioned solely in the script (Josef and Karl). In the movie, they are nameless soldiers emblematic of "the Nazis."[59]

The soldiers are also made of porcelain but totally smooth, polished, and well-nourished. They are complete—they have no cracks.[60] Seeing the carrot moving, one of them inserts his pistol into the hole and pulls the trigger indifferently, fully aware of the fact that he killed someone. The final sequence is a series of shots in which birds swirl in the sky.[61] Thus without words, the tragedy of the Jews in the Warsaw ghetto is manifested.

In this movie, there is no catharsis at the end, no consolation in bravery, the triumph of the human spirit, or small acts of humanity, reflecting what Langer termed an un-redemptive memory of the Holocaust.[62] There is darkness, death, cruelty, and brutality towards the innocent. In this rare representation of horrors within a non-redemptive Holocaust story, even the movie's title emphasizes the atrocities. These are only seven minutes

---

[56] Ibid., 32.
[57] Ibid., 19–20.
[58] Ibid., 21.
[59] Ibid., 24.
[60] Steir-Livny, "An Interview with Johan Oeslinger."
[61] Raskin, "Seven Minutes," 25–26.
[62] Langer, *The Afterdeath of the Holocaust*, 37–61.

Figure 4.4   7 Minutes in the Warsaw Ghetto *(Johan Oettinger, 2012)*

in the Warsaw ghetto. The story of one family. Around 450,000 Jews were imprisoned in the ghetto for years. If these seven minutes are so horrific, the story of the Warsaw ghetto as a whole is an assemblage of unending atrocities. Raskin felt it was important not to have a happy end:[63]

> Feature movies portraying the Holocaust tend either to conceal the true horror (*Life Is Beautiful*) or to show glimpses of that horror but concluding nevertheless with a reassuring ending (*Schindler's List*, *The Pianist*). In either case, the moviemaker's intention is a noble one: to keep the memory of the Holocaust alive, and to inscribe that memory in a life-affirming story. And in either case, the viewer is left feeling good at the end, even if the movie journey included unbearable moments. [*Seven Minutes in the Warsaw Ghetto*] violates a major convention of Holocaust cinema (and one of my own principles of storytelling more generally) by not offering the viewer a feeling of relief at the end. This is not a gratuitous defiance of conventions. Well aware of the risks involved, I want the viewer to experience a striking image of the Holocaust that leaves him or her with an undiluted sense of loss and despair. The final moments of this movie are deliberately left unbearable.[64]

---

[63] Steir-Livny, "An Interview with Johan Oeslinger."
[64] Raskin, "Seven Minutes," 27.

Raskin cites Elie Wiesel's famous article in *The New York Times* that was published in reaction to the broadcast of the series *Holocaust* on NBC at the end of the 1970s. It was the first TV series to present a fictional narrative of the Holocaust, was watched by millions in the Western world, and is considered to be one of the most influential texts on the Holocaust of that period. Wiesel criticized the series, stating that works of fiction about the Holocaust are "misleading, exploitative, voyeuristic, and trivializing by nature."[65] Raskin argues that even though his movie is based on a real story

> it is nevertheless a work of fiction [...] no birds, drawings, apartment, family members, feathers or levitating stones are mentioned in the source of the story and have all been added in the movie as embellishments to the narrative.[66]

His statement thus rekindles the debate on the "real" in animated documentaries.

KARSKI AND THE LORDS OF HUMANITY

Karski and the Lords of Humanity is a feature-length partially animated documentary that tells the story of Jan Karski[67] (1914–2000), a Polish Catholic who worked in the Polish Ministry of Foreign Affairs in the diplomatic corps in the 1930s. After World War II broke out, he joined the Polish underground movement *Armia Krajowa*. Thanks to his exceptional visual memory, he was chosen to be a courier and an emissary to the exiled Polish government. Part of his mission was to inform the Allies of Nazi crimes against the Jews in Poland. Two members of the Jewish underground (Leon Feiner from the Bund and another Zionist activist whose identity is unknown),[68] asked Karski to sneak into the Warsaw Ghetto and a camp and then convey his eye-witness report of the atrocities to the exiled Polish government, Britain, and the United States, hoping that it would awaken the conscience of these powerful leaders, or—as he would later call them—the Lords of Humanity.[69]

The movie is a Polish, Israeli, German, and US co-production.[70] Grunberg is an award-winning director and the producer of over forty documentaries

---

[65] Raskin, "Art and the Holocaust," 223–226.
[66] Ibid.
[67] His original family name was Kozielewski. Karski was his nickname in the Underground. See: "Jan Karski," *Yad Vashem* [Hebrew], https://bit.ly/3mjHWBh
[68] Daniel Blatman, "A Testimony About the Holocaust which Deserves a Special Attention," *Haaretz*, May 27, 2014 [Hebrew], https://bit.ly/2YoKBS1
[69] "Karski & The Lords of Humanity," *Facebook*, https://bit.ly/3FcSAlR
[70] "Karski and the Lords of Humanity," *Kickstarter*, https://bit.ly/3a2Azsc

and a Guggenheim Fellow. His movies have been broadcast on major TV stations and have won prestigious awards.[71] As a part of the pre-production of this movie, extensive research was done at the Hoover Institution at Stanford University in Palo Alto, CA, which houses the Jan Karski archives. Dozens of photographs and over forty hours of audiovisual materials were scanned or transferred from VHS to DVD. These included numerous American, British, and Polish programs and movies featuring Karski, interviews with him, as well as roughly eight hours of never-broadcast interviews made by the movie's production crew.[72]

About 15 to 20 per cent of the movie is animation. According to the directors, animation was used to visualize what was not filmed, such as how Karski was able to sneak into the Warsaw Ghetto.[73] Grunberg said that what inspired him to choose animation over fictionalized reenactments "was the fabulous movie *Waltz with Bashir* which I saw a few years ago."[74] No wonder the animation in *Karski and the Lords of Humanity* was headed by Yoni Goodman, the director of animation of *Waltz with Bashir*.[75]

Karski was one of the many interviewees in Claude Lanzmann's *Shoah* (1985).[76] In 2010 Lanzmann devoted an entire documentary to his testimony (*The Karski Report*), and included scenes that were cut out of *Shoah*. The movie begins with Karski's interview with Lanzmann, in which he says that during all his years as a lecturer he never discussed his role in the Holocaust. It includes the famous scene in which he tries to describe what he saw in the Warsaw ghetto but chokes up, begins to cry, and leaves the room. Later he discusses some of the things he saw, and this scene makes it obvious that words can only partially convey the historical truth.

Karski and the Lords of Humanity combines "talking heads" including interviews with professors at Georgetown University where he taught, interviews with Karski himself talking about his life, interviews with historians (such as Martin Gilbert, Ephraim Zuroff), people who interviewed him, archival movie footage (Lodz where he was born, Nazi footage, World War II footage but also scenes from the 1942 Nazi movie *Das ghetto*, which represented the Warsaw ghetto without stating that it was a Nazi propaganda movie), documents, still

---

[71] Many of the previous movies were broadcast on PBS, HBO, and many international television networks. See: "Karski," *Kickstarter*.
[72] "Karski," *Kickstarter*.
[73] Ibid.
[74] Ibid.
[75] Ibid.
[76] Andy Webster, "Review: In 'Karski & the Lords of Humanity', a Holocaust Spy," *The New York Times*, November 26, 2015, https://nyti.ms/3l34pTr. The interview took place in 1977.

pictures (his mother, Karski in his youth, Warsaw ghetto hunger, death on the streets, mass graves, *Muselmanner*). The atrocities appear in live action, still pictures and animation.

The animation in the movie is mimetic, and in the 1940s scenes aims to represent what was not filmed. The people, like in *Waltz with Bashir*, are drawn in a very realistic manner, but sometimes the movement in the animation is fantastic to highlight the moment. The animation depicts his meeting with the two Jewish leaders who asked him to sneak into the Warsaw ghetto to report what he saw. It is animated in a continuous pan movement, during which the protagonists turn from realistic figures into silhouettes, as though they were part of a cruel shadow play. As in other parts of the movie, the animation is intertwined with real-life interviews of Karski from Landsman's documentaries. This combination loads the animation with authenticity. It is an integral part of the testimony and visualizes what he says.

"Never in my life did I think that I would see what I saw in the ghetto in September-October 1942," says Karski, while scenes are shown from the Nazi propaganda movie *Das Ghetto*. One episode is animated as Karski talks about seeing an old man staring blankly ahead. Karski says he asked his Jewish guide what the man was doing. "He is just dying," was the response. "Starvation, degradation, death [...] stench, dirt everywhere, suffocating, nervousness, tension." The scene returns to the interview with Karski in his living room. He gazes downward, suggesting that he is once again seeing these images in his mind.

Another specific incident represented through both animation and live action shows Jews fleeing, while scenes from *Das Ghetto* are intertwined in animation. Karski says that he suddenly saw Jews running and did not understand why. His guide grabbed his arm, and they hid in a house. From the window, Karski saw two boys from the Hitlerjugend. The animation shows what happened: one of them takes a gun and shoots at a window, and a scream is heard. The slow-motion movement shows the Jews running, the two boys, the gunfire is red as the broken window opens to show a woman shot in the chest. The camera returns to a live action interview of Karski in *Shoah*. He is crying: "It was not a part of humanity [...] I had never seen such a thing [...] this kind of reality [...] I was told these are human beings. They didn't look like human beings."

In his efforts to provide the Western world with evidence about the situation of the Jews, Karski also entered a transit camp disguised as an Estonian camp guard. At the time he believed it was the Bełżec death camp, but historians think it was a transit camp.[77] The camp is shown through stills and video

---

[77] Karski accepts this theory. See: Blatman, "A Testimony."

(that were not necessarily taken in this specific camp) and animation depicting the Nazis and collaborators pushing Jews into the train. The pan reveals beatings. Karski talks about a baby being taken from a woman and thrown in the air "like a piece of meat." A woman is beaten on the head. The blood covering her head is animated in slow-motion against a background of sounds of shots and blasts "never again in my life did I see this kind of scene. As soon as I left the camp I started to vomit." The animation shows a hand pressed over his mouth while he was in the camp, to prevent him from screaming.

Karski and the Lords of Humanity is one of the few exceptions that deals successfully with topics found in the other movies: the human spirit, bravery, rebellion, and courageous adventures,[78] yet still presents the atrocities. Almost all of the horrors are represented through the stills and the Nazi footage, and reinforced by the interplay between the animation, the stills, the live action interviews, and Nazi footage. The horrors are represented through the stills and the Nazi footage and reinforced by the interplay between them, the animation, and the live action interviews.

---

[78] Andy Webster, "Review: In 'Karski & the Lords of Humanity,' a Holocaust Spy," *The New York Times*, November 26, 2015, https://nyti.ms/3mhRzQJ

Part II

The Life After

Research on emotional responses to trauma emerged gradually over the course of the twentieth-century. Part II (Chapter 5) draws on studies dealing with Post-Traumatic Stress Disorder (PTSD)[1] and its manifestations in Holocaust survivors[2] to analyze how animated documentaries visualize the visible and invisible components of post-trauma. Aesthetic techniques are crucial to depicting these facets of the aftereffects of trauma in all its complexity and ambiguity. The chapter discusses different modes of dealing with the past, testimonies, and their representations. It shows how animated documentaries can serve as a vehicle for fostering new relationships between the viewer and the documentary text.

---

[1] Judith. L. Herman, *Trauma vehachlama* [*Trauma and Healing*], (Tel-Aviv: Am Oved, 1994) [Hebrew]; Cathy Caruth, *Unclaimed Experience: Trauma, Narrative, and History* (Baltimore: Johns Hopkins University Press, 2016); "PTSD," *Diagnostic and Statistical Manual of Mental Disorders* (DSM 5th ed.) (Arlington, VA: American Psychiatric Publishing, 2013), 271–280.

[2] See, for example: Dov Shmotkin, Amit Shrira, Shira C. Goldberg, and Yuval Palgi, "Resilience and Vulnerability among Aging Holocaust Survivors and their Families: An Intergenerational Overview," *Journal of Intergenerational Relationships* 9, no. 1 (2011), 7–21; Inbar Lebkovitz, "Bein hosen vepgiut: nizolei shoah mizdaknim beisrael" [*Between Resilience and Vulnerability—Holocaust Survivors are Aging in Israel*], *Hebrew Psychology*, April 18, 2012, accessed October 1, 2018, https://bit.ly/3zfqlip

CHAPTER 5

The Face of Post-Trauma

The term "concentration camp syndrome" first appeared in the 1960s. Studies at that time ascribed it to survivors imprisoned during the Nazi era. Over the years, the psychological research of Holocaust survivors has expanded. It acknowledges that individuals who survived the Nazi era cope in different ways.[1]

The term Post-Traumatic Stress Disorder first appeared in *The Diagnostic and Statistical Manual of Mental Disorders* (DSM), published by the American Psychological Association (APA) in 1982. According to the DSM, PTSD can occur after exposure to an event or a series of traumatic events that involve a real risk to individuals or those around them. These events include wars, terrorist incidents, death, forced labor camps, natural disasters, serious accidents, acts of assault and robbery, rape, physical and sexual abuse, and others. Not everyone who has been exposed to trauma develops post-traumatic stress disorder. Sometimes symptoms appear after the event and vanish soon after. Post-traumatic stress disorder is only diagnosed when the symptoms last more than a month.[2]

Currently, different types of symptoms meet the criteria for the diagnosis of PTSD in the DSM-5 and the DSM-5-TR, updated in 2022. These include

---

[1] "Concentration Camp Syndrome," *APA Dictionary of Psychology*, American Psychological Association, https://bit.ly/3quZ7Ch. See also: Jan Bastiaans, "The Kz-Syndrome. A Thirty-year Study of the Effects on Victims of Nazi Concentration Camps," *Rev Med Chir Soc Med Nat Iasi*, Jul–Sep, 78, no. 3 (1974): 573–578; Ryn Zdesilaw, "The KZ-Syndrome and its Evolution through the Generations," *Medical Review Auschwitz: Medicine behind the Barbed Wire Conference Proceedings* 2018, 85–92, trans. Teresa Bałuk-Ulewiczowa; Robert Jabłońskia, Joanna Rosińczukb, Jerzy Leszekc, Izabella Uchmanowiczd, and Bernard Panaszek, "The Progressive Nature of Concentration Camp Syndrome in Former Prisoners of Nazi Concentration Camps—Not Just History, but the Important Issue of Contemporary Medicine," *Journal of Psychiatric Research* 75 (April 2016): 1–6; Antoni Kępiński, "The So-called 'KZ-Syndrome': An Attempt at a Synthesis," *Medical Review Auschwitz*, August 21, 2017, https://bit.ly/3QDaliy

[2] "PTSD," *Diagnostic and Statistical Manual of Mental Disorders* (5th ed.) (Arlington, VA: American Psychiatric Publishing, 2013), 271–280; Judith. L. Herman, *Trauma vehachlama* [Trauma and Healing] (Tel-Aviv: Am Oved, 1994) [Hebrew]; Cathy Caruth, *Unclaimed Experience: Trauma, Narrative, and History* (Baltimore: Johns Hopkins University Press, 2016).

intrusive symptoms and trauma re-experiencing, lucid dreams, flashbacks, intrusive memories during the day, or moments when individuals encounter triggers that make them feel they are in the midst of a traumatic situation while living in the present.[3] Sometimes the symptoms involve expressions of avoidance of anything related to the trauma. Hyperarousal, such as difficulties sleeping, outbursts of anger, hypervigilance, untimely reactions, and difficulties in concentration and memory, are also included. Other well-known characteristics of post-traumatic reactions are symptoms of depression, anxiety, alcohol and drug abuse (which is sometimes attributed to "self-treatment" of mental distress), psychosomatic sensations (such as pain), feelings of guilt ("victim's guilt"), and others. The symptoms of PTSD interfere with daily functioning and disrupt everyday life and routine.[4]

Scholarly debates on post-trauma in Holocaust survivors have developed since the 1980s. Current views suggest that there are numerous differences between survivors in terms of the ways they deal with trauma, such that they should not be treated as a homogenous entity. Different survivors experienced a range of situations under different conditions in terms of age, family, the duration of exposure to the trauma, and their incarceration conditions (ghetto, hideout, labor camp, et cetera). Most recent works acknowledge the long-term suffering of the victims, but there are contradictory opinions as to the impact of the Holocaust on the survivors' lives.[5]

This chapter first focuses on a cinematic rendering of strategies for survival of an orphaned child who suppressed her memories and pain. It then turns

---

[3] On the specific diagnosis of PTSD see: "DSM-5 Criteria for PTSD," National Center for PTSD, US Department of Veterans' Affairs, https://bit.ly/2vOFuZK

[4] Judith Lewis Herman, *Trauma and Recovery* (New York: Basic Books, 2005 [first published 1992]); Richard F. Mollica, *Textbook of Global Mental Health: Trauma and Recovery: A Companion Guide for Field and Clinical Care of Traumatized People Worldwide* (Cambridge: Harvard Program in Refugee Trauma, 2011); "Clinical Practice Guideline for the Treatment of Posttraumatic Stress Disorder (PTSD) in Adults (2017)", Post Traumatic Stress Disorder, APA, https://bit.ly/3xj66Sw; Yael Lahav and Zahava Solomon (eds.), *Restoration of Memory, Treatment of Mental Trauma* (Tel-Aviv: Resling, 2019); "PTSD", *Diagnostic and Statistical Manual of Mental Disorders* (5th ed.) (Arlington, VA: American Psychiatric Publishing, 2013), 271–280; Judith. L. Herman, *Trauma vehachlama* [Trauma and Healing] (Tel Aviv: Am Oved, 1994) [Hebrew]; Cathy Caruth, *Unclaimed Experience: Trauma, Narrative, and History* (Baltimore: Johns Hopkins University Press, 2016); "PTSD Post-Traumatic Stress Disorder: Symptoms, Diagnosis and Treatment," *Tamir Institute for Psychotherapy*, https://bit.ly/3d7dQQW

[5] See, for example: Dov Shmotkin, Amit Shrira, Shira C. Goldberg, and Yuval Palgi, "Resilience and Vulnerability among Aging Holocaust Survivors and their Families: An Intergenerational Overview," *Journal of Intergenerational Relationships* 9, no. 1 (2011): 7–21; Inbar Levkovitz, "Bein hosen vepgiut: nizolei shoah mizdaknim beisrael" [*Between Strength and Venerability: Aging Holocaust Survivors in Israel*], *Hebrew Psychology*, April 18, 2012, accessed October 1, 2018, https://bit.ly/3zfqlip

to lost identities and how they re-emerge later in life. It discusses movies that specifically explore the lives of survivors after the Holocaust and their traumatic memories. It draws on recent research in sociology, psychology, and history to better understand the subjective meanings witnesses attribute to these events, since the survivors build their responses and resilience around this interpretation.[6] The movies analyzed in this chapter explore how animated documentaries capture the broad range of PTSD symptoms by finding ways to show what cannot be seen by the naked eye.[7] Their departure from indexical documentation enables viewers to experience the depth of suffering, repetition compulsion, and the inability to let go of the trauma. The movies analyzed are *Silence* (England, Silvie Bringas and Orly Yadin, 1998), *Broken Branches* (Ayala Sharot, 2014), and *A Trip to the Other Planet* (Israel, Tom Kless, 2014), as well as parts of *Noch Am Leben* [*Still Alive*] (Anita Lester, 2017), *Eva Kor: The Holocaust Survivor who Forgave the Nazis* (Anna Humphries and Amelia Chiew, 2020), and *Kishon* (Eliav Lilty, 2017).

IMPOSED AND SELF-INFLICTED SILENCE IN *SILENCE*

Silence (see also Chapter 3) depicts the Holocaust and its aftermath in Sweden through the perspective of Tana Ross, a child Holocaust survivor who tells her story for the first time fifty years after the Holocaust and explains her long silence. Hers is a story of trauma and post-trauma, memories and forced forgetfulness, self-imposed silence, and attempts to work through the past. *Silence* has been shown worldwide on TV, at movie festivals, in high schools, and in museums.[8]

Between Trauma and Post-Trauma

As discussed in Chapter 3, the movie begins with blurred archival footage of Berlin and then shifts to animation. Walden argued that "archive imagery is expressed with particularly pronounced graininess and fadedness suggesting that such photographs, which are often construed, however inaccurate this may be, as objective, historical evidence of the past, reveal lacunae that can never show us a true sense of the experience of living in that time and

---

[6] Dan Bar-On, *Hapsychologia shel hashoah* [*The Psychology of the Holocaust*] (Ra'anana, Israel: Open University Press, 2006).

[7] Ohad Landesman and Roy Bendor, "Animated Recollections and Spectatorial Experience in *Waltz with Bashir*," *Animation: An Interdisciplinary Journal* 6, no. 3 (2011): 353–370.

[8] Yadin Orly, "But is it Documentary?," in *Holocaust and the Moving Image: Representations in Film and Television since 1933*, eds. Toby Haggith and Joanna Newman (New York: Wallflower Press, 2005), 168–172, https://bit.ly/3xf0mcD

space."⁹ Thus the pivotal moment in Tana Ross's life—the disappearance of her mother and the deportation to Theresienstadt, which ripped her away from her normal world—is symbolized through the abrupt transition from live action scenes to animation. The movie never returns to the "live action" world, even after the Holocaust. This aesthetic technique is a powerful way to convey that trauma can change the victim's life forever and does not cease when the traumatic event ends. It can remain, even if the victim is forbidden to discuss it.

The suitcase in the movie is a leitmotif. It symbolizes detachment, wandering, the lack of a real home, and her imposed silence (the suitcase was one of her hiding places in Theresienstadt). Later it becomes a symbol of being an outsider in Sweden. When Ross discusses growing up in Sweden, the suitcase reappears as Ross says she is twenty and still "the best in hiding." Copley suggested that the suitcase becomes an onscreen signifier of both trauma and post-trauma, and a metaphor for Ross's continuous return to the bounded space of the unspoken and the unseen.[10]

The Act of Remembering

Dori Laub argued that survivors do not always report "empirical historical facts" but rather feelings and emotions.[11] Similarly, James Young noted that "it is not the experiences that are being transmitted in testimony but the special understanding of them that only survivors can have." This special memory must be preserved.[12] Tim Cole calls this "a different kind of truth" that reveals individual perspectives.[13] *Silence* is not a historical documentary about the Holocaust but rather about the traumatic memory of a survivor. The period in Berlin and in Theresienstadt is portrayed in a gritty black and white style that animator Ruth Lingford compares to woodcuts. Animator Tim Webb portrayed the period in Sweden in a very colorful style which takes its inspiration from the work of Charlotte Salomon, a Jewish artist who hid

---

[9] Victoria Grace Walden, "Animation: Textural Difference and the Materiality of Holocaust Memory," *Animation Studies*, 2014, https://bit.ly/3B6x690

[10] Jessica Copley, "Modes of Representing."

[11] Dori Laub, "Bearing Witness on the Vicissitudes of Listening," in *Testimony: Crises of Witnessing in Literature, Psychoanalysis and History*, Shoshana Felman and Dori Laub (London: Routledge, 1992), 57–74; esp. 62.

[12] James E. Young, *Writing and Rewriting the Holocaust: Narrative and the Consequence of Interpretation* (Bloomington: Indiana Univ. Press, 1988), 171.

[13] Tim Cole, "Please Mind the Gap: Integrated Histories and Geographies of the Holocaust and Holocaust Memory," paper presented at the Beyond Camps and Forced Labor Conference, Birkbeck, University of London, January 10–12, 2018.

during the war in Southern France and drew her life story in color before she was murdered in Auschwitz.[14] The visual difference between the two periods also helps define the post-trauma: in the Sweden scenes, when memories take over, flashbacks in black and white penetrate the colorful present. Yadin comments that[15]

> We decided that the film would have two main sections with visual styles to echo the two locations of the film: Theresienstadt and Stockholm. We chose to work with two animators whose work we knew: Ruth Lingford, with her black and white woodcut style images (reminiscent of Käthe Kollwitz) for the camp scenes, and Tim Webb for the colorful, crowded, Swedish part of the story [...] We then worked on a storyboard [...] and a rough voiceover guide [...] we set about hiring our team—animators and painters to flesh out the film. We only recorded Tana's reading of the script after the picture was locked.[16]

The memories that penetrate the present are animated like a nightmare. The language of the scenes is poetic and Lingford commented that this poetic language could only be achieved through animation: "a subtle and more concentrated portrayal of the situation would not have been possible using live-action drama ... using animation makes it clear that this is a subjective account."[17]

In his research on trauma, Dominic LaCapra draws on Freudian theory to distinguish between two forms of memory. The first is termed acting out, where the past is not construed as a distant memory and internalized, but rather is reborn and experienced as though integral to present-day social and cultural life rather than to remote events. The second form is working-through, where clear boundaries are maintained between past and present, and there is an awareness of the differences between then and now. There is less identification with the traumatic period. While there is also a return to the past in working through, it is accompanied by conscious control of the past, a critical distance from it, and perspective-taking. Working-through is used as a mechanism guarding against post-traumatic repetition compulsion; i.e., returning to the trauma while blurring the boundaries between past and present and thus re-experiencing it. This repetition causes suffering and works against the desire of the sufferer not to be flooded with the past.[18]

---

[14] Copley, "Modes of Representing."
[15] Ibid.
[16] Yadin, "But is it Documentary?"
[17] Aaron Kerner, *Film and the Holocaust* (London: Bloomsbury, 2001), 248.
[18] Dominic La Capra, *Writing History, Writing Trauma* (Baltimore: Johns Hopkins University Press, 2000), 37–74.

Tana Ross's new life in Sweden begins in color.[19] She and her grandmother are on a train on the way to Sweden, where "my great uncle and aunt will be waiting for us." The landscape from the window is light green and light blue, with a little brown and yellow. The train rattles through acres of open, bright fields, the complete opposite of the Theresienstadt scenes. But in the space of a second, this wonderful scenery turns black again as memory takes over, making it a train to death in Nazi Europe rather than a train to freedom. As in many cases of acting out, it disappears as quickly as it came, and the scene returns to the colorful train with its bright hues. The past bursts through again when the conductor opens the door politely for them. Ross's grandmother gets off first, but when the conductor goes inside to help Ross, his image is morphed into the image of a Nazi officer trying to grab her hand. As she backs off, he turns back into the Swedish conductor. Ross runs to the safety of her grandmother's arms.

Cathy Caruth defined the return to a traumatic event as a return to the moment when things could conceivably have changed; in other words, when the event could still have been prevented. She suggests that the incomprehensibility of traumatic events makes it impossible to integrate the trauma into a narrative memory of the past. The inability to formulate a comprehensive story from the trauma leads back to the initial trauma in an endless cycle.[20] Maureen Turim suggested that cinematic flashbacks can represent a juncture between present and past that implies memory and history, images of memory, and "the personal archives of the past" of subjective memory.[21] In her view, a flashback is "an image or a filmic segment that is understood as representing temporal occurrences anterior to those in the images that preceded it." It is a representation of the past that intervenes within the present flow of movie narrative,[22] where flashbacks and nightmares escape full consciousness. They provide "a form of recall that survives at the cost of willed memory or of the very continuity of conscious thought."[23] This form of traumatic remembrance can be mimicked cinematically in a nonlinear life

---

[19] On female Holocaust survivors who were sent to Sweden as part of a humanitarian mission after World War II, see: Victoria Martinez, "Afterlives: Histories of Survivors of Nazi Persecution in Sweden," Linköping University, https://bit.ly/3QFmRhM

[20] Cathy Caruth, *Unclaimed Experience: Trauma, Narrative, and History* (Baltimore: Johns Hopkins University Press, 2016), 13; Cathy Caruth, "An Introduction: Recapturing the Past," in *Trauma: Explorations in Memory*, ed. Cathy Caruth (Baltimore: John Hopkins Univ. Press, 1995), 151–157.

[21] Maureen Turim, *Flashbacks in Film* (London: Routledge, 1989), 1–20.

[22] Turim, *Flashbacks*.

[23] Cathy Caruth, "Recapturing the Past: Introduction," in *Trauma: Explorations in Memory*, ed. Cathy Caruth (Baltimore: John Hopkins University Press, 1995), 151–153.

story. Turim suggested that "the flashback is introduced when the image in the present dissolves to an image in the past, understood either as a story being told, or a subjective memory."[24] Other less obviously marked forms of flashback have also been used in movies.[25] In *Silence* these transitions are not accompanied by a blurring of the frame such as fade or dissolve. Rather, the flashbacks abruptly penetrate the present without warning and without any accepted visual or auditory cue.[26] This cinematic choice strengthens the imprecision between past and present and points to the repetition compulsion of the traumatized individual.

PTSD research considers flashbacks a symptom of post-trauma. A flashback is a vivid experience in which one relives some aspects of a traumatic event and feels like it is happening in the present. It can include seeing full or partial images of what happened, sensing sounds, smells, or tastes connected to the trauma, and experiencing pain or anxiety. Specific places, people, or situations can trigger a flashback where unconscious processes link places, events, sounds, smells, or people to the memory of the traumatic event.[27] The movie shows that along with the obvious (a train in Sweden that triggers a flashback of the train to Theresienstadt), even seemingly neutral places or events can cause a traumatic flashback. For example, in one instance, she is watching the St. Lucia's day parade. The animation first shows what everybody sees: pretty angelic girls singing and a devilish character at the end of their row. This archetypal Christian figure is then shown from Ross's perspective, where he resembles an antisemitic caricature of a Jew, which then morphs into a rat (an antisemitic image often used in Nazi propaganda).

Depression and a reduced capacity for enjoyment are characteristics of PTSD. During her time in Sweden, the movie never shows Ross smiling. "I had become a Swedish child," she says as she looks in the mirror as if lying to herself, because everything else hints that inside she is still the girl from

---

[24] Amos Goldberg, *Trauma beguf rishon: ktivat yomanim betqufat hashoah* [*Trauma in the First Person: Diary Writing during the Holocaust*] (Or Yehuda: Dvir, 2012), 78–103 [Hebrew].

[25] Turim, *Flashbacks*, 1–20.

[26] This cinematic blur also appears in later films that feature intrusive flashbacks that haunt a Holocaust survivor, such as *The Pawnbroker* (Sidney Lumet, 1964), *High Street* (Rue Haute & Andre Ernotte, 1976), and *Sophie's Choice* (Alan J. Pakula, 1982); see Joshua Hirsch, "The Pawnbroker and the Posttraumatic Flashback," in *Afterimage: Film, Trauma and the Holocaust* (Philadelphia: Temple University Press, 2003), 85–110; Annette Insdorf, *Indelible Shadows: Film and the Holocaust* (Cambridge: Cambridge University Press, 2003), 27–42; Henry Gonshak, *Hollywood and the Holocaust* (Maryland: Rowman and Littlefield, 2015), 117–130, 163–174.

[27] "Post-Traumatic Stress Disorder (PTSD)," *Mind*, https://bit.ly/3QFmEez

Theresienstadt: "I was eight, I was twelve, I was twenty years old." As she counts, her image twirls in the air in a way that resembles the vortex at the beginning of the movie above the roofs of Nazi Germany. The voiceover incorporates counting in German, just as she counted the number of children pushed into the cattle car being sent from Theresienstadt to Auschwitz. As she flies in the air, props from her past appear, including the laundry basket she hid in. These scenes create a rich, consistent, and trustworthy sense of Ross's inner world for viewers because of their unique aesthetic choices and the mixing of reality with fantasy. The movie's departure from indexical documentation and its shift towards subjective perception and phantasmagorical imaginings augment the depiction of complex events by visualizing what cannot be seen by the naked eye.[28] By combining subjective and fantastic animation modes and by using the metonymic mode of witnessing, the movie increases the audience's knowledge and viewers' ability to identify and sympathize with the survivor and her pain.

The Imposed Silence

Repetition compulsion does not end there. The family that welcomes Ross and her grandmother does not give Ross a sense of warmth. Ross's great-uncle hugs her grandmother, and other figures appear, circling her grandmother, but the frame is white and empty. When Ross leaves the circle, nobody pays attention as she heads towards a suitcase, as if ready to hide again. The voiceover states, "They are curious to see the survivors, especially the miracle child." A relative follows her and joyfully lifts her in the air, but his body, which becomes gigantesque as he approaches, is intimidating rather than comforting. When he lifts her, she imagines she is flying over rooftops just like her flight from Berlin to Theresienstadt, only this time in color—the past is there again.

The movie depicts two rooms in her uncle's home: the large living room in red, and Ross's room, in blue. The contrast creates two separate spaces as though Ross is not an integral part of the household. The uncle, a former concert conductor, performs for his friends in the red room. In the blue room, a color associated with cold and sadness (another meaning of blue), Ross's aunt brushes her hair and whispers: "Don't tell, don't tell, we don't ever want to know. Promise?" she insists before she tucks her into bed. The small child looks lost in the big bed. "I knew how to keep silent," Ross says as she and the animation go back in her imagination to Theresienstadt, to the basket in which she was hidden, suggesting how enforced muteness is

---

[28] Landesman and Bendor, "Animated Recollection," 353–370.

possible only towards the outside. On the inside, the post-trauma cannot be silenced.

The flashback/nightmare ends in the morning when her aunt enters the room and opens the curtains. "Today is another day, my aunt used to say," Ross states, referring not only to the new day but to her new life in Sweden. The "old day," the Holocaust, must not be mentioned. "You must forget the past," her aunt tells her, as she dresses her in the big blue room. In keeping with the sadness infused by the aunt's behavior, the backdrop of the animation is always blue as her aunt does the housework.

These scenes represent how the older Ross, the narrator, perceives her aunt, who in one sense, completely misunderstood Ross's need to talk, share, and unburden herself, and locked her in a circle of silence that lasted years. Conversely, the older Ross grasps that her aunt meant well and thought she was helping her. Director Yadin supports this perception visually in that the aunt is not represented as evil. When Ross recalls her aunt's warnings, her voice is tender. The visuals show that she takes care of Ross well. This combination of assistance and avoidance was not unique to post-war Sweden.[29] The movie describes the aftermath of the war, a time when information on PTSD did not exist. In this sense, the aunt's need for enforced silence seemed reasonable to many people. It is possible that at the bottom of her heart, her aunt felt guilty for not doing enough during the Holocaust to save her family. Her way of coping was trying to avoid everything connected to the past. She could not avoid Ross, but she could avoid her stories by imposing silence. The fact that she does have a name might signify that she represents a wider phenomenon.

When Ross grows up, she leaves her uncle's home on another train to freedom, this time escaping her aunt's demand for silence. But can she talk? Her aunt and uncle give her a box containing desperate letters her mother wrote to them, pleading to arrange a visa for her and her family since her attempts in other countries had failed. As Ross's voiceover reads these letters, the animation shifts between black and white scenes of her mother writing in Berlin, bent over a desk, and the comfort of the red living room in Sweden

---

[29] See, for example: Dina Porat, *Café haboker b'reach ha'ashan* [*Smoke-Scented Morning Coffee*] (Jerusalem: Yad Vashem: Am Oved, 2011); Liat Steir-Livny, *Shtei panim bamar'a* [*Two Faces in the Mirror*] (Jerusalem: Eshkolot-Magnes, 2009); Jeffry Shandler, *While America Watches: Televising the Holocaust* (New York: Oxford University Press, 1999); Lawrence Baron, "The Holocaust and American Public Memory, 1945–1960," *Holocaust and Genocide Studies* 17, no. 1 (2003): 62–88; Hasia R. Diner, *We Remember with Reverence and Love: American Jews and the Myth of Silence after the Holocaust, 1945–1962* (New York: New York University Press, 2009); Beth Cohen, *Case Closed: Holocaust Survivors in Postwar America* (New Jersey: Rutgers University Press, 2017).

where her aunt is playing the piano. The calmness of the living room in Sweden creates dissonance and discomfort. The hint is sub-textualized but clear: they did not go out of their way to help her. They read the letters, lived their lives, stored the letters in a drawer, and her uncle continued to conduct an orchestra. The red living room takes on metaphorical meaning as the red of blood: "It took me 50 years to tell that story," Ross finally says.

In this parallel editing, the colors sometimes overlap, such that in one sequence, Ross's mother's striped dress is reflected on her uncle's body. Later, when the animation returns to Berlin, the uncle is animated for several seconds in black and white. Yadin says:

> We wanted to question the wartime role of her Swedish relatives through the full range of Tana's emotions, but without assigning blame that could not be proven [...], We tried to construct the images in such a way as to imply all this without having to spell it out. Animation is very useful for saying a lot in very few frames and saying it ambiguously enough for the audience to form its own interpretation and bring its own experience to the screen.[30]

Without any clear finger-pointing (thus creating another unresolved silence), these scenes constitute a muffled accusation that the uncle and aunt did nothing when her mother tried to save her family. Yadin says that since the movie presents several forms of silence, she and her colleagues initially thought of calling the movie *Silences*. "Eventually, we decided that one generic 'silence' would stand for more than the plural of the word."[31] In the movie, Ross breaks her silence and tells her story, but as Sara Horowitz noted concerning representation in *Maus*, "The space of the told story is framed by untold stories."[32] It provides only bits and pieces of a fragmented past that could never be stitched together after fifty years of silence.

EMOTIONAL DETACHMENT IN *BROKEN BRANCHES*

Scholars have voiced concern that the ubiquity of animated documentaries in the twenty-first century may lead to superficial exploitation of animation as a mere visual accompaniment to the soundtrack. By contrast, *Broken Branches* shows how a director uses animation not only to reflect the Holocaust survivors' stories, point of view, and mental state, but also to subvert them and deal with the director's emotional understanding of these stories in ways that sometimes contradict the protagonists' attitudes, feelings, and beliefs.

---

[30] Yadin, "But is it Documentary?"
[31] Ibid.
[32] Sara R. Horowitz, *Voicing the Void: Muteness and Memory in Holocaust Fiction* (Albany: State University of New York Press, 1997), 3.

Figure 5.1 Broken Branches *(Ayala Sharot, 2014)*

The movie's protagonist is Michla Rechter (later Michal), who grew up in Sinewca, Poland. She and her siblings were members of the Gordonia Zionist youth movement that operated youth camps for children throughout Poland. Children who were fit to immigrate to Palestine were chosen, and in 1936, Rechter was one of them. Her father encouraged her to go in the hope that the rest of the family would sell the family farm and follow her. Her mother objected to sending a fourteen-year-old alone and wanted to wait until the whole family could immigrate together. However, Rechter's father decided they should send her immediately: "The sooner we act, the better." Rechter, together with other adolescents, was sent to the Ben-Shemen Youth Village in Palestine. At the end of 1940, she stopped receiving letters from her family. Later she found out they had been shot, along with the rest of the village's Jews, in 1941.[33]

The director, Ayala Sharot, is Rechter's granddaughter. She studied animation in Israel and later moved to London to complete her MA in communication design. According to Sharot, her grandmother never referred to herself as a "Holocaust survivor," and neither did she. In a country like Israel that is steeped in horrific stories of Holocaust survivors who were in occupied Europe during World War II, Rechter's story is somewhat out of the ordinary. Even though Rechter left Poland three years before the onset of the war, Poland in 1933 to 1936 was dominated by the rise of Nazism in Germany. Her years in Palestine were haunted by the letters she received from her family and by the realization that they were all shot and interred in

---

[33] List Steir-Livny, "An Interview with Ayala Sharot," August 5, 2016.

mass burial pits. Sharot did not realize the significance of her grandmother's tragic story in the context of Holocaust remembrance and commemoration until she told non-Israelis in London about it.[34] This revelation sparked *Broken Branches*, a hybrid combining live action and animated documentary.

A Hybrid Movie

The movie is composed of Sharot's interviews with Rechter. It reflects what movie scholar Bill Nichols called "the interactive mode," in which the moviemaker is part of the movie in that he or she looks, listens, speaks, and reacts on camera (and not only in voiceover) to the actors. Since the moviemaker interacts, questions, and provokes situations, her impact on these situations becomes an integral part of the movie.[35] Sharot is not seen on screen, but her voice is heard from behind the camera, and her close ties with her grandmother produce informal and casual exchanges. The movie does not present a "talking head" describing the past but rather two women discussing Rechter's life story. To highlight this freewheeling, intimate atmosphere, Sharot inserts ongoing dialogues into the movie. For example, the soundtrack at the beginning of the movie includes dialogue such as "Are you shooting right now? Just a minute, I'm trying to set the focus" as the titles fade. When they meet Rechter's friend Sarah Berman, who was sent with Rechter to the Ben Shemen Youth Village, Sharot inserts the small talk before the interview, where Berman urges them to eat something, and Rechter asks Sharot if she has eaten breakfast.

Rechter dominates the scenes: she is filmed, heard, and shown in live-action and still pictures. She is also morphed into an animation that often overtakes the scenes and represents her unfilmed past, thoughts, and emotions. Sharot chose to tell Rechter's story with various animation techniques, "some of which I invented specifically for the movie."[36] Alongside its cartoon style-animation and other genres, the movie is clearly inspired by Marc Chagall's oil paintings.[37] For example, the Polish scenery is influenced by Chagall's paintings of pre-World War II Polish shtetls in East Europe that depict tiny houses on crowded off-kilter hills in dream-like surroundings with

---

[34] Ibid.
[35] Bill Nichols, *Representing Reality: Issues and Concepts in Documentary* (Bloomington: Indiana University Press, 1991), 32–75; Bill Nichols, *Introduction to Documentary* (Bloomington: Indiana University Press, 2001), 142–211.
[36] Barry Davis, "Mending 'Broken Branches'", *The Jerusalem Post*, August 6, 2014, accessed September 6, 2014, https://bit.ly/3978bok
[37] Daniella Kopler, "Meet the Creator: An Interview with Ayala Sharut for her Upcoming Movie 'Broken Branches,'" *Moonfash*, May 1, 2015 [Hebrew], accessed May 5, 2015, https://bit.ly/3k5kk3k

peasants and Jewish icons like *Klezmer*,[38] *Challah*,[39] and Hebrew letters flying in the sky. The animation sometimes appears in separate scenes from the live action segments, or "intervenes" in the live action scenes, thus creating hybrid moments.

The Role of Animation: The Two Perspectives

Sharot claims that animation should primarily serve the story and the stylistic choices should always derive from the content. Animation in her movie is used to represent historical facts in an innovative way.[40] At the beginning of the movie, in the first interview with Rechter about her childhood, Sharot provides biographical details through animation. Rechter sits in the middle of the frame while illustrations, names, and numbers are animated around her, giving her fragmented memories a more concrete context. These include information such as her maiden name (Michla Gelfand), date of birth (1922), her status (retired teacher), and number of children, grandchildren, and great-grandchildren. Sharot does the same when she introduces Berman, Rechter's friend and former classmate at Ben Shemen. This enables her to avoid standard expositions and presentations of the protagonists' biographical information.

In some scenes the animation complements Rechter's statements.[41] When Rechter reads out loud from an article she wrote as a child in Poland where she talks about looking forward to winter and riding on a sleigh, a happy little girl is animated on a sleigh. When Rechter reads from a poem about hoping for spring to come, happy children play outside.

Sharot claims that animation is best suited to dealing with difficult and challenging topics and considers that the story of a girl who was orphaned after her family was murdered fits this description. However, Rechter is laconic. She delivers pieces of information in what Amir refers to as a "metaphoric mode of witnessing." In this mode, the traumatic events are not only repeated but are also represented from a distance, enabling the formulation of new meanings.[42] Most of the time, Rechter maintains an emotional distance from the events (even the most horrific ones). This is unacceptable to Sharot, who is more emotional and perceives her grandmother's stories differently. Sharot uses animation to compensate for what she cannot get from her grandmother, namely, a more dynamic description of the past and her inner

---

[38] Jewish musicians specializing in Jewish music. They were entertainers, especially in Eastern Europe.
[39] Traditional braided loaf of bread for the Sabbath.
[40] Davis, "Mending 'Broken Branches.'"
[41] Ibid.
[42] Amir, *Bearing Witness*, 10–11.

world. She imagines what Rechter's reactions must have been as a child and her feelings into the frame, thus adding another stratum to the story. As a result, the story is told from three perspectives: the elderly Rechter who recollects, the young Rechter, and Sharot.

During their meeting with Berman, Rechter reminisces about her arrival in Palestine. Sharot adds entertaining animations to highlight what she believes was the girls' perspective of their encounter with the new land and its people. When Rechter talks about the Arabs they saw in the Jaffa harbor, she says they had "wide trousers. We looked at these odd people. The trousers they wore," Sharot combines an animation of an Arab with two humorous depictions of Rechter and Berman as young girls. One points at him while a comic strip balloon comes out of her mouth, saying, "Look! An Arab!" while the other girl's caption reads, "Oh dear!" As Rechter and Berman go through the still pictures from Ben Shemen, the two cartoon-like little girls pop up again, pointing at the still pictures with amazement. Their dialogue balloons laugh as they comment, "Look at those shorts" and "They are all so tanned." Sharot also brings the stills to life by having animated bees, the symbol of life in an agricultural youth village, buzzing around the people in the pictures.

Animation also enables Sharot to dissect her grandmother's perspective. According to Dori Laub, there are two main ways of bearing witness: being a witness to a trauma, such as the victims who experienced the Holocaust who can testify to what happened to them, and witnesses to the trauma witnesses (the listeners or interviewers). Laub discusses the strong emotional influence of testimony on the listener: "Through his very listening, he [the hearer] comes to partially experience trauma in himself."[43] *Broken Branches* shows that the "witness to the witness" can prompt an interpretation of the testimony, which may not match the way the witness represents events. Sharot says this is why she loves animated documentaries:

> You can bounce back between ideas. The content and the visuals engage in a kind of dialogue [...] What interests me most about combining documentary and animation is not that you can add animation to the movie or fill in the gaps, but rather create a dual perspective. My grandmother has a way of seeing things. There are times when Grandma thinks one thing, and I understand it differently, so I use animation to present my point of view.[44]

---

[43] Dori Laub, "Bearing Witness on the Vicissitudes of Listening," in *Testimony: Crises of Witnessing in Literature, Psychoanalysis and History*, Shoshana Felman and Dori Laub (London: Routledge, 1992), 57–74.

[44] Daniella Kopler, "Meet the Creator: An Interview with Ayala Sharot for her Upcoming Movie 'Broken Branches,'" *Moonfash*, May 1, 2015 [Hebrew], https://bit.ly/3hrYKEf; Steir-Livny, "An Interview with Ayala Sharot."

When Rechter talks about her first days in Ben Shemen, she says that she had packed pajamas and two nightgowns but quickly realized that in Ben Shemen, nobody wore nightgowns, so she hid them. She tells this as a funny anecdote, but Sharot sees it in a more serious, tragic-dramatic manner. As Rechter speaks, Sharot paints a suitcase with pajamas and nightgowns. But the suitcase also contains other objects that, according to Sharot, Rechter had to do without in her new life and identity: a piano, an elegant teacup, and a can of sardines. She did not merely put away the nightgowns; she surrendered her entire Polish identity.

Rechter describes her welcome in Ben Shemen nostalgically ("They enveloped us in a warm atmosphere."). Even the process of name-changing, which was traumatic for many newcomers to Palestine (and later, to Israel), is described in simple, laconic terms ("during this time we felt we had to do everything like the Eretz-Israelis"). She saw no harm in it ("So since then, I am Michal. O.K. Michal"). Sharot, in her animation, makes it clear that the name change was a much weightier process. Through animation, she erases Rechter's still picture and inserts a new picture of Rechter as a child with a different haircut and the typical Eretz-Israeli hat in its place. Her Polish identity is gone. Sharot animates Rechter's transformation by mimicking Zionist propaganda posters of the 1930s and 1940s that depicted the iconic young *Sabra* in khaki shorts and the *kova tembel* [a hat] that became a national symbol. She does not draw her grandmother as an individual. Rechter's image is multiplied to highlight the expectation that everyone should dress and act according to the norms of the new country. Thus, while Rechter summarizes this transition very casually ("even though we [the children in Ben Shemen] were lonely, we were happy"), Sharot takes a more critical stance.

The two talk about the changes in hygiene that the Polish children had to adapt to in Palestine. Ayala enlivens the stories by filling the frame with impressions of 1930s and 1940s commercial hygiene posters. Rechter describes a specific incident in which Hava Lubianiker, the house mother, took one of Michal's classmates, Ze'ev Koviasky, into the shower, scrubbed him vigorously, and told him in Yiddish, "you are an old bear" (meaning you are old enough to know how to get clean). Rechter tells this story as though it was a very funny incident. She says Lubianiker was warm to them, and wanted to help the young boy. She describes Lubianiker as "courageous." When people said, "How can a woman get in the shower with a grown boy?" Lubianiker replied, "I have already seen such things." Sharot sees it differently: "From my point of view, I saw it as something very sad and represented it in a mixed style, using a combination of cut-out and manual animation. Together with suitable music and scene design, it takes a more mournful and more critical approach."[45] In the scene, Sharot portrayed Koviasky as a big bear who sheds a tear when a tiny woman forcibly washes him. There is nothing funny about it, and the contradiction between Rechter's voiceover and the visuals enables the viewers to reflect on their views of the incident.

Rechter maintains the metaphoric witnessing mode and does not burst into tears or manifest hardship, even when reading aloud the last letters she received from her family. To highlight the tragedy, Sharot inserts the voice of a young actor who reads the letter Rechter received from her younger brother Naftaly, and then the voice of a young actress who reads the letter she received from her sister Dvora. Naftaly was too young to understand the political situation. His letter is childish and is accompanied by childish animation. In contrast, Rechter's sister's letter is more mature and depressed. She sees the future in dark colors and asks Rechter to try to save them. Sharot animates a sad young woman drawn in white against a black background and adds dark abstract figures resembling blood, which spreads all over the letter.[46] This is the first and only time that Rechter tears up a bit, explaining that she was a child and did not know what to do. "Maybe I should have asked the teachers, told them to help, or ... I don't know ... but ... maybe she even demanded that the school here accept her. I don't know ... but perhaps ... I have often thought that maybe I should have done more, but I don't know what I could have done." Her real-life image dissolves into her animated sister's depiction. The pages of the letter fall and dissolve into a campfire, a popular group activity among Eretz-Israeli youth. The fusing of these elements confirms that, in Sharot's perspective, Rechter's distant and detached storytelling manner is a defense mechanism intended to protect her from "survivors' guilt."[47]

While sitting in front of the camera in another scene, Rechter attempts to explain her emotional remoteness from the horrific events, claiming that she and others like her do not have nightmares because they did not experience the disaster. "We were not damaged by the catastrophe because we didn't go through it ourselves; we didn't experience it." As home videos of Rechter as a young mother with her new family appear, Rechter continues, "You start a family, you live here ... a person cannot go through life constantly thinking about these problems even though it was my immediate family. You weren't there with them, so you didn't experience it." But Sharot persists and asks,

---

[45] Steir-Livny, "An Interview with Ayala Sharot."
[46] Davis, "Mending 'Broken Branches.'"
[47] Bonnie Sue Fisher and Steven P. Lab (eds.), *Encyclopedia of Victimology and Crime Prevention* (London: SAGE, 2010), 33.

"But you did experience that you were suddenly alone in the world?" Rechter does not change her expression or tone and responds, "That I was a girl who was all alone in this world? I realized that long before." Her live action figure dissolves into her animated image showing the young Michal, the ship behind her, and the sea in front of her. The blue waves resemble the flames of the Chagall paintings and fade into a notebook with a popular Polish song. This montage captures Sharot's constant struggle with Rechter's metaphoric mode of witnessing. She refuses to accept this emotional distance and keeps on inserting the tragedy in Poland into the Eretz-Israeli narrative.

The Horrors as Symbols

Berman, Rechter's friend, also maintains an emotional distance when recounting the events of her life. She describes the shooting of her family in a detached manner: "In my hometown, there was a beautiful park, Radziwill Park. So, they dug a big pit in the middle of the park and threw all the Jews in alive … dead." Sharot considers that since Rechter and Berman maintained an emotional distance, "all the emotion comes from the animation."[48] As the two friends discuss the faith of their families during the Holocaust, the frame turns black, and a menacing scarecrow is positioned near a tree. The sound of broken branches is heard as the scarecrow seems to be holding an eye it took from one of the murdered people in its mouth.

In another scene, Rechter talks about the murder of her family. In a live action scene, Ayala gently asks her grandmother if she knows when the Nazis took her family. "It was on the Day of Atonement. They rounded up all the people in the village and made them stand in line. They had to dig their graves, and then a group of soldiers shot them, and they fell into the grave, and the grave was covered. That's it. That was the story." Sharot animated this as a duck range at a country fair, but the images in the booth are Rechter's family, taken from her family photo album. Sitting ducks with targets on their bodies are in the foreground, and her family members with targets on their bodies are in the background. Sounds of shots are heard, and their bodies are covered in blood. The combination of real photos of her family members in the animated sitting duck booth turns the incident into something more concrete: actual human beings were slaughtered there. She does not depict horrors, but the image of the sitting ducks is chilling.

As Rechter's story ends, a red curtain with Nazi symbols comes down as though what the viewers saw was a part of a grotesque play. The curtain rises again, revealing the youth of Ben Shemen standing smiling in front of the

---

[48] Steir-Livny, "An Interview with Ayala Sharot."

camera. At first, the sitting ducks remain, but then they disappear, and familiar symbols of Eretz-Israel appear, such as palm trees, the desert, a camel, the bright sun, plowed land, and fruit. They symbolize how Rechter distances herself from memories of her family, puts an emotional barrier between herself and their faith, and sticks to her new Eretz-Israeli identity.[49]

At the end of the movie, Rechter sings a song from her childhood that she says she has not sung for seventy or eighty years. In a choking voice, she sings "Please tell me, my dear child, please tell me, my beloved, how will you travel? How will you travel to the Land of Israel?" As the camera centers on Rechter's hands holding the notebook, all the animated elements which Sharot considers to represent her grandmother's life story from Poland and Eretz-Israel are animated together: the Chagall-style houses of the shtetl, the klezmer, the piano, the teacup, Eretz-Israeli fruit, the sun, her classmate the bear, and the Eretz-Israeli scenery. They circle the Eretz-Israeli sun and vanish into the pages. Rechter closes the notebook, and the movie ends. Rechter tries to close the door on the past; Sharot refuses. The animation enables the past in Europe to filter into Eretz Israel, and Rechter's life story encompasses the two places that will forever be intertwined within Rechter's identity, even though she perceives a clear chronological boundary between the two.

Depressing the Depression[50]

In the hybrid *Kishon* that depicts the famous Israeli author and Holocaust survivor Efraim Kishon (see Chapter 3), Kishon claims he was "raised and educated by the Holocaust." In a live action interview with Kishon's daughter Renana, she says she does not doubt that "the school of the Holocaust, World War II, shaped major parts of his personality. The sarcasm, the skepticism, the sense that we are not standing on solid ground […] in our lives he went back there every day." She and his two adult sons, Raphael and Amir, cite examples showing that a person who seems to be in control and working through the trauma is actually shaped in the present by his traumatic past, which, many times, acts out in various ways. When Kishon ate his meals, for example, he would place all the food around him, and if someone dared take something from his "territory," he would slap them on the wrist.

Individuals who suffer from PTSD can try to avoid the triggers that remind them of the trauma. If these triggers are everyday occurrences, avoidance can

---

[49] List Steir-Livny, "An Interview with Ayala Sharot."
[50] "Kishon," *Go2Films*, https://bit.ly/3d8LINf

crimp a person's lifestyle. On the other hand, others unconsciously look for content and places that remind them of the event and have difficulty letting go. Both avoidance and compulsive searching are attempts at dealing with difficult memory.[51] Kishon's children talk about his compulsive interest in Nazi materials and symbols. Before he went to bed, he used to stomp his feet to imitate the Nazi soldiers' goosesteps and said "Heil" with a Nazi salute. He would play audio cassettes in the car with speeches by Hitler and other high-ranking Nazis as they drove down the streets of Tel-Aviv. Amir says he found it funny. As children, they did not know it was supposed to be frightening. The directors screen home videos of cute children in the car with Kishon, with the speeches in the soundtrack. The contrast between the naïve faces of the children and the sound is overwhelming.

This compulsion was mixed with sarcasm and black humor. Freud[52] saw humor as a pivotal defense mechanism. He believed that when people use humor in situations that provoke fear and anxiety, they gain a new perspective on the situation that helps them avoid experiencing negative emotions. Through humor, people can thus avoid or reduce their emotional suffering and grief. More recent studies[53] view humor as a defense mechanism that helps alleviate stress, cope with negative feelings and tough situations, mitigate suffering, temporarily dissipate feelings of anxiety, and endow people with a sense of power and control in situations of helplessness. Humor can help those coping with unpleasant memories and enable trauma victims to lessen their tension and anxiety. It also helps people maintain emotional distance from the trauma by creating a "comfort zone." As a defense mechanism, humor takes two forms: black humor and self-deprecating humor. Black humor deals with anxiety-producing subjects. The therapeutic importance of black humor and self-deprecating humor for traumatized individuals has been frequently studied in a wide range of contexts (among victims of abuse, crime, disasters, et cetera), particularly in the context of Jewish humor.[54] Black humor has been presented as an effective tool for an oppressed minority to withstand attacks by their oppressors; in the Jewish

---

[51] Yael Lahav and Zahava Solomon (eds.), *Restoration of Memory, Treatment of Mental Trauma* (Tel-Aviv: Resling, 2019).

[52] Sigmund Freud, *The Psychopathology of Everyday Life* (1901) (New York: W. W. Norton and Company, 1990).

[53] See, for example: Itamar Levin, *Mibaad la-dmaot* [*Through the Tears: Jewish Humor under the Nazi Regime*] (Jerusalem: Yad Vashem, 2004), 13–36; Haya Ostrover, *Lelo humour hainu mitabdim* [*If Not for Humor, We would have Committed Suicide*] (Jerusalem: Yad Vashem, 2009), 63–104.

[54] Avner Ziv, "Psycho-social Aspects of Jewish Humor in Israel and in the Diaspora," in Avner Ziv (ed.), *Jewish Humour* (New Brunswick: Transaction Publishers, 1998), 47–76.

context, it constitutes the defense mechanism of an entire people.[55] Thus, these scenes point to the very interesting phenomenon of acting out (compulsion) while activating mechanisms that are presumed to create a mental buffer between the traumatized person and the past. Renana talks about how black humor and the absurd was a therapeutic tool for her father, "otherwise, a dam would break, and he wouldn't have been able to survive."

The animation highlights his blurred identity between past and present in hybrid scenes in which elderly images of Kishon and journalist Yaron London, who interviews him, dissolve into 1940s footage of Jews being marched down one of the main streets of Budapest. The dissolve is another cinematic device to signal acting out. The elderly Kishon's image is combined for a few seconds with the 1940s scenes of Jewish humiliation and fear. It is an integral part of his identity, both visually and mentally. The Jews with their yellow badges walk down the street, raising their hands in surrender, while the "camera" pans slightly to the side to show the animated elderly Kishon and London walking near them. Dogs are barking in the background.

These scenes were probably partially inspired by Lanzmann in *Shoah*, who sometimes walked with his interviewees in places that were once filled with death but in the present are green and pleasant, as though nothing bad had ever happened there. The horrific story completely contradicts the pleasant scenery. Animated documentary enables the viewer to enter Kishon's mind as he walks down memory lane, literally into the visuals (which Lanzmann felt should not be used) to demonstrate the hold of the traumatic past in the present.

The movie suggests that Kishon became increasingly drawn to Germany, where he became a great success in the 1980s while his popularity was declining in Israel. Israeli taste in humor had changed; Kishon's third movie, *The Fox in the Chicken Coop* (1977), was a failure, and he felt he was marginalized. Whereas in these years, outside Israel, his books were translated into numerous languages, his plays performed across Europe, and the Germans adored his work.

The animated figures of Kishon and London discuss his changing attitude towards Germany. In 1952 he wrote in one of his columns that he opposed screening German movies in Israel (which was the consensus in Israel then). He knew it was not logical to ban the cultural output of an entire people, but claimed that his sense of logic had been cremated in Auschwitz. This all

---

[55] Joanna Sliwa, "Jewish Humor as a Source of Research on Polish-Jewish Relations," in Leonard Greenspoon (ed.), *Jews and Humour* (West Lafayette: Purdue University Press), 67–82; Ruth Wisse, *No Joke: Making Jewish Humour* (Princeton: Princeton University Press, 2013), 59–103.

changed in the 1980s. An animated Kishon fills the screen as an animated German flag unfurls behind him and then morphs into the animated flag of the European Union, and then flags of other European countries, as he explains his stance: "If you don't go to Germany, you cannot travel to Europe at all," since almost every country took part in one way or another in the annihilation of the Jews. Amir, his son, backs up his attitude as videos of Kishon at a very successful book signing in Germany are shown: "Father said to me that 'the children of the executioners stand in line for hours, waiting for me to sign their book.'" He appears to have made peace with the past. "Both sides fell in love with each other," laughs Amir. In the last few years of his life, after his second wife Sara died of cancer, Kishon met Lisa, an Austrian non-Jew many years his junior. They got married in 2003 and lived together in Appenzell, Switzerland, in a German-speaking canton since their language of communication was German.

However, the movie shows that PTSD is a much deeper experience and external changes cannot heal it. In Israel, he carried a gun, and in Switzerland, he carried a kit he called his "murder bag" everywhere with him. He needed to have it with him at all times, even when he watched TV. Lisa opens the kit in front of the camera: it consisted of a small, handsome bag that contained a gun, cyanide pills for Kishon and herself, candy ("so I would not fall asleep in case of an emergency"), an alarm to contact the security company he hired ("when he pressed it, a security guard would come"), earplugs (so gunfire would not startle him), and a flashlight camouflaged as a pen. Lisa explained that the kit was in preparation for an abduction. "He didn't want to be a prisoner who could be tortured, he didn't want to be helpless. He wanted to make his own decisions."

Depression is another characteristic of PTSD and is examined in animated documentary scenes when the animated figures of London and Kishon walk together in a stunning Swiss landscape. "Do you fight your depression?" asks London. "All-out war. I don't give in," says Kishon, "I lash out at that idiot Ferike." The fact that he refers to his childhood name highlights that the roots of his depression go back to the Holocaust. Kishon says that fighting "Ferike" means forcing himself to start working, take medication, learn to dive, play chess, and flip through channels on TV. "In short, I'm trying to depress my depression. Sometimes it works. Sometimes it doesn't."

His son Amir explains his depression and the murder bag. "He went back *there*," he says as the scene shows Kishon's animated figure walking near the Jews huddled in Rackutzy street in Budapest. In earlier scenes, London's animated figure walked beside him. Now Kishon is alone, walking near them, looking at them as Amir states "In terms of the narrative of his life, the Holocaust was the first chapter and the last chapter. The classic narrative in which the end connects with the beginning." As the camera zooms in on a still picture of the elderly Kishon, Amir suggests that "As you get old, the psychological muscles that stop the Holocaust get weaker. It that sense it all came out." The camera returns to the scene of the home movies of the children sitting in the car listening to Hitler's speeches that Kishon used to play during their drives. It stayed with him his entire life.

FORGIVENESS IN *EVA KOR: THE HOLOCAUST SURVIVOR WHO FORGAVE THE NAZIS*

As noted in Chapter 4, the first three minutes of the movie *Eva Kor: The Holocaust Survivor who Forgave the Nazis* tell the story of Eva and her twin sister Miriam, who were deported to Auschwitz and subjected to Mengele's horrific experiments on twins but survived. The rest of the movie deals with Eva's unique mechanism of dealing with her trauma.

"Six months after (the liberation from Auschwitz), we were home," says Eva in her voiceover. She and Miriam stand on a hilltop overlooking their home but as they go inside, the peaceful countryside disappears when they discover no one in the family survived. The way Eva opens the door is animated in an oblique angle to make it awkward for the viewers to see. Personal belongings are scattered on the floor. "Only three crumpled pictures" were left of their family.

The titles state that Eva married and started a family in the US. Her sister had health issues due to the Nazi experiments. In 1987, Eva donated her a kidney, "but she died in 1993." Miriam's image fades from the frame as though being blown away by the wind, and Eva is left alone, standing and crying, falling to the ground, as the ground begins to crack, symbolizing Eva's mental state: "I was devastated. She was the only one from our family that was alive."

Outbursts of anger are characteristic of post-trauma. When her sister was alive, it was marginalized. Upon her death, these feelings burst out. Anger can be about why an event happened to a person. Alternatively, there can be anger about one's reaction during and after the event or one's reaction in the present. Anger can also be directed at the world for its unfairness or lack of understanding on the part of others. The amount of anger accumulated in a person and its intensity can be overwhelming.[56] The black cracks tie her up like ropes, and the frame turns black as Eva says, "I was angry." The darkness fills her.

---

[56] "PTSD—How Do You Recognize a Post-Traumatic Reaction? Post Trauma Signs and Treatment Methods," Dr. Tal Center, https://bit.ly/3qBg2Dm

A candle burns in the dark frame as the titles explain this darkness and light: "As the years passed, Eva tried to heal herself from her traumatic past. She took the unusual step of contacting a Nazi doctor named Hans Munch." She is animated in a train, as the title gives the date "August 20, 1993." In the scenes that described her previous life, there were no specific dates, only years. This precision indicates the importance of this life-changing day. "I was headed to Germany to meet a Nazi doctor. I was unbelievably nervous and scared." As she is invited in, no symbol connects this location with evil: the house is in the countryside, surrounded by greenery, and the man who welcomes her looks like a nice elderly individual. There is no threatening music or dark images: "Dr. Munch at that time was 82 years old. He greeted me with kindness, respect and consideration." Coffee is poured into cups in elegant chinaware, and the two of them sit on the balcony. "I was blown away. A Nazi treating me with respect." The "camera" shows a picture of him in his youth on the wall, which is also not intimidating. He is drawn as a good-looking, kind young man: "Dr. Hans Munch was a bacteriologist at Auschwitz," Eva comments as the frame dissolves to him in Nazi uniform next to a barbed wire fence as she says, "but he also had a second job, since he was stationed outside the gas chambers." He is portrayed looking through a small round window in a door. The animation shows what he sees: piles of corpses, gray and obscure through the round window: "When people were dead, he would sign one death certificate, no names, just the numbers of the people who were murdered." Here, as in the entire movie, she expresses herself with clear emotional remoteness. Her tone does not change when she talks about the last time she saw her mother, the fact that she almost died from the experiments, or the duties in Auschwitz of the doctor, whom she decided to forgive. Eva and the director go so far as to identify with his trauma. He tells her: "This is my problem; this is a nightmare that I live with." The camera dissolves to the elderly Munch, who looks nice and kind and has the same sad face. These scenes show how the directors embrace Eva's perspective. They could have subverted her testimony (as Sharot did in *Broken Branches*), but they did not. They accept it and reinforce it through the animation and the touching music in the scenes that symbolize the immensity of the moment when Munch agrees to go to the Auschwitz memorial museum with Eva.

The animation zooms along the famous train tracks to Auschwitz as though riding on them: "I asked him if he was willing to go with me to Auschwitz and make the same statement that he made to me, and he said he would love to." The titles appearing on a white screen (to symbolize that the darkness in her life is over) state that Munch revisited the gas chambers with Eva and signed a document confirming they existed. "Eva wanted to thank him." She is drawn in her home next to a wall with a picture of her and

Miriam. The picture dissolves into earlier scenes that depicted Auschwitz, including their separation from their mother, and then the elderly face of sad Munch: "I knew that was a crazy idea to thank a Nazi, a survivor of Auschwitz to thank a Nazi, people would think that I have lost my mind, I tried to figure out how to thank him, and after ten months a simple idea popped into my head."

She seems exhilarated. Her hand writes on a piece of paper, "I forgive you," as she talks about her idea. "A letter of forgiveness from me, the survivor of Auschwitz. I knew that that was a meaningful gift for him, but what I discovered for myself was life-changing: that I had the power to forgive." Her hands are shown handcuffed. "No one could give me that power. No one could take it away," she says as she moves her hand, and the handcuffs shatter and disappear. The power of forgiveness marginalized the post-trauma that shaped her life and filled her with anger. However, this was not the end of the change.

"To challenge myself, I decided even to forgive Mengele, the person who had put me through hell." Mengele disappeared after the war, and it is claimed he drowned in Brazil in 1979, so her forgiveness could only be abstract. The animation lets the viewers enter her mind as she visualizes what would have happened if she had encountered him: Eva stands before him as a child in Auschwitz, wearing the same red dress she wore when she arrived there. Mengele, a young man in white scrubs, is looking at her. They stand in a dark room against a brick wall. She walks towards him, confident. She is the active one now, not his victim. He is animated from a low angle to mimic a child's perspective, which appears to magnify him. Unlike Munch, who was depicted positively, Mengele has a harsh, evil face. She knows he is a monster and does not want or need to embellish it, but it does not undermine her willingness to forgive because it helps her. "It wasn't easy, but I felt an enormous weight had been lifted from me." The animation visualizes this by reversing the difference in heights. He is morphed into a tiny creature while she turns into a very tall woman: the elderly Eva looking down at him, tiny and insignificant. He has lost all his power to intimidate and control her life. The bricks in the room where she was imprisoned tumble down: "I finally felt free." Instead of being locked in her post-traumatic past, she stands on the beach looking at the sea. The frame is open, with the relaxing sound of the waves in the background as she explains how she refused to surrender to post-trauma: "Who decided that I, as a victim, must be sad, angry, feel hopeless and helpless for the rest of my life? I refuse." Her bare feet are in the sand at the water's edge. "You can never change what happened in the past. All you can do is change how you react to it." The waves wash everything away, and her feet are sparkly clean. She walks up a hill near the shore as she talks about her life and her sister's life that were destroyed in the Holocaust.

Her climb is the opposite of her difficult description of the ways her life was destroyed, but this contradiction mirrors the process she has undergone. She does not let the past push her down or drown her; rather, she stands firm on the ground and climbs, despite the past. Standing on the hilltop, looking towards the future, she says, "I have the power to forgive, and so do you," hinting that other survivors or people who suffer from PTSD may find solace by forgiving their perpetrators.

Nevertheless, the movie, which supports this way of dealing with post-trauma, fails to mention two crucial pieces of information. The first is that she forgave others, including Oskar Gröning, the Auschwitz accountant who was brought to trial in his nineties. Survivors were there to testify about the atrocities committed by the Nazis in Auschwitz-Birkenau. Eva went to court, shook his hand, and urged him to confess and persuade former Nazis to admit to their acts in a world of Holocaust denial. In return, he kissed her.[57] The second is that Eva's decisions and actions created turmoil. Even though she stated that she was acting in her name alone and did not represent other survivors, it infuriated many survivors and others.[58] The movie does not show any of these critiques since the directors opted to cling to her perspective and used animation to visualize her inner feelings, her journey, and her success in fighting post-trauma.

THE PSYCHOTIC IN *NOCH AM LEBEN*

As noted in Chapter 4, director Anita Lester's narrative in the movie *Noch Am Leben* corresponds to what Amir called the psychotic or excessive mode of witnessing. In the movie, she visualizes the life of her great aunt Eva Nagler, who survived a death march in which her sister was shot into a pit while shielding her, and later she was sexually abused by the Nazis. The parts of the movie that discuss Nagler's life after the war tell the story of her post-trauma. In this mode, the language collapses into rhetoric. The linguistic excessiveness does not create a vital link with the trauma but rather fixates on the traumatic object while pushing the reflective subject to the margins.[59] Lester, who embraces her great aunt's perspective, is the one using this mode to describe her aunt's PTSD symptoms.

---

[57] "Why a Holocaust Survivor Forgave the Nazis | The Girl Who Forgave The Nazis," *YouTube*, November 27, 2018, https://bit.ly/3xj9Jb8

[58] See, for example: "Eva Kor", The Forgiveness Project, https://bit.ly/3RJ97Us; "I Survived The Holocaust Twin Experiments," *YouTube*, September 16, 2017, https://bit.ly/3UhpcT8; "Victim of Nazi Twin Experiments in Auschwitz | DW Documentary," *YouTube*, January 26, 2020, https://bit.ly/3daT16U

[59] Amir, *Bearing Witness*, 14–16.

Lester uses unrealistic animation to tell Nagler's story. Nagler's emotional problems are represented in the opening scene as a white image on a black background that approaches a door. Lester states in the voiceover that the last time she saw Nagler, she opened the door dressed in nothing but a blouse and an apron so short it revealed her genitals. In the movie, when Nagler opens the door, it is not Lester who enters but a wave of redness. This is Nagler's perspective. She cannot see reality, and the viewers are subjected to her perspective. The red is like a wave threatening to drown her. "Although small, I felt as though she towered over me, her eyes flickering as if catching the view through train windows," says Lester in the voiceover, explaining that the images Nagler sees are from the past (the trains in the Holocaust) and not the present (her great niece entering) as two images are screened: the small black figure of Lester sitting and a large white figure of Nagler making strange dancing movements while handing a bowl to Lester. "She sat me down and handed me my legacy in the shape of a cereal bowl full of cigarettes."

Lester moves between the personal and the more general as white images of women with their heads wrapped walk bizarrely into the frame. She comments that although some survivors managed to rebuild their lives, others could not. Nagler is only one of them. While they fill the frame, she talks about the many sides of Nagler: "Eva. The old woman. Eva. The kind aunt. The obsessive collector. Eva. The actress. Eva. The survivor. Eva. The receiver of shock therapy. Eva. The maniac."

Lester talks about Nagler's inability to rehabilitate after the Holocaust. "Eva was crushed. She was broken," her voiceover says as the image of Nagler as a young woman smoking appears, but this smoke that dominates the frame is also the smoke from the burning of her relatives' bodies in the death camps.

Lester talks about her mother telling her that Nagler is a fragile woman obsessed with order that enables her to resist the volcano in her mind. Nagler's image mimics gigantic waves or a volcano erupting in red and black. The animation shows Nagler holding her head and moving uncontrollably as Lester describes her midnight screams. The soundtrack is very dramatic, loud, and frightening. There is no relief, no calming sounds. The music is a way for Lester to enter Nagler's mind and represent her nightmares. In her dreams, Nagler would return to the beach on the Baltic shore where her sister was murdered. Nagler's elderly image leaning on a cane stands next to her young image as a young girl in the Holocaust while "she met herself" in her nightmares "where she watched her sister pass away."

According to Amir,[60] women who went through traumatic experiences and sexual abuse consider that staying alive is not victory but rather defeat.

---

[60] Amir, *Bearing Witness*.

The root of the unbearable is not the trauma itself but survival. In this sense, Nagler had two deaths and two defeats. After the war, she experienced a third: "Years after the war when she became pregnant," Lester says, but this is not depicted as the start of a new life in that Nagler's image is back-lit horizontally in the white frame as if dead, touching her body. "She was forced to remove the child planted in her body by the grace of a god she barely believed in." In this scene, Lester combines the loss of faith after the Holocaust and the immaculate conception. Lester does not explain how Nagler got pregnant or who the father was. In Nagler's case, no son of God is born, and Nagler is forced to have an abortion. Nagler's image continues to lie still as Lester describes the abortion as "knowing it was a kind of murder, understanding that murder is a part of life, only then to mourn that child, that she buried in the waters of the sewers, just as she'd watched her mother sink into the blood-stained snow, swallowed by her fellow dead." Nagler's living image disappears, leaving the white frame like the snow that swallowed her dead parents.

There is no sense of closure at the end of the movie. The animation shows an old woman crumpled in bed, clutching white sheets against a black background. "Towards the end of her life, she slept alone in an asylum." Her screaming, disheveled face fills the screen as Lester describes her deteriorating condition: "As the memories she so feverishly attempted to suffocate descended on her failing body, she became tiny [...] she attacked those who loved her and loved those who attacked her."

Lester noted in an interview that "when people talk about the Holocaust, we so often hear a happy end. I ran away from these kinds of stories. I saw other things: chain smokers, alcoholics, and people who suffer from depression." This subject is dealt with explicitly in the movie. "I did not want to talk about triumphs," she says. "There are those who triumphed, and there are those who lived, but they did not really survive."[61] The movie is a strong visualization of severe post-trauma that overpowers the survivor, who cannot live in the present because her mind is buried in the past.

HALLUCINATIONS, PHANTASMS, AND MEMORIES IN *A TRIP TO THE OTHER PLANET*

A Trip to the Other Planet is an animated portrait of a hallucinatory journey experienced by Jewish writer Yehiel De-Nur (Ka-tzetnik) during psychiatric treatment with LSD in the Netherlands. The movie tackles post-trauma by entering De-Nur's inner world and visualizing PTSD from within.

---

[61] Liat Steir-Livny, "An Interview with Anita Lester," November 8, 2019.

Who was Ka-tzetnik?

Yechiel Fajner (De-Nur), also known as Karl Tsetinski[62] (1909–2001), was a Jewish-Polish writer from Sosnowiec in Poland. His family was Hasidic, and he studied in a yeshiva in Lublin but slowly abandoned Jewish orthodoxy. He began writing between the two world wars, and in 1931 published a volume of poetry in Yiddish. During World War II, he and his family were imprisoned in the Sosnowiec ghetto. According to his testimony at the Eichmann trial, his relatives abroad attempted to provide him with a Uruguayan passport. Eichmann, who was at a meeting in Gestapo headquarters in Katowice, tore up his papers and sent him back to the ghetto.[63] De-Nur and his family were sent to Auschwitz in August 1943. His family was murdered, but he survived. In the aftermath of World War II, while recovering in Naples, Italy, he wrote his first novel, *Salamandra*, under the pen name of "Ka-tzetnik"—slang for a prisoner in a camp—thus indicating that he took it upon himself to represent the Holocaust victims as a whole.

De-Nur immigrated to Israel and became one of the few writers who wrote about the Holocaust in the 1950s and 1960s. Most of his books were hyper-realistic and concentrated on the horrors. In many, there are stark depictions of physical and sexual violence, sadism, prostitution, and cannibalism. Most readers considered the texts to be authentic documentation.[64] Rapidly, however, other literary critics cautioned that his books were not pure documentation but rather prose, which cast doubt on their historical veracity.[65] In the 1990s, researchers raised more questions and suggested that his works were nothing more than pornographic kitschy fiction. To this day, the historical value of his books is still hotly debated.[66] The literary historian Yehiel Sheituch claimed that De-Nur documented what he saw and argues for the historical accuracy of his books.[67] De-Nur's real identity was revealed during the Eichmann trial (1961). In his brief testimony, he made it clear that he spoke in the name of those murdered. His testimony is one of the most famous in the trial since he fainted on the stand.

---

[62] It is unclear when he changed his last name to De-Nur.
[63] Yechiel Szeintuch, *Salamandra: Myth and History in Katzetnik's Writings*, (Jerusalem: Carmel, 2009), 28–29.
[64] See Imanuel Ben-Gurion, *Davar*, April 12, 1953.
[65] See Nahor Asher, "Beit habubot" ["House of Dolls"], *Herut*, March 6, 1953 [Hebrew], https://bit.ly/3ZYxmTf
[66] Dan Miron, "Bein sefer le'efer" ["Between a Book and Ash"], *Alpaim*, 1994, pp. 196–224; *Stalags*, Ari Liebsker, 2007.
[67] Szeintuch, *Salamandra*, 22–68.

Figure 5.2   A Trip to the Other Planet *(Israel, Tom Kless, 2014)*

In 1976, with the encouragement of his wife, De-Nur went to the Netherlands and was treated by Dutch psychiatrist Jan C. Bastiaans, who specialized in the administration of hallucinogens such as LSD. De-Nur documented his experience in *Zofen E.D.M.A* (1987, English translation 1989). Unlike many of his previous books, De-Nur refrained from using a fictional alter-ego and referred in the first person to his own experiences during the treatment. In 1988 he agreed to a very rare interview with journalist Ram Evron, in which he discussed his change in perspective after treatment. The voiceover in *A Trip to the Other Planet* is excerpted from this interview.

The movie combines live action scenes and animated scenes. The live action scenes are taken from documentaries filmed by the Red Army during the liberation of Auschwitz (1945), the Eichmann trial (1961), and his interview with Ram Evron in 1987. The animation allows viewers to enter into De-Nur's mind and relive his tortured perception of everyday life, and his emotional journey under the influence of LSD. "The other planet" is thus De-Nur's mind: a place he enters under the influence of the drug, but also the phrase he coined in the Eichmann trial when he called Auschwitz "another planet." The meshing of these genres is a metaphor for the complexity of the image where the cinematic aesthetic highlights De-Nur's multifaceted personality. To further underscore De-Nur's complexity, the movie is not chronological. It begins with a typewriter clicking (which later will be shown in De-Nur's study in Tel-Aviv), shifts to 1976 in the Netherlands, jumps to documentary scenes from the Eichmann trial in 1961, returns to Tel-Aviv, enters his mind, and vice-versa. This aesthetic hints at a form of acting out. The composition aims to reflect the stream of consciousness of an individual suffering from PTSD for whom the past and the present are intertwined.

Visualizing Acting Out

De-Nur first appears in the movie in footage from the Eichmann trial in which he explains to prosecutor Gideon Hauzner that Ka-tzetnik is not a pseudonym and that he does not consider himself a writer "who writes literature" but rather someone who provides "a chronicle from the planet called Auschwitz." The decision to start the movie with this scene gives the audience a real view of De-Nur before turning to the animated scenes. In so doing, these initial scenes strengthen the documentary facet of this animated movie. This beginning also propels De-Nur's famous labeling of Auschwitz as "another planet" to the forefront. One of the most important outcomes of his LSD treatment is later revealed to be the change in his notion of another planet that had been embedded in his mind since World War II.

Director Kless depicts De-Nur as either melancholy or engaged in acting out. This is done by showing him roaming the streets of Tel Aviv as an animated figure in a realistic world and by using animation to represent his inner world. "The decision to represent him as an animated figure in a realistic world came out of the desire to represent visually the way he perceived himself in the world, the way I understand it," says Kless:

> He was always a stranger, anomalous in the world. He didn't feel at home in Israel. Throughout his life, he was torn apart by his two identities—the identity of Yehiel De-Nur, the man who had a family and a career in Tel-Aviv, and Ka-TZetnik, the Holocaust survivor who remained in Auschwitz. He was a figure from the past roaming in the present and I tried to demonstrate this discrepancy through animation.[68]

De-Nur's inability to differentiate between past and present is rendered in scenes in which Kless links De-Nur's voiceover and acts with Holocaust symbols. For example, when he sees cars coming towards him, their headlights gleaming in the dark, his voice is heard telling that after he was released, and went walking on busy roads, "all I saw were the pairs of eyes rising up towards me, the headlights of the trucks shuttling endlessly back and forth to the crematorium." The visuals show trucks and cars in Tel Aviv. When he glances at a giant commercial billboard, he no longer sees the advertisement but rather sees his own testimony at the Eichmann trial.

When he stops to look at shoes in a window display, the audience does not need an explanation for what he sees in his mind: the infamous piles of shoes found at Auschwitz. When a dog barks, he flinches. In De-Nur's mind, the dog is not in downtown Rabin square in Tel Aviv, but a Nazi dog in a camp.

---

[68] Liat Steir-Livny, "An Interview with Tom Kless," April 4, 2018.

The temporal intersection reaches its high point when standing in line for a movie in Tel Aviv. There is parallel editing between this scene and scenes of De-Nur's testimony from the Eichman trial, when he explained that the past came back to him and he then fainted: "I see them looking at me," he mumbled, "I see them, I see them in line, I remember." The line at the cinema is the line to the gas chamber, and there is no distance between then, and now, so he runs away in fear.

Entering De-Nur's Mind

Since the movie is narrated from the perspective of someone suffering from PTSD, there are no fully live action scenes of the treatment. The audience hears but does not see Prof. Batians. The montage shows De-Nur's feet as he lies on the couch, the large tape recorder making recordings of the sessions, Bastians' hand and his figure in a white coat as he draws a curtain. These scenes are out of focus, as though from De-Nur's perspective, under the influence. Kless then presents a series of animation scenes visualizing what he may have experienced with LSD.

De-Nur's treatment lasted five sessions before he chose to stop, despite Dr. Bastian's entreaties to continue. As described in *Tzofen Adama*, sensory impressions are perceived more strongly, colors are brighter, and sounds like the ticking of clocks, that one would not normally hear, become strikingly audible under LSD. When the eyes are shut, swirling patterns of colors and shapes are seen. The relationship between current sensory impressions and past experiences is eliminated so one sees things as they were for the first time. Hallucinations, ranging from familiar images to the unreal, are common. Finally, and most importantly, memories and experiences that have been deeply repressed may be released and experienced as reality.[69] Kless uses animation to imitate the effects of the drug. The blue and red, and the different shapes in the animated scenes, are so vivid that they almost leap out of the frame.

De-Nur's description of Auschwitz as "another planet" characterized the Holocaust as something that happened in a different space, and was carried out by monsters, not humans, because humans are not capable of doing these things. "The meaning of the term 'another planet' is repression," says Kless. "It is a psychological estrangement. It is like saying: I cannot deal with what happened in Auschwitz, so it was carried out elsewhere, on another planet, by monsters, not humans, because humans cannot do these things. This was De-Nur's perception."[70]

---

[69] Szeintuch, *Salamandra*, 80–86.
[70] Steir-Livny, "Interview with Tom Kless."

Under the influence of LSD, De-Nur had a life-changing experience. In his hallucinations, he returned to Auschwitz, stood facing a Nazi officer, and saw him yawn. This made De-Nur see the Nazi for the first time as a human, and possibly even weak. He suddenly saw him as tired, hungry, and cold. He identified with the perpetrator, his victimizer, through this weakness and then had a revelation that everyone and anyone could be in this position, even himself. Kless represents this insight by replacing the animated image of the Nazi with the animated image of De-Nur in the same spot in the frame. "I could have been him. It is I—a person, who created Auschwitz," says De-Nur, thus affirming that humans were responsible for building this terrible place. The understanding that he and the Nazi could have traded places in an alternative version of history altered his perspective. From dealing with his own personal trauma, he turned to dealing with universal issues of the essence of human evil, and each individual's responsibility to choose good and not bad.

Kless then plunges into LSD experience through animated visuals of the inside of a machine. The movie shows pipes and hoses that swirl to mimic a machine processing all this new information. The animation visualizes a beating heart to suggest that even the most horrific place is man-made. The scenes show a pumping heart that turns out to be the innards of a typewriter. People created this place. Other people write about it. These scenes enable the viewers to identify more strongly with the protagonist, since they have gotten to know him as deeply as they can by witnessing the moment that changed his life from the inner depths of his mind.

Partial Redemption

This change was so dramatic for De-Nur that at the end of the movie, Kless combines documentary segments from homemade videos of children playing and segments from De Nur's television interview with Ram Evron. De-Nur states, "When you went into a kindergarten, you could see that out of the 50 children, there was one child called Adolf Hitler. Hitler was not Satan. He was a man." Then and only then, the daylight of Tel Aviv is finally shown. However, this redemption is partial. The blue sky is filled with airplanes, and for the viewers, it is obvious that De-Nur does not see the Israeli air force but planes during World War II. These animated military airplanes fly over the streets of Tel-Aviv, showing that this insight did not free him from acting out: present-day Tel-Aviv is still submerged in the Holocaust. On the other hand, even when referring to the past, the planes symbolize the possibility of freedom.

"Auschwitz is not another planet like I thought," says De-Nur. "If you say it was another planet or the devil, it is an escape, then you've learned nothing.

It is you, the human, who can choose. Pay attention and choose life." In these scenes, De-Nur changes from an animated image, torn from the real world, into a real image in the real world. The visual decision to shift from animated documentary to documentary is a clear influence of the Israeli animated documentary *Waltz with Bashir* (see Chapter 6). This esthetic choice reminds the viewers that this is not fiction but rather the documentation of a real man's experiences. It hints that De-Nur's insight about Auschwitz enabled him to be a part of the real world. The movie ends as De-Nur states, "The choice is in your hands. Choose life," and fades to black, to let the viewers contemplate this universal lesson.

Part III

Secondary Trauma, Postmemory, and Wishful Postmemory

Part III deals with the representations of survivors' descendants. The post-Holocaust generations are exposed to stories and recollections of trauma they did not experience and can only imagine.[1] Based on a wide range of scholarly research on the second and third generations and their ways of dealing with the traumas of their parents and grandparents, this section explores how animated documentaries depict secondary traumatic stress.[2] By combining the aesthetics of animated documentaries that make it possible to visualize the unfilmed past, the inner worlds, and modes of "witnessing to the witness,"[3] animated documentaries can lead to a greater comprehension of the transgenerational transfer of the trauma.[4] Animated documentaries

---

[1] For example, Victoria Aarons and Alan L. Berger, *Third-Generation Holocaust Representation: Trauma, History, and Memory* (Northwestern University Press, 2017), 3–39.

[2] Charles Figley, ed., *Compassion Fatigue: Secondary Traumatic Stress Disorder from Treating the Traumatized* (New York: Brunner/Mazel, 1995), esp. 1–20.

[3] A term coined by Dori Laub to describe interviewers of Holocaust survivors. See Dori Laub, "Bearing Witness on the Vicissitudes of Listening," in *Testimony: Crises of Witnessing in Literature, Psychoanalysis and History*, Shoshana Felman and Dori Laub (London: Routledge, 1992), 57–74.

[4] See, for example: Nurith Gertz, *A Different Choir: Holocaust Survivors, Aliens, and Others in Israeli Cinema and Literature* (Tel Aviv: Am Oved and Open University, 2004) [Hebrew], 78–102; Liat Steir-Livny, *Two Faces in the Mirror: The Representation of Holocaust Survivors in Israeli Cinema* (Jerusalem: Eshkolot-Magnes, 2009), 96–204; Yosefa Loshitzky, *Identity Politics on the Israeli Screen* (Austin: University of Texas Press, 2002), 32–71; Aaron Kerner, *Film and the Holocaust* (London: Bloomsbury, 2001), 195–242; Brad Prager, *After the Fact: The Holocaust in Twenty-First Century Documentary Film* (London: Bloomsbury, 2015).

can point outward and visualize the unfilmed childhood of the descendants while at the same time pointing inwards and plunging into the unconscious in scenes that evoke thoughts and feelings. Visualizing these invisible aspects of life through animation, often in an abstract or symbolic style, enables the viewers to imagine the world from the offspring's perspective.

CHAPTER 6

Struggling with the Parents' Memories

This chapter discusses movies made by and about the second generation. It reflects the way animated documentaries can visualize new aspects of secondary trauma by combining mimetic, non-mimetic, and evocation. Animated documentaries can depict what eludes live action documentaries: the unfilmed past and the inner worlds of the second generation. The movies analyzed are *I Was a Child of Holocaust Survivors* (Ann Marie Fleming, 2012), *German Shepherd* (Nils Bergendal, Sweden, 2014), and *Waltz with Bashir* (Ari Folman, 2009).

SECOND GENERATION: THE PSYCHOLOGICAL DEBATE AND REPRESENTATIONS IN THE WESTERN WORLD

The term "second-generation" was coined by Canadian psychoanalysts as a clinical concept, and today is commonly used to denote the children of Holocaust survivors. In the 1960s, when the issue was first studied, it became clear that second-generation survivors had certain mental health problems that unified them as a group. Since then, hundreds of articles have been written on the issue of the intergenerational transmission of Holocaust trauma from survivors to their children. These are based on research indicating that post-traumatic syndromes can emerge in individuals who did not experience trauma directly. Secondary traumatic stress can be found in friends and relatives of traumatized individuals as well as in wider circles.[1] There are differences in opinion on the transfer of trauma from the survivors to their descendants that can be divided into several schools of thought.

The first suggests that second-generationers have clear, specific characteristics. The Holocaust impacts them on a deep, subconscious level, which inevitably leads to symptoms and characteristics that distinguish them from

---

[1] Charles Figley, ed., *Compassion Fatigue: Secondary Traumatic Stress Disorders from Treating the Traumatized* (New York: Brunner/Mazel, 1995), esp. 1–20.

the general population and other groups in their age.² The second school of thought holds that the second-generation has no significant psychological disorders and that the Holocaust had no long-term consequences on the survivors' offspring. Thus, the notion of intergenerational transfer to the second generation is a misconception because the findings are based on case studies that do not represent the vast majority of the second-generation.³ The third school of thought acknowledges the specificities of interactions between Holocaust survivors and their offspring, which is expressed in many different ways.⁴ Eva Hoffman, for instance, suggested that the term "second generation" attributes homogeneous features to what is a very diverse group.⁵ Finally, the fourth school of thought argues that the diverse experiences of subgroups among Holocaust survivors may impact whether there is secondary traumatization among the survivors' descendants and its specific characteristics.⁶

---

² See, for example: Dina Wardi, *Nosei hahotam* [*Memorial Candles*] (Jerusalem: Keter, 1990), 14; Carol Kidron, "Hahavnaya hahevratit shel hador hasheni lashoah" ["The Social Construction of Second-Generation Survivors: Support Group Narratives of Wounded Bearers of Memory"], in *Yaldut b'tzel hashoah: yeladim-nitsolim vedor sheni* [*Childhood in the Shadow of the Holocaust: Child Survivors and Second Generation*], ed. Zehava Solomon and Julia Chaitin (Tel-Aviv: Hakibbutz Hameuchad, 2007), 261–285; Julia Chaitin, "Yeladim v'nechadim shel nitzolim mitmodedim im hashoah" ["Children and Grandchildren of Holocaust Survivors deal with the Holocaust"], in *Yaldut b'tzel hashoah: yeladim-nitsolim vedor sheni* [*Childhood in the Shadow of the Holocaust: Child Survivors and Second Generation*], ed. Zehava Solomon and Julia Chaitin (Tel-Aviv: Hakibbutz Hameuchad, 2007), 304–336.

³ See, for example: Yoram Hazan, "Dor sheni lashoah: musag besafek" ["The Second Generation of the Holocaust: A Questionable Concept"], *Sihot: Israel Journal of Psychotherapy* 1 (1987): 104–108; Hillel Klein, "Hipus nitzolei hashoah ahar mashma'ut v'zehut" ["The Survivors' Search for Meaning and Identity"], in *Nazi Concentration Camps: Lectures and Discussions at the 4th Yad Vashem International Historical Conference of Holocaust Researchers*, ed. Israel Gutman and Rachel Manber (Jerusalem: Yad Vashem, 1980), 543–553; Abraham Sagi-Schwartz, Marinus H. van IJzendoorn, and Marian J. Bakermans-Kranenburg, "Does Intergenerational Transference of Trauma Skip a Generation? No Meta-Analytic Evidence for Tertiary Traumatization with Third Generation Holocaust Survivors," *Attachment and Human Development* 10, no. 2 (June 2008), 105–121.

⁴ See, for example: Iris Milner, *Kirey avar* [*A Torn Past*] (Tel Aviv: 2004), 19–35; Eva Hoffman, *After Such Knowledge: A Meditation on the Aftermath of the Holocaust* (London: Vintage, 2004), 28; Dan Bar-On, *Bein pahad letikva: sipurei haim shel hamesh mishpahot nitsolei shoah shlosha dorot bamishpaha* [*Fear and Hope: Three Generations of the Holocaust*] (Tel-Aviv: Beit Lochamei Haghetaot and Kibbutz Hameuchad Press, 1994); see also Milner, *Kir'ei 'avar*, 23–25.

⁵ Eva Hoffman, *After Such Knowledge: A Meditation on the Aftermath of the Holocaust* (London: 2004). 28.

⁶ Yael Aviad and Diana Cuhenca, "The Effects of Gender and Survival Situation of the Parent Holocaust Survivor on Their Offspring: An Attachment Perspective," *The Israel Journal of Psychiatry and Related Sciences* 55, no. 2 (2018), 15–22.

Since the 1980s, the representation of the second-generation Holocaust survivors has become one of the main themes in Holocaust commemorations. Marianne Hirsch suggested that the Holocaust, as represented in the works of second-generation survivors, is an indirect affinity structured on inherited imagination and memory. This is what she terms "postmemory," which characterizes the experiences of those controlled by events that happened before they were born, and who apply their imagination to places they cannot remember.[7] Alison Landsberg coined the term "prosthetic memory" to characterize memories of historical events that people take as their own even though they did not actually experience them.[8] These notions have been examined in cultural texts on and by children of Holocaust survivors.[9]

In the Western world, the lives of the children who grew up in the shadow of their parents' trauma have been represented in literature, poetry, theater, and movies, which depict the ways it has affected them and been incorporated into their identities. Second-generation survivors first entered the cultural sphere in the 1980s and have contributed to increasing Holocaust awareness by making their stories known through literature, poetry, popular music, autobiographies, art, graphic novels, various cinematic genres (experimental, fiction, documentary), TV, social media, and others.[10] In their cultural works, second-generationers position the survivors and themselves as protagonists. Their works portray the new lives the survivors created for themselves, but also their emotional scars, the transgenerational transfer of the trauma to the second generation, and the complex relationships between these parents and their children.

According to moviemaker and researcher Jeffrey Skoller, animated documentary can rejuvenate older forms by exhuming them from worn-out clichés

---

[7] Marianne Hirsch, "Past Lives, First Memories in Exile," *Poetics Today* 17, no. 4 (1996): 659–667.

[8] Alison Landsberg, *Prosthetic Memory: The Transformation of American Remembrance in the Age of Mass Culture* (New York: Columbia University Press, 2004).

[9] For an overview of this field of research see Liat Steir-Livny, *Remaking Holocaust Memory: Documentary Cinema by Third-Generation Survivors in Israel* (Syracuse: Syracuse University Press, 2019).

[10] See Yosefa Loshitzky, *Identity Politics on the Israeli Screen* (Austin: Univ. of Texas Press, 2002), 32–71; Nurith Gertz, *Makhela aheret: nitzolei shoa zarim v'aherim* [*A Different Choir: Holocaust Survivors, Aliens, and Others in Israeli Cinema and Literature*] (Tel Aviv: Am Oved and Open University, 2004); Moshe Zimmermann, *Al tigu li bashoah* [*Don't Touch My Holocaust*] (Haifa: Haifa University Press, 2002); Michal Friedman, "The Double Legacy of Arbeit Macht Frei," *Prooftexts* 22, nos. 1–2 (Winter–Spring 2002): 200–220; Régine-Mihal Friedman, "Witnessing for the Witness: 'Choice and Destiny' by Tsipi Reibenbach," *Shofar* 24, no. 1 (Fall 2005), 81–93; Steir-Livny, *Two Faces in the Mirror*, 96–127, 150–165.

and moribund cinematic forms.[11] Classic second-generation Holocaust documentaries produced since the 1980s tend to recycle aesthetic notions in that the survivors either talk directly to the camera or engage in conversations with their offspring or friends in their homes or while wandering through the survivors' childhood homes, and former ghettos, concentration camps, and mass killing sites. In these movies, the second-generationers talk about the anxieties that were transmitted to them, the horrible stories that were part and parcel of their childhoods, or silent houses shrouded in dark secrets.[12] The movies below take a different tack.

THE HOLOCAUST AS A DRUG IN *I WAS A CHILD OF HOLOCAUST SURVIVORS*

I Was a Child of Holocaust Survivors was the first animated documentary devoted solely to the way a second generationer experienced growing up in the shadow of the Holocaust. The movie is based on the graphic novel of the same name by Bernice Eisenstein (2006), in which she describes growing up in the 1950s in Toronto's Kensington Market neighborhood in the first person. Eisenstein took an active part in the movie's production, and she also narrates it.

The movie reflects what Charles Figley referred to as 'secondary traumatic stress disorder'; namely, indirect exposure to trauma that affects those who were not themselves involved in the traumatic events. Secondary traumatic stress can manifest in friends and relatives of the traumatized persons, as well as in wider circles.[13] By visualizing Holocaust-related fantasies, dreams, and hallucinations; the movie enables a deeper understanding of what Rony Alfandary refers to as "postmemorial work": the realization that people can be affected by events they did not experience and be haunted by patterns of behavior, forms of relationships, and emotions that cannot be explained solely in terms of their individual history.[14] Director Fleming, who is not a member of the second generation, and Eisenstein, who is completely aware

---

[11] Skoller, "Introduction," 208.

[12] See, for example: Nurith Gertz, *A Different Choir: Holocaust Survivors, Aliens, and Others in Israeli Cinema and Literature* (Tel Aviv: Am Oved and Open University, 2004) [Hebrew], 78–102; Liat Steir-Livny, *Two Faces in the Mirror: The Representation of Holocaust Survivors in Israeli Cinema* (Jerusalem: Eshkolot-Magnes, 2009), 96–204; Yosefa Loshitzky, *Identity Politics on the Israeli Screen* (Austin: University of Texas Press, 2002), 32–71; Aaron Kerner, *Film and the Holocaust* (London: Bloomsbury, 2001), 195–242; Brad Prager, *After the Fact: The Holocaust in Twenty-First Century Documentary Film* (London: Bloomsbury, 2015).

[13] Figley, *Compassion Fatigue*, 1–20.

[14] Rony Alfandary, *Postmemory, Psychoanalysis and Holocaust Ghosts: The Salonica Cohen Family and Trauma Across Generations* (London: Routledge, 2021), 12.

of the Holocaust's effect on her life, harnessed this medium to explore post-memorial work in an attempt to uncover the sources of Eisenstein's cyclical repetitions.

Subjective Memories of Un-filmed Events

To return to the past, the movie alternates between the mimetic and the non-mimetic without signaling these transitions. Although the images are human, the colors (black and white dominate, with touches of yellow, blue, and red in some scenes), the often deliberately unrealistic camera movements, and the constant blurring of real events, dreams, fantasies, thoughts, and hallucinations strengthen the non-mimetic quality. This produces a type of aesthetic that calls on the audience to consider a new way of dealing with reality and truth. It echoes animator Orly Yadin's claim that animated documentary is the most honest form of documentation because there is no pretense of reflecting reality. Instead, it affirms itself as a representation of subjective memory.[15]

The movie openly represents the intimate world of Eisenstein's parents, their relatives, and herself, in which the trauma prevents both generations from experiencing complete happiness. Scholars have suggested that animated documentary is less exploitative of its subjects than live action documentaries because it conceals the identity of its protagonists.[16] The animation enables a profound look into a family and a community's traumatic experiences, but without being voyeuristic, because it shields the characters through animation. In so doing, Eisenstein and Fleming "defend" not only Eisenstein, but also her parents and relatives whom they represent. They are there, their stories are visualized, but they are unrecognizable. This is not only an aesthetic choice but an ethical stance as well.

In the scenes depicting parties with friends and family, the guests greet each other with the familiar phrase in Yiddish *"auf Simches,"* which is used on celebratory occasions but also when offering consolation. This impossible yet very vivid combination is strengthened when the party turns into a scene showing a concentration camp inmate standing on a small stage behind barbed wire saying *"auf Simches."* As the animation morphs from a swastika to the entrance to Auschwitz to the image of two frightened inmates in striped uniforms, Eisenstein's voiceover explains that its dual meaning is symbolic of the family's life, in which even the happy occasions are marked with constant grief mingled with trauma.

---

[15] Yadin, "But is it Documentary?"
[16] Landesman and Bendor, *Animated Recollection and Spectatorial Experience*, 359.

The acting out of this trauma is visualized in other scenes in which the camera moves between family members as Eisenstein briefly summarizes their past in her voiceover ("Norman had a wife and a young child before the war, but they died in a concentration camp. [...] Rose saved my mother's life when they were both in Auschwitz [...]"). A close-up of another family friend has a background soundtrack of train noises ("On a transport [...] Carola was able to jump out of the moving train"). The present is always mixed with the past. It is also there in the representation of her seventh birthday party. A cake with seven candles appears, bringing a touch of yellow light to the black and white animation. But in the soundtrack, Eisenstein also deals with the past. As the "camera" focuses on the face of an old man, she says:

> My mother's father had been taken from his home in Benjen, Poland, to a labor camp. My grandmother found him after the war in Sweden. She and the rest of the family had been taken to Auschwitz. Their son Lemel didn't survive.

I Was a Child of Holocaust Survivors also uses black humor to present how Eisenstein learned to use her parents' past as leverage. When a classmate pulled her hair, she yelled at him to stop because "My parents were in Auschwitz"; when sitting around a bonfire with friends, no one could top her story ("My parents were in Auschwitz"), and as an adult visiting a therapist, she used the same phrase to explain her problems.

Evocation: Representing Thoughts, Dreams, and Hallucinations

Representations of the inner world are a dominant part of the movie. Although the movie is based on an autobiography, the title intimates a collective story by suggesting that the children of Holocaust survivors are different from others, thus echoing the first school of thought, which claims that the second generation differs from other groups in society. The teaser starts with melancholic music. An animated image appears of a child sitting naked on a rock on which the names of the Jewish communities in Europe have been carved. In a zoom-out, the scene shows that the rock is positioned on top of the globe. This scene suggests that the child was born from this rock, and from the memory of the Jewish communities that were destroyed in the Holocaust. Since the movie is presented from Eisenstein's perspective, this signifies that in her view, the entire world was created from Jewish ashes. The rock that commemorates the Jews who perished in the Holocaust is the center of the world in this child's eyes and represents the world she knows. In the next scene, as the Earth turns, Eisenstein reflects on her life, stating "I'm lost in memory." Since this is the voice of a woman and not a child, this double perspective clarifies that she is telling a story in which awareness of the Holocaust has been the center of her world her entire life.

Eisenstein appears with the sad, serious face of a grownup in the body of a child, as though the secondary trauma had deprived her of her childhood. From the moment of birth, an adult emerged from the ashes. This is apparent when she explains that the *sloshim*[17] is a "time of transition for the mourner" as her own image changes from a child to a teenager, to a wrinkled old woman. As the eternal mourner, she cannot be a normal teenager. The memories of her parents' past that she inherited do not allow her to be young and free. She is forever suspended in this child-adult limbo.

The reason for the constant sadness is explained as the opening titles appear. The music changes from melancholic to frightening. The visuals include a frightened child hugging a doll animated from a high angle that minimizes her even more, as a shadow takes over the frame threatening to swallow her up. The movie's titles mimic B-movies of the horror genre from the 1950s. This tribute appears again later in the movie, as a constant reminder that the Holocaust is always there, threatening and creating constant anxiety.

Animation and Postmemory

Fleming argued that "It's really about a state of mind almost, and how you deal with this in a family: how you deal with horrific events that have shaped a generation's lives."[18] The combination of mimetic and non-mimetic forms is used to represent the familial past she experienced and her postmemory.[19] Animation visualizes parts of her parents' Holocaust stories as well as how she imagines them. For example, she tells the story of her mother's ring in a sequence of black and white scenes in which the ring is singled out in a yellow zoom-in. Eisenstein tells her mother's story in the voiceover as the animation visualizes her postmemory of Auschwitz-Birkenau as she imagines it. The scene focuses on inmates in "Canada" (where gas chamber victims' clothing and belongings were sorted by inmates and sent to Germany). Her mother is shown sorting the belongings and finding a coat. Eisenstein recounts that her mother told her that one day she was so cold she asked the guard if she could wear one. Her mother's head is not seen in the scenes as though she has no image. Her daughter cannot imagine what she looked like in the camp, so her head cannot be animated. When her mother puts on the coat, the scene is depicted in color, since this is the coat that brought her warmth and good luck. Without a temporal transition,

---

[17] *Sloshim*: In Jewish bereavement customs, the thirtieth day after burial.
[18] Dallian, "I Was a Child of Holocaust Survivors."
[19] Hirsch, "Postmemory."

the scene shifts to one where her mother and father are shown together, happy, hugging after the war, while Eisenstein says that her mother gave the ring she found in the coat to her father when they were married. The scene ends emblematically as in silent movies, by turning into a small circle that closes in on the figures until the screen goes black, as Eisenstein says that this was the only thing she had to give him, and he wore it forever.

In other scenes, animation is used to portray Eisenstein's postmemory of her father's Holocaust experiences. Eisenstein remembers that as a child, after her father ate dinner, he would lie in bed and watch TV. She segues from the horses shown on TV to tell his history:

> When war began, my father was drafted into the Polish cavalry. After his horse was wounded, he went back to his family in Michałów, only to be taken to a labor camp with his brother. Eventually they were separated, and my father was sent to Auschwitz.

The animation morphs from a horse to a hand patting a horse, to silhouettes of men with their heads lowered who are climbing a hill to the entrance of Auschwitz. "His mother, father, and two sisters didn't survive. He was not able to save them," she concludes as the gates of Auschwitz turn into a moon and stars, like a metaphorical night encompassing the family, which then morphs into an eye, possibly her eye, as she "sees" the past in her memory.

Wishful Postmemory

The movie shows how, by using animation, one can expand Hirsch's postmemory and represent what I term "wishful postmemory"; i.e., what Eisenstein wishes could have happened. For example, after representing the postmemory of her father's Holocaust experiences, in subsequent Holocaust scenes, the horse comes back, this time in a different form. Her father, who became a fan of Westerns after he immigrated to Canada, rides the horse, this time as the town's sheriff, and the yellow badge the Nazis forced Jews to wear now becomes his sheriff's badge as he throws open the gates of Auschwitz in a dramatic gesture. Through his cosmic powers, he opens a vast pit in the ground, an inferno that swallows up all the Nazi soldiers. He lifts the barbed wire, allowing the inmates to escape and at the end winks at the "viewers," tipping his hat in a gesture reminiscent of Westerns, as he rides off into the sunset with the woman he has saved (who is dressed in a striped uniform) while cowboy music plays in the background. These scenes, dominated by blue and yellow, bring smidgens of color into their black and white trauma-filled lives. In her sad-ridden life, the second-generation doesn't only try to imagine what happened, but also what could have happened, which gives her a little comfort.

Visualizing Holocaust Obsession and the Effects of Secondary Trauma

Dominic La Capra[20] suggested that second-generation survivors may sense a missing link in their identity due to the obliteration of places, people, communities, and memorabilia. This "ontological absence" can create an obsession with the past and the Holocaust that is aimed at endowing this eradicated past with a representation, language, and story. According to Iris Milner,[21] an imposed disconnect with the past can lead to a compulsive obsession with forbidden knowledge, and a longing and desire for it. The need to know the "causative" or "formative trauma" has an unceasing influence on the present. This unending quest for the missing link affects the very foundations of identity.

The animation breathes life into this longing and enables the viewer to plunge into Eisenstein's consciousness by visualizing her growing obsession with the past. The Eichmann trial in 1961[22] was the catalyst for her Holocaust obsession: "Knowing that the Holocaust happened wasn't enough. I needed to know what it had done to my parents," she says. From that point on, she became addicted. "Suddenly I'm injected with the white hit rush of a new reality: the Holocaust is a drug, and I've entered an opium den."

This change brought is illustrated as a dark vortex pulling her in, as the child falls deeper and deeper with a look of terror. This scene appears between two sequences depicting the family watching the trial, thus enabling the viewers to understand the trial's deep emotional effect. "I've been given my first taste [of the drug] for free from everyone here," she says in a voiceover as the animation zooms out of the drawings of the adult family members, dissolving to her parents and relatives pulling up their long sleeves, showing her and the audience, the numbers tattooed on their arms. The numbers turn into a rope that turns into barbed wire, behind which the blurred images of concentration camp prisoners can be seen. "This is when my addiction takes hold. [...] There is no end to the dealers I can find for just one more hit." She defines her obsession as "One more hallucinatory entry into the world of ghosts," into a world that is both intimidating and intoxicating at the same time.

Scene after scene visualizes her "addiction" where the "H" (the Holocaust, but also heroin) gives her a "high." This metaphor takes on mythical power as the child is shown pleading with an old man who stands, like the biblical

---

[20] La Capra, *Writing History, Writing Trauma*, 47.
[21] Milner, *A Torn Past*, 19–35.
[22] Adolf Eichmann was one of the most high-ranking Nazi officers. He oversaw the logistics of the mass deportation of European Jews to the concentration and death camps in Poland. After World War II he escaped to Argentina. He was captured by the Israeli Mossad in 1960, tried in Israel in 1961, and hung in 1962.

Moses, on top of a mountain holding the letter "H" instead of the tablets of the covenant. Everything around him is black, and only the letter "H" stands out in white, surrounded by a halo. This image turns the Holocaust not only into the most important part of her Jewish identity, but into the constitutive event for the entire Jewish people. The child jumps over the dark pit of the Holocaust and lands in a movie theater as Holocaust books appear on screen, while her emotionless voice describes how this desire to know sends her "out of my home, alone, to the cinema, to the library, where I can see any movie and read any book." Suddenly, the little girl from the first scene reappears, but this time instead of sitting on top of the world, she is perched on top of a pile of books. Some of them are written by survivors and others by members of the second generation, such as *Night* by Elie Wiesel (1960) and *Nothing Makes You Free* edited by Melvin Jules Bukiet (2003), which introduces writings by descendants of Holocaust survivors. She is still naked, as though born from these books.

Like any other addiction, her obsession is visualized as mixed with a desire to get clean. In later scenes, the little girl appears pushing a big rock up a hill. The rock falls, crushes her, turns into the Sun, and then becomes a ball she rolls in her hands. "Here I am, some Jewish Sisyphus, pushing history and memory up the hill, wanting to stand in front of my parents and say "Here, take it, I don't want it. It's yours." However, her father sits with his hands in his lap, as though unwilling to take it. The little girl is, therefore "stuck" with the transgenerational transfer of the trauma and the perception that the Holocaust is the center of the world, like the Sun. No wonder she refers to Eli Wiesel and Primo Levi as the "forefathers of memory." They take her hand and guide her gently through the dark door of memory.

The circle is the leitmotif of the movie. The circle is Eisenstein's father's wedding ring, the hole in her soul, and the pretzel she eats as she talks about

Figure 6.1 I Was a Child of Holocaust Survivors *(Ann Marie Fleming, 2012)*

her Holocaust addiction and Holocaust craving. The shtetl, Holocaust survivors, and the trauma cannot be organized into a linear narrative in a world where the imagined past constantly bursts into the present. "There is no center to be found in memory," she says in a scene in which she is portrayed as a child throwing pebbles into the water. The pebbles create ripples in the water, which grow larger and take over the frame.

The circle also appears in the final scenes, which highlights the fact that Fleming did not yield to "the temptation of closure."[23] These scenes represent Eisenstein's son's circumcision ceremony, which took place after Eisenstein's father died. Her husband is seen holding the baby, flanked by his brothers, who are soon encircled by a ring drawn by an invisible pen, which morphs into the wedding ring, this time topped by her father as an angel watching from above. The men are soon replaced by an image of the crying baby, which turns into the naked child sitting on the globe; the same image is shown at the beginning of the movie. The globe rotates as Jewish music plays and the movie fades out. This is the circle of life, which captures the second generation and the next, the third generation, in an endless traumatic memory that clutches onto the children and grandchildren, locking them within. Even though time marches on and the children grow up and the elderly die, the circle lives on while paralleling linear developments.

INHERITANCE IN *GERMAN SHEPHERD*

David Paul's vision of Germany and Germans as he grew up in Baltimore was shaped by Holocaust stories. Later in life, he reflects on whether it is possible to overcome this history. This movie poses difficult questions about the human capacity to forgive evil acts and is based on a forty-five-minute interview Bergendal recorded with his friend Paul in 2009 in New York. Paul is a judge and a Jewish entrepreneur who is involved in efforts to connect Jewish organizations and young Germans, such as *The Reconciliation Service for Peace*.[24] The interview was not planned. Bergendal says it was "a spontaneous impulse. I knew about his obsession with Germany, and it was just the perfect time to figure out some more."[25]

---

[23] Saul Friedländer, "Trauma, Memory, and Transference," in *Holocaust Remembrance: The Shapes of Memory*, ed. Geoffrey Hartman (Oxford: Basil Blackwell, 1994), 252–264.

[24] "The Hart of New York Show with NYC Judge David Paul, discussing the Holocaust", *YouTube*, January 22, 2020, https://bit.ly/3rSvnQu

[25] "'German Shepherd' Intro—Director Nils Bergendal," *YouTube*, September 23, 2014, https://bit.ly/3RX9IBa "German Shepherd en DocumentaMadrid 2015," *YouTube*, June 8, 2015, https://bit.ly/3TeiSdG

Figure 6.2 German Shepherd *(Nils Bergendal, Sweden, 2014)*

Initially, Bergendal shot *German Shepherd* as a live action short where Paul walks past various historical sites in Berlin, while contemplating the past and the present. However, after seeing the result, Bergendal thought it was "visually quite poor." After he returned to Sweden, he decided to create an animated documentary even though he had no experience in the field. "After many rejections, I finally got a budget and advice from the Swedish Movie Institute on how to animate the whole thing myself. It was a time-consuming process but turned out to be quite rewarding."[26] Bergendal had worked as a still photographer and moviemaker since 1990, and *German Shepherd* was his first animated work, which he and Paul edited together.[27] It has been screened in over fifty festivals and has won several awards.[28] The movie was also one of forty considered for Oscar nomination.[29]

Paul's voiceover accompanies the movie. The animation is illustrative and non-mimetic as Paul discusses his attitude towards the Germans and his thoughts about humanity as he grew up. Even as a child, he perceived the Germans as absolute evil. The image of his mother is shown pacing in the house, holding a picture and placing it on the mantel with other pictures of murdered relatives as Paul explains the attitudes he grew up with:

---

[26] Rob Munday, "German Shepherd," https://bit.ly/3TgaR7V
[27] "The Hart of New York Show with NYC Judge David Paul, Discussing the Holocaust," *YouTube*, January 22, 2020, https://bit.ly/3SYxL49
[28] Cinequest (Best Animated Short), NYC Shorts (Best Documentary), Pixel Movie Festival (Best Movie, Best Music), Heartland Movie Festival (Award Winner), DOC NYC (Special Jury Prize). See: "German Shepherd," *Vimeo* (no date), https://vimeo.com/79479302; "German Shepherd," https://bit.ly/3SZcJCe
[29] "The Hart of New York Show."

> My mother, you know, she hates Germans and Germany and everything it stands for. She thinks they are born to hate Jews [...] My mother thinks that Germans are just evil people. It's not rational and I don't challenge her, don't blame her, it's like a whole wave swept her family away and they were gone. I think that's why she has an obsessional connection with dead relatives. She always talked to her dead relatives at night, whenever my father wasn't around, in Polish or Yiddish.

Throughout the movie, Paul is depicted without facial characteristics. At times, he resembles a Montessori puppet that has no features, permitting universal identification. In other scenes, he appears as a black silhouette. This visual generalization, like the title in *I Was a Child of Holocaust Survivors*, turns a personal biography into a much more generalized story of a generation. Similarly, it rejects the premise that the second generation has no specific characteristics and suggests that growing up in a house of Holocaust survivors created a "second generation" that differs from others because the Holocaust was an integral part of their identity.

The scenes highlight David's mother's influence on him. He talks about his biggest fears in his childhood. This scene shows him sitting on a bed and then zooms on his legs swinging back and forth as he reads. "When you grow up with scary stories, you are afraid something under the bed is going to grab you. For me, it was the Germans. When I go to sleep, they might get me, grab me and take me away like my mother's relatives." The animation visualizes his fears: two human hands inching forward from under the bed, grabbing his legs. The movie portrays him growing up filled with questions, and his unwillingness to accept this dichotomous view. He pulls up his legs and the hands disappear: "and I thought there have got to be some nice Germans."

As a young adult, he is determined to find them. The animation shows a plane in flight and a stamp on a passport indicating his arrival in Berlin, where he goes to face his postmemory. His silhouette walks down the streets, encountering other silhouettes on crosswalks and in the windows, as he notes that he has been going to Berlin for over twenty years and has made many friends ("I think I have more friends in Berlin than I do in my home in New York"). Nevertheless, the past is part of his relationship with the Germans he encounters. "Germans have an extra layer; they have to work to be my friend and it is all around the grandfather question," he says as the image of an elderly man with a cane stops at a crosswalk, waiting for the traffic light to change. His silhouette symbolizes his generation, the generation who were young men during the Nazi era.

Paul says he asks every German he meets what their grandparents did during the war, "and if I don't know I cannot be friends with them." The elderly man suddenly shoulders his cane like a rifle. He turns into a Nazi in contemporary Berlin, suggesting that for Paul, there are no boundaries between the past and the present. "I don't mind if they were SS executioners if they are willing to talk about it, but I cannot get to normalcy before I discuss the Nazi thing." The elderly man crosses the road, as Paul's silhouette crosses to the other side looking at him as though wondering what crimes he committed.

The title serves a similar function, since the German Shepherd was the Nazis' favorite breed and today is a Holocaust icon, or visual shortcut to refer to Nazi brutality. Tammy Bar-Yosef suggested that for many years many Israelis did not have German Shepherds as pets for this reason.[30]

Just as the elderly man fades into the past, Paul's silhouette walks towards a movie theater showing "The Human Condition," but he keeps on walking. He enters the Berlin sports arena through its open doors and surveys the empty stadium. The soundtrack switches to shouts of "Heil Hitler" during Nazi rallies. "There were hundreds of thousands of people who were involved and millions more who did nothing." The stadium changes into a movie theater. David's silhouette walks down the stairs: "My view on the human condition, what we are made of, what we are naturally inclined to do ... because of that experience it is all negative, it is all like we are inclined to do nothing good." The camera pans over the numbers on seats, 177 and 178, lingers on 179, and then zooms out to show that all the other seat numbers are also 179, to highlight Paul's pessimistic view of human nature—they are all the same. "[...] people whom you think should be naturally good will do the most horrible things for vanity, for competition, for advancement."

The protagonist in *I Was a Child of Holocaust Survivors* called the Holocaust a drug. Paul (who is not mentioned by his name in the movie) is seen sitting alone in a movie theater where he watches the same Holocaust movie several times. Paul is depicted as a black silhouette. He marches right onto the stage, with his back to the viewers as he discusses what he terms his addiction to Holocaust information: "When I go to a Holocaust movie like *The Pianist* or *Schindler's List*, it's very sad, but in a weird way it's like a high to me. I'm like, can't get enough of it." He goes up to the screen and looks at it closely as the limping character on the screen walks towards the horizon in a scene that resembles *The Pianist* when protagonist Vladislav Shpilman limps through the ruins of the Warsaw ghetto. In *German Shepherd* there are no surroundings, only the limping man against the backdrop of the white screen because this is what Paul focuses on.

---

[30] Bar-Yosef, "Nazis, Dogs and Collective Memory." For more on this Holocaust icon, see the analysis of the movie *Silence* in Part 1.

I want it to be ten hours long, because for a moment ... I'm there, I'm that little boy, I am this persecuted person, and in a way, I can't say the words "I enjoy it," but it's like a high, it is like I'm on something and it makes me in a weird way happy cause it gets me a little bit closer to feeling what they felt.

Paul's image jumps into the screen and enters the frame as in Woody Allen's *Radio Days* (1987), blending real and fantastic, past and present. The animation fulfills his dream of reuniting with the past. "Then it is such a letdown." Paul looks small and lost in the big screen that spins around him. This pessimistic worldview is reinforced by the black screen depicting his tiny silhouette as though from a helicopter hovering above him, overlooking dark surroundings. Blobs like colorful bombs thrown into the water emerge as he talks about the negative features of human nature: jealousy, envy, competition, resentment, and indignation. "If you are allowed free reign, you do the bad things, not the good things [...]."

The movie deals very honestly with the way individuals want to see themselves and the shattering of these beliefs. Paul is sketched standing on a speaker's box with a microphone, talking to the crowd the way he wants to think he would have behaved if he had been a German in the 1930s and 1940s: "I would have been a resistance fighter, I would protest, I would leave the country." The crowd applauds. As he stands on the box, he is no longer in gray or black, but has brown hair, a blue shirt, and trousers. Vibrant colors enter his persona as he talks about his "wishful postmemory" but he ends on a totally different note as he confesses: "But you know—I might be like everyone else." He is left with nothing, and is animated walking away, tiny and miserable, in an extreme long shot. The only thing left in the frame is the German Shepherd, and the past that continues to haunt him and shape his pessimistic worldview.

Director Bergendal describes the movie as the story of a second generationer but also one that deals with universal topics: a "personal coming-of-age story with a universal message," "a private reconciliation," or "how to liberate oneself from one's parents and how to conquer a more true view of the world based on your own observations in a more straightforward manner."[31] He considers that "it boils down to questioning the world your parents and teachers present to you."[32] Paul himself refers to this as a combination of his personal story and a universal story of moral choices.[33] His ability to free himself from negative determinist perceptions of the Germans stems partly from developing negative perceptions of the human race.

---

[31] "'German Shepherd' Intro."
[32] "German Shepherd."
[33] "German Shepherd en DocumentaMadrid 2015."

THE LEBANON WAR AND HOLOCAUST ASSOCIATIONS IN *WALTZ WITH BASHIR*

The feature-length movie *Waltz with Bashir* is not about the Holocaust or growing up in a survivors' home. It depicts young Israeli soldiers' experiences and post-trauma stemming from the 1982 Israel-Lebanon war and the IDF's indirect involvement in the Sabra and Shatila massacre, where Christian Phalangists in Lebanon murdered hundreds to thousands of civilian Palestinians in these two refugee camps. This was done to exact revenge for the murder of the Christian Lebanese president (and their former commander) Bashir Gemayel. The Phalangists claimed that they entered the camps to find terrorists, but they also murdered women, children, and the elderly. While the massacre was taking place, Israeli soldiers surrounded the area, and many of them saw and knew what was going on. The Israeli army halted the massacre three days later (16–18 September 1982). The movie has won numerous prizes[34] and fueled a stormy debate in Israel and abroad.

Director Folman uses the movie to tell his autobiographical story about repression, misremembering, and delayed recollection. In his journey into his past, he meets with his former army buddies to find out whether they have dealt with their post-trauma. Research on documentaries has discussed how a moviemaker's subjective experience is inevitably inscribed in the processes of conceptualizing, shooting, and editing a movie. More broadly, studies have adopted the conventional notion in the visual arts that the artist's inner emotional life can penetrate beyond the surface of the work to inhabit that surface.[35] These notions are concretized in movies where the director is also the protagonist, who tells the story in the first person.

The movie presents a dual journey in parallel time zones. In the present, Folman sets out on a journey to restore his memory that involves trying to understand why he suffers from memory loss. He fills in the black holes in his biography by interviewing friends and journalists who covered the events. The second journey goes into the past to depict fragments of his memories of his whereabouts as a young soldier in the war. The first journey is linear in that Folman meets up with acquaintances, friends, and therapists,

---

[34] The movie has been very successful internationally and has won numerous awards, some in the category of fiction and others in the category of documentary, thus reflecting the hybrid nature of this genre. See: Joseph A. Kraemer, "Waltz with Bashir (2008): Trauma and Representation in the Animated Documentary," *Journal of Movie and Video* 67, no. 3–4 (Fall/Winter 2015): 57, https://bit.ly/3rXrDNr; "Waltz with Bashir," *Israeli Cinema Book*, https://bit.ly/3g63odh

[35] Steve Fore, "Reenacting Ryan: The Fantasmatic and the Animated Documentary," *Animation: An Interdisciplinary Journal* 6, no. 3: 277–292.

Figure 6.3 Waltz with Bashir *(Ari Folman, 2009)*

collecting information until he regains his memory. The narrative of the past is incoherent, blurred, and interrupted by stories of other soldiers, dreams, hallucinations, and fantasies. Both journeys are suffused with his identity as a second-generationer and how those images from 1982 Lebanon merge with his postmemory of the Holocaust.

The movie combines mimetic and non-mimetic animation. It operates within the interstitial space between memory, trauma, dreams, and real historical events.[36] When Folman was asked why he chose animation, he replied that a journey into memory and attempts to remember could not have been achieved through a live action documentary. Animated documentary enabled him to create a documentary that represents his inner world, nightmares and hallucinations.[37] In another interview Folman stated that he used animation "to return to being who I am, to understand myself [...] I had to be drawn and in that way to find my true self again, understand who I am."[38] This unresolved tension between dream and reality, misremembering and reality, delusions and truth could only be shown through animated documentary, which can slip from the outer to the inner, what people misremember or disremember, what people really saw and what they dream or fantasize.

---

[36] Paul Ward, "Animating with Facts: The Performative Process of Documentary Animation in the Ten Mark (2010)," *Animation: An Interdisciplinary Journal* 6, no. 3: 295; Nea Ehrlich, "Animated Documentaries as Masking," December 22, 2011, *Animation Studies*, https://bit.ly/3fSDcTo

[37] Ohad Landesman, "Paint as Much as You Want, as Long as you Don't Movie…Walz with Bashir and the Animated Reproduction of War's Memory," *Takriv*, no date [Hebrew], https://bit.ly/2LE43ie

[38] Dvorit Shargal, "Waltz with Bashir," https://bit.ly/3SZMr2L

The animation also enabled individuals who wished to remain anonymous to confess.[39] The notion that animated documentary is less exploitive because the protagonists' real images are not seen on the screen may be crucial to post-traumatized individuals. Meital Zvieli, the movie's researcher, interviewed more than 100 soldiers who served in Lebanon. Out of hundreds of hours of documented interviews, only six interviews appear in the movie, four of which are completely authentic (thus maintaining indexical acoustic and mimetic animation),[40] and two with concealed identities and dubbed (actor Micky Leon as Boaz Rein-Buskila and actor Yehezkel Lazarov as Carmi Cana'n combined with mimetic animation). The interviews constituted the visual references for the animation.[41] Rather than using rotoscoping, a popular animation technique where the image is directly painted over to create movement,[42] Folman used the videos as a visual reference for a stand-alone process of animation. The images were produced from scratch by ten animators employing the "cutout" technique, which turned more than 2,000 drawings (which were based on the interviews, photos from the Lebanon War, descriptions of the war and the imagination) into animation.[43] Thus the movie is composed of layers of live action testimonies, animated testimonies referencing the true ones, and imaginary scenes (the unfilmed past, memories, dreams, delusions).[44] The animation masks the protagonists, which enables them to express themselves freely.

Many scenes in the movie are mimetic representations of objects and spaces, creating what Steven Fore referred to as "illusions of material reality, and especially those portraying human figures and movement."[45] The characters are visually introduced twice: once in the present as they discuss the past and then as younger versions of themselves when the animation visualizes the unfilmed past of the Lebanon War. The interviews are represented in a very realistic manner, using the "talking heads" technique familiar from live action documentary movies as though an imaginary camera had been positioned facing the interviewees. At the same time, the memories, dreams,

---

[39] Landesman, "Paint as Much as You Want."
[40] Shmulik Duvdevany, "As Long as You Draw and Not Movie it's OK," *Mikan* 13 (October 2013): 50–67.
[41] Shargal, "Waltz with Bashir"; Landesman, "Paint as Much as You Want."
[42] According to Dvorit Shargal, Folman wanted to purchase this technique from director Richard Linklater, who used it in his movie *Waking Life* (2001), but he refused, so he had to draw in a different way. Shargal, "Waltz with Bashir."
[43] Nirit Andenman, "The Animation behind Walz with Bashir", *Ha'aretz*, June 12, 2008 [Hebrew] https://bit.ly/3EDfMM9
[44] Kraemer, "Waltz with Bashir."
[45] Fore, "Reenacting Ryan," 280.

and delusions are hyper-realistic, merging realistic aesthetics with hallucinations (a giant naked woman swimming in the ocean, dogs from Hell running down the streets in a dystopic Tel-Aviv, the Beirut airport, et cetera) taking on a more spectacle-like quality.[46] The unfilmed past and the inner worlds are not depicted through different forms or textures of animation. The color scheme changes, and so does the sound, but the animation style is similar (Folman does not shift to puppet animation or other forms), which contributes to the movie's representation of the way the past merges with the present. In the dreams, nightmares, and hallucinations, Folman uses what Fore calls "the imaginative license of animation "mirroring the discourse of delirium."[47]

The Postmemory of the Holocaust Beneath the Trauma of the Lebanon War

Nurit Gertz and Gal Hermoni draw attention to the ways that traumatic memory can conceal another trauma. They refer to research suggesting that traumatic memory is constructed as a chain of traumas, where each visible trauma may mask a hidden trauma. The discovery of the traumatic event can thus be seen as a signifier of another trauma, which is expressed through it. Gertz and Hermoni analyze the cinematic representation of cases in which the original traumatic event derives from the historical continuum of the psyche, which emerges in the present in a way that does not enable it to be identified since is marked by another marker or markers. *Waltz with Bashir* is an example of a movie that does not only discuss the trauma of the Lebanon War but the much earlier trauma of the Holocaust, through the eyes of a member of the second generation. It reflects unwillingness to be a victim, the inability to accept the role of the perpetrator (and/or enabler), and the huis clos of a person who finds himself caught between the two.[48]

The interviews reveal post-traumatic memories including experiencing the death of comrades, the sight of wounded humans and animals, the pressure to kill children who attacked them with RPGs,[49] and devastating fears of the unknown. The movie uses Holocaust associations to depict the way Folman relates to the Israel Defense Forces as the new perpetrators in Lebanon and

---

[46] Landesman and Bendor, "Animated Recollection."
[47] Fore, "Reenacting Ryan," 287.
[48] Nurith Gertz and Gal Hermoni, "Between Lebanon and Hirbat Hizah: On Trauma, Ethics and Revival in Israeli Cinema and Literature" [Hebrew], https://bit.ly/3g4cCqE
[49] Children who were sent by the PLO to fight the IDF and attack the soldiers with RPGs.

the Palestinians in the refugee camps as the "victims of the former victims." These comparisons have been a well-known theme in Israeli culture and cinema since the late 1970s, which correspond to political, sociological, and cultural upheavals in Israel. From the late 1940s until the late 1970s, Israeli culture drew a direct parallel between Arabs and Nazis. Wars against the Arab nations were seen as wars to prevent a second Holocaust that could strike Israel at any moment, and Arab leaders were described as Nazi successors. Demonizing the Arabs and forging links between the past and the present helped unite the ranks in Israel and create immediate empathy for Zionism in the Western world. Whereas in the past the Allied forces had fought the Nazis, today it was their duty to subjugate the Arabs.

However, from the 1970s onwards, the association between the Holocaust and the Israeli-Arab conflict underwent a reversal. Although the memory of the Holocaust was and remains a crucial factor in cultural representations of the Israeli-Arab conflict, perceptions of victimization have become more ambivalent and complex. The right-wing continues to recycle the "Arabs are Nazis" equation. In contrast, left-wing politicians, journalists, and artists use the Holocaust to create the antithetical equivalency in which Jewish-Israelis in general, and IDF soldiers in particular, are equated with Nazis.

These left-wing comparisons are especially patent in cinema and literature, and are related to local political and social trends. The 1970s was a period of crisis for the left-wing Labor movement that had governed Israel since its founding. The debate over the occupied territories, the Yom Kippur War (1973) and the Commission of Inquiry that followed it, and the illegal dollar account held by Leah Rabin (the wife of then Prime Minister, Yitzhak Rabin) that was discovered in Switzerland, were all emblematic of the fall of the moderate left. The rise to power of the right-wing movement—the Likud (1977)—was the first time that the left had been ejected from political power hubs. As right-wing attitudes spread throughout the Israeli public, and new militant groups sprang up from the nationalist religious right, the Left lost effective impact on the political establishment. Instead, its dominance increased in intellectual life, art, literature, and academia. The Lebanon War in June 1982, the start of the first intifada (1987), the second intifada (2000), and the emergence of post-Zionist researchers who opposed the Zionist narrative of the Israeli-Arab conflict, further entrenched this critical tendency. Culture became the mouthpiece of the left-wing and radical left-wing circles to voice their sorrow over Israel.

In journalism and in public debates in the last three decades, both narratives coexist. One continues to compare Arabs to Nazis, whereas the other criticizes the former narrative and compares the Holocaust to the Nakbah (the Arab catastrophe of 1948) and/or Jewish-Israelis in general, and IDF soldiers to Nazis. In the cinema and literature there is a clear and obvious dominance of the latter narrative.[50]

According to Raya Morag, *Waltz with Bashir* "proposes a new direction in cinema studies to deal with national traumas that for the first time recognizes a shift from trauma suffered by victims to that suffered by perpetrators."[51] She considers it to be an example of the "new wave of perpetrator cinema" in contemporary Israeli documentaries, which attests to the difficulty of Israeli documentary cinema in dealing with Israeli soldiers' amoral acts in a state which maintains its self-image as a victimized Jewish society.[52] According to Morag, these Holocaust manifestations are a variant of Hirsch's postmemory. Folman and the second generation are tortured because they grew up with Holocaust postmemory and as adults must deal with their own identity as perpetrators by proxy in Lebanon.[53] Thus they refuse to acknowledge their deeds because the past haunts them in various ways. Loss of memory is one way of shielding the psyche.

The "perpetrators" are represented in the movie as confused young men. They are not redolent with hate and barely understand what they are doing there. The myth of fearless Israeli soldiers is deconstructed. In the movie, there are no acts of bravery, just aimless shooting, the dead and casualties, lives that were taken or saved chaotically. The movie portrays the blurred boundaries between victims and perpetrators since Israelis are also injured and killed by Palestinians. This random killing is represented as completely arbitrary because the context of war is not mentioned, nor its reasons, nor who the fighting parties are. The senseless violence and the absurdity of war are highlighted by the intentional jarring use of uplifting, cheerful music in the killing scenes. The dissonance between sound and image creates a surreal atmosphere.[54] What the viewers see is Israelis and Palestinians killing one another. The soldiers are represented as terrified, very young men ("I was 19, I hadn't even begun to shave") with juvenile ways of thinking (Folman recalls he wanted to die so his girlfriend, who dumped him a week before, would feel guilty her entire life), who were thrown into a war they did not understand and did things they never thought they would do.

---

[50] Liat Steir-Livny, "From Victims to Aggressors: Cultural Representations of the Link between the Holocaust and the Israeli-Palestinian Conflict," *Interactions: Studies in Communication and Culture* 7, no. 2 (7.2) (September 2016): 123–136.

[51] Raya Morag, *Waltzing with Bashir: Perpetrator Trauma and Cinema* (New York & London: I. B. Tauris, 2013), 3.

[52] Morag, *Waltzing with Bashir*, 130.

[53] Morag, *Perpetrator Trauma and Israeli Intifada Cinema* (Tel-Aviv: Resling, 2017) [Hebrew], 185–197, esp. 188.

[54] Landesman and Bendor, "Animated Recollection."

The movie shows that each one of the young soldiers deals with post-trauma in a different way. Boaz Rein-Buskila had recurring nightmares, Carmi Can'an escaped geographically to avoid bumping into old army buddies. Although he was a brilliant mathematician and was considered a candidate for the Nobel prize, he moved to the Netherlands, made a fortune selling falafel, and settled in a rural area where he lives with his family on a 40-acre plot, in complete isolation, smoking pot. Ronny Dayag, the only one who was saved when his tank was attacked, lives with survivor's guilt that he could not save his crewmates.

Alongside the hinted equation between Nazi perpetrators and Israeli soldiers, the movie explores soldiers' post-traumatic memories while echoing the Holocaust. In some scenes, this is made explicit. For example, the opening scene is an audio-visual spectacle representing various modes of time and reality contrasted with memory, fantasy, and imagination. The movie begins with a vicious black yellow-eyed dog that looks straight at the viewers and runs down the streets of ruined Beirut, which a few seconds later blur into the familiar streets of Tel-Aviv (Rothschild Boulevard), which however looks like the city after an apocalypse since it is gray, partly deserted with a yellow sky and dark buildings, echoing the Beirut war landscape. As the seconds go by, more and more dogs chase the yellow-eyed dog, creating a frightening pack of hounds, ruining whatever is in their path, accompanied by loud rock music in the soundtrack combining 102 different sound channels (which also includes lions, wolves, and tigers). Finally, the dogs stop in front of a building and start to bark. A man stares at them from a window. In the next scene the man—Boaz Rein—is shown talking with Folman, explaining the dream to him, saying that twenty-six dogs came to kill him, demanding "the head of Boaz Rein." At this point the viewers understand they have seen a dream sequence. The camera zooms out to show that the images of Folman and Rein are in a bar, drinking and talking. "Every night the same dream." Rein connects it to Lebanon and to the nights they entered villages to look for wanted Palestinian men and had to kill dogs to prevent them from barking to alert the Palestinian of the IDF's whereabouts. The animation "follows" Boaz into the flashback, showing him shooting twenty-six dogs. "I remember each and every one of them." More than twenty years later they come back to haunt him in his dreams. He says he called Folman in the middle of the night because he saw how he had achieved closure in his life through his movies and suggested that perhaps now was the time to discuss Lebanon. Rein considers that movies are therapeutic for the director, but perhaps also for the other protagonists and viewers who took part in this or similar traumatic events.

Cathy Caruth[55] suggested that the belatedness that characterizes trauma, the inability to comprehend what happened and the way it haunts the person, is symbolized by the dogs. Rein is haunted by an event that happened during the war. Still, these dogs are also the memories of war in general, which haunt the moviemaker, many others who served in Lebanon, and by extension, Israeli society as a whole. No one wants to face frightening memories which threaten to swallow up and destroy society. Since the dogs are also a Holocaust icon, they serve as a double symbol of what Israeli society fears.

At some point during his search (in the movie), Folman feels he has reached a dead end since he is unable to find anyone who was with him the night of the Sabra and Shatila massacre. "All I'm left with is the delusion." "But the delusion is real," his friend Uri Sivan explains to him. Sivan considers that Folman's interest in the massacre is derived from another massacre. His interest in what happened in Sabra and Shatila is what happened in "*these* camps" (with a gesture signaling the past and the concentration, extermination, and labor camps during the Holocaust). "Your parents were in the camps?," "Yes," "They were in Auschwitz?," "Yes." "It is from there, from your childhood."

Sivan tells Folman to find out what really happened on that day in Lebanon ("through the factual details, maybe you'll recover your memory"). After meeting with numerous individuals, Folman's memory returns. The animation visualizes this by showing Palestinian civilians taken out of the camp, and marched away in long lines while the Christian phalanges yell at them and put them on trucks that drive them to a stadium. These representations clearly resemble similar scenes from Holocaust movies: lines of poor, frightened people, mothers holding their babies, the guards with their rifles threatening them, and a child's sad face looking through the holes in the truck.[56] The yellow of the dog's eyes in Rein's dream in Tel-Aviv corresponds to the yellow of the flares the Israelis launched at night when the massacre was taking place. This time the Israelis are the bystanders/enablers, and this is a story of collaboration The movie implies that this burden was so heavy on the second generation that their defense mechanism was to repress and forget. After Folman remembers that he was there on a roof with the soldiers who launched the flares "who helped people below to kill," Sivan explains to him that he did not remember because he felt guilty "at 19, you were cast to play the role of the Nazi against your will. You were there. You launched the flares, but you did not commit the massacre."

---

[55] Cathy Caruth, "Introduction," in *Trauma: Explorations in Memory* (Baltimore: John Hopkins University Press, 1995), 4.
[56] Gertz and Hermoni, "Between Lebanon and Hirbat Hizah."

Folman and Sivan are not the only ones who explain the massacre through Holocaust associations. Ron Ben Yishai was a military reporter who spent a considerable amount of time in Lebanon. When he heard rumors about the massacre, he telephoned Ariel Sharon, the minister of security at the time, to let him know. Ben Yishai states that Sharon thanked him for the information and went back to sleep. Yishai tells Folman that he woke up his crew at 5:30 AM and headed towards the camps: "Do you know the picture from the Warsaw ghetto? The child with his hands raised his in the air?" "Yes," Folman replies. "It was exactly like that: a convoy of children, women, the elderly, being marched." The visuals show beaten, hunched-over people walking slowly with their hands up in the air. After Ben Yishai describes what he saw and the visuals illustrate the ruined camp, the dead in the yards, the piles of corpses, the scene shifts to women who come out of the camp, who appeared in Folman's "delusion." This is the fourth time they appear, but this time they highlight Folman's remembering. This is the only time the movie turns to live action—Folman shows eighty seconds of footage of the crying, yelling women who survived the massacre. The live action scenes depict the dead, in very graphic scenes that include children. This is also the last scene in the movie. The memory is unveiled. It is alive. No more masking.

Audiences' reactions to the movie help shed light on whether animation creates a distance between the viewers and the themes.[57] For many viewers, the movie evoked strong emotional responses. Men who served in Lebanon reported that watching the movie brought repressed memories of the war to the surface. Some stated that watching the movie provoked somatic and physical responses (crying, seeing scenes from the war in their minds, smelling the burned corpses, shaking, and feeling as though they had been struck by bullets). Others felt it was a therapeutic experience that helped them to deal with their trauma from that war.[58] The animation was the sensory stimulus for memories despite the lack of verisimilitude.[59] Nea Ehrlich, who interviewed former Israeli soldiers about the movie, found that for them the animation made these depictions accurate and realistic, since there was really no way to present the bizarre and unreal sensations of the experiences of war.[60]

Critics' reactions to the movie and the use of animated documentary combined with the transition to the live action scenes at the end were mixed.

---

[57] Honess Roe, "Against Animated Documentary."
[58] Kobi Ben Simhon, "Waltz with Bashir Awakens the Traumas," *Ha'aretz*, February 6, 2009 [Hebrew], https://bit.ly/3fSDZ6O; Landesman, "Paint as Much as You Want."
[59] Landesman and Bendor, "Animated Recollection."
[60] Ehrlich, "Animated Documentaries."

After the release of *Waltz with Bashir* in Israel, and when it was short-listed for an Academy Award, some left-wing and radical left-wing Israeli moviemakers, intellectuals, and researchers protested against what they termed the "shooting and crying syndrome," in other words, the coverup of crimes by recalling victimization traumas. For example, journalist Gideon Levy argued that "The *Waltz* is founded on two principles: we shot and we cried, oh, how much we cried, and it wasn't our hands that spilled the blood. A few Holocaust memories [...] a pinch of victimization, and here you go, here is the tricky portrait of Israel of 2008."[61]

Joseph A. Kraemer criticized the shift to the live action scenes, arguing that by doing so, Folman ignored the elusiveness of the trauma, and fell into the trap of "the pornography of the real," by turning the Palestinians into objects, as though their trauma could be understood. The movie leaves the Palestinians voiceless and betrays Folman's own claim throughout the movie that archival footage cannot maintain the event.[62] Kobi Niv was critical of telling this story through animation. He suggested that animation distances viewers from the horrific reality and hence distances the ethical failings that could/should stem from the event. Animation provides no objectivity, no truth, and no responsibility, but only a stream of consciousness in which memories and hallucinations merge and create a story that is just a story. He argued that the eighty seconds when there is no soundtrack are too little and too late in a movie in which the Israeli soldier is shown to be the victim, and where the animation, according to Niv, creates a spectacular false fantasy that helps Israelis shake off the stain of the Sabra and Shatila massacre.[63]

On the other hand, Landesman and Bendor argued that *Waltz with Bashir* establishes a new relationship between the viewer and the documentary text. The movie produces a rich, consistent, and thus trustworthy sense of reality for its viewers because of, rather than despite, its unique aesthetic choices and the mixing of reality with fantasy. The aesthetic strategies are essential to its disclosure of reality in all its complexity, ambiguity, and multifacetedness. The movie's departure from indexical documentation toward subjective perception and phantasmagorical imaginings can enhance the richness and density of the depiction by showing viewers what cannot be seen by the naked eye.[64] Shmulik Duvdevani considered that animation is an aesthetic that seemingly distances but actually enables one to come closer and deal with a traumatic

---

[61] Laliv Melamed, "Book Review: Waltzing with Bashir: Perpetrator Trauma and Cinema," *Historical Journal of Movie, Radio and Television*, September 5, 2014, https://bit.ly/3fSErSy
[62] Kraemer, "Waltz with Bashir."
[63] Niv Kobi, *Look Back into the Future* (Tel-Aviv: Olam Hadash), 2014, 94–129.
[64] Landesman and Bendor, "Animated Recollection," 353–370.

event. In his view, by using animation Folman disconnected the situation from its realistic associations and turned reality into a hallucination. The simplicity of the images makes it easier to deal with them. The animated anesthetization beautifies the horrific, which is why Folman turns to live action scenes at the end of the movie to remind the viewers of reality.[65] Raya Morag claimed that the transition to live action endows the movie with the values of "truth," "real," and "proof" that are supposedly absent from animation.[66]

However, the shift from animation to live action horrific footage may have been meant to shake the viewers as it shook Folman himself when his memory returned. He realized that for years he had repressed the fact that he was a witness to a massacre enabled by the Israeli IDF. This constituted a slap in the face for Folman, who had been struggling with his identity as a second generationer and was now forced to become an enabler/perpetrator. The move to live action allows the viewers to go through the same mental breakpoint as this transition: it is there, it was real. Some studies have claimed that this scene is an "awakening" or "truer" than the animation, a reasoning that implies that animation cannot "awaken."[67] In fact, viewers' responses to the animated scenes were just as strong. Orly Yadin, the director of *Silence*, commented that "one of our main concerns was not to spell everything out and allow the viewer to put something of themselves into what they saw and heard."[68] Folman does the same thing. By ending the movie with these scenes, he leaves the viewers with their thoughts on shame, guilt, accountability, and the resemblance between past and present. This is a movie, not a political manifesto or a propaganda tool, and Folman is not obligated to teach the viewers a lesson. Just as Folman forces himself to remember, he forces Israeli society to remember, to deal with accountability, to look at this part of history that many Israelis wish to forget, and contemplate its connection to the trauma of the Jewish people during the Holocaust.

---

[65] Duvdevani, "As Long as You Draw."
[66] Morag, *Perpetrator Trauma*, 197.
[67] Landesman and Bendor, "Animated Recollection."
[68] Copley, "Modes of Representing."

CHAPTER 7

The Memories Don't Let Go

The third generation began to be studied in the 1980s, when psychologists in the United States who were treating a seven-year-old boy, the grandson of Holocaust survivors, claimed that the effects of the Holocaust affected him strongly and that the issue deserved comprehensive treatment in the psychiatric community.[1] Since then, psychologists and psychiatrists have debated the term "third generation" and its characteristics. Some researchers claim that the trauma of the Holocaust is transferred to members of the third generation. Some claim that the third generation, as a group, does not have distinguishing traits relative to trauma and that there is no difference between the biological grandchildren of Holocaust survivors and other groups whose grandparents are not Holocaust survivors. Others note the wide spectrum of reactions to trauma that does not justify viewing the third generation as one group. Various books and movies in the last two decades have drawn on third-generation narratives from several continents and highlight the diversity of inherited memory and the transgenerational transfer of trauma, as well as the elements common to members of this group.[2] Since the late 1990s, the third generation in the Western world have related to the Holocaust in various cultural fields.[3]

This chapter deals with the depiction of the third generation and how third generation directors use animation to show how they perceive trauma, memory, postmemory, and their effects on them. By combining subjective, fantastic, and postmodern animation modes and employing various ways of dealing with traumatic events, they inform audiences and enhance their ability to identify and sympathize with the survivors' grandchildren. In so doing, they explore the weight of these memories and the role of Holocaust memory in the present. The movies presented in this chapter highlight the ways the Holocaust is remembered, misremembered, and debated in various contexts,

---

[1] Perihan Aral Rosenthal and Stuart Rosenthal, "Holocaust Effects in the Third Generation: Child of Another Time," *American Journal of Psychotherapy* 34, no. 4 (1980): 572–580.
[2] See Steir-Livny, *Remaking Holocaust Memory*, 20–22.
[3] Liat Steir-Livny, *Let the Memorial Hill Remember* (Tel-Aviv: Resling, 2014) [Hebrew].

and how it has shaped the lives of the grandchildren and their relationships, not only with their surviving grandparents but also with their parents—the second generation. The movies analyzed are *2nd World War 3rd Generation* (Elad Eisen, Gil Laron, and Shahar Madmon, 2013); *Noch Am Leben* (Still Alive, Anita Lester, 2017), *Sketches from München* (Shahaf Ram, 2013), and *Compartments* (Daniella Koffler and Uli Seis, 2017).

Epigenetics in *Noch Am Leben*

As analyzed in Chapter 5, *Noch Am Leben* is the story of director Lester's recollection of her Holocaust survivor great-aunt, Eva Nagler, who was shot with her sister into a mass grave and watched her sister die in front of her eyes. Later she was raped multiple times and never recovered mentally. Nagler was treated for psychosis and was interned towards the end of her life.

In the movie, Lester tells her great-aunt's story from her perspective after Nagler passed away, based on Nagler's writings and Lester's personal recollections. According to Lester:

> It was not intended to be a narrative from my perspective. Through extensive research, I found that the protagonist of my movie (my great aunt Eva), was not in fact triumphant in her survival, but broken by it. […] My family members advised me to tell her story from my perspective, which would also enable me to discuss epigenetics, the genetic memory in the family. My mom, a second generationer, always had horrible nightmares about her father's trauma, and I believe my brother and sister are affected as well. My brother is obsessed with it, and my sister has night terrors and has gone to Poland many times. I don't have nightmares, but I believe it is part of my story as well.[4]

Lester considers the Holocaust for the descendants as a legacy of post-trauma and madness. In one scene when she goes to Nagler's house, the cereal bowl Nagler gives her is not filled with cereal, but with cigarettes, as though she is handing over her madness. Lester's image trembles. The dancing image of Nagler grows bigger and bigger, her movements stronger as she takes over the screen, which turns white as though swallowing Lester's image. The fear of this legacy of inherited post-trauma and mental illness dominates the scene.

In her voiceover, Lester discusses her inability to understand Nagler's world, and the nightmares she had when she was a child. She grew up in a world that was "too comfortable": she could not grasp that there had been a time that was not filled with the sweet smell of eucalyptus, ice cream, and children's healthy bodies. She talks about herself, but delves more deeply into

---

[4] "Salute Your Shorts 2018—*Still Alive/Noch Am Leben*," *We Are Moving Stories*, https://bit.ly/3CxhlIL; Liat Steir-Livny, "An Interview with Anita Lester," November 8, 2019.

other generations' inability to understand a trauma they did not go through, but which influences them. The childhood Lester cannot fathom is represented as she talks, when the image of Lester the child is portrayed in the main square of a city next to deported Jews' belongings. They are shown as black images against white houses. A car appears, its blood-red lights run over Nagler and fill the screen with red.

Towards the end of the movie, after Lester describes Nagler's life in the asylum, white hands reaching towards the sky appear and turn into stumps as Lester says she wanted to tell a different story about Nagler, something different about her family. These stumps do not represent growth. Red flashes fill the frame from behind and cover "these struggles and historical pains that find threads between each generation." The imagery is of a woman in white clutching her face in pain. "Somehow this thread that I found was genetic memory in the form of madness." Whiteness pops from the woman's eyes and fills the screen, leaving the images of two women's heads drawn in black. "Why are we like this?" asks one of them. "It is our legacy," answers the other, and they disappear. The scene lets the viewers reflect on the question of the genetic and maybe epigenetic transfer of trauma "and whether we can inherit pain."[5]

THE HOLOCAUST, YOUNG ISRAELIS AND YOUNG GERMANS IN *2ND WORLD WAR 3RD GENERATION*

This short animation was submitted as a final project in the animation section of the cinema department at Sapir Academic College, in Israel. The soundtrack is made up of interviews with young Germans and Israelis during which the directors explore how echoes of the Holocaust influence today's younger generations. The faces of the interviewees are not seen and there are no captions indicating their names, ages, or whereabouts. Their voices suggest they are in their twenties or thirties. The monologues are intertwined to reveal the complex attitude of both sides towards each other. The viewers can only tell who is Israeli and who is German from the language spoken.

The monologues are visualized using mimetic, non-mimetic, and evocation animation: some portray reality and others depict dreams, thoughts, and nightmares. Between the different images the frame always returns to a stylized Lego robot in a large dark room, whose walls are made of compartments containing white bricks/boxes that the robot is filling. Sometimes, the visualization is screened from within one of the bricks. This gives the movie a hi-tech flavor corresponding to the modern world, but the past drags it

---

[5] *"Still Alive/Noch Am Leben."*

backward as both sides talk about how events that took place almost eighty years ago influence their personalities and lives in the present.

Director Eisen says the idea for the movie came from a need to resolve the tension. "My grandmother's family perished in the Holocaust, and the other directors have similar stories. On the other hand, one day we could all move to Berlin. The film arose from this conflict."[6] According to Eisen, their generation is open to many perspectives, not only the Israeli narrative. "I have traveled with Germans, and on Facebook, it is very easy to connect with people and hear what they say. In addition, the time has passed, and I think we (the younger generation) have worked through the topic in a way."[7] The movie provides an opportunity to hear the young Germans' side. The Israelis' monologues do not describe ways of working through the trauma, but rather how it is continuously being acted out. The past is also there for the young Germans.

Israelis in Berlin

Prior to the 1990s, only a small number of Jewish Israelis lived in Berlin. More began to settle in the city during the 1990s, and this trend has continued to intensify. In 2017, approximately 10,000 Israelis were living in Berlin. This choice corresponds to the post-national cultural globalization since the turn of the millennium that challenges national and cultural borders.[8] There are larger Israeli communities in other locations, such as New York City, Los Angeles, Silicon Valley, et cetera. Still, the Berlin community has attracted the most attention because of its symbolism.[9] This thriving community is now home to many artists, which in itself has elicited great interest in Israel.[10]

Some Israelis see contemporary Germany, and especially Berlin, as disconnected from the past: "In my opinion, Berlin today is an amazing city. Perhaps the best city for young people in the world. Half of Tel-Aviv's and Jerusalem's youngsters live in Berlin," says one against a backdrop of two people in a coffee shop and a young girl bicycling. "You can't keep on reliving your own pain, because you'll bump into it all the time, and surely you can't relive your grandmother's pain," says another.

---

[6] Toker, Ina. "The Y Generation Makes Holocaust Movies." *YNET*, April 24, 2017, https://bit.ly/3Vmpvwh

[7] Toker, "The Y Generation."

[8] Horng-luen Wang, "Mind the Gap: On Post-National Idea(l)s and the Nationalist Reality," *Social Analysis: The International Journal of Anthropology* 46, no. 2 (2002): 139–147; Yehuda Shenhav, "Identity in a Postnational Society," *Theory and Criticism* 19 (2001): 5–16.

[9] Gad Yair, *Love Is Not Practical* (Tel-Aviv, 2015); Fania Oz-Salzberger, *Israelis, Berlin* (Tel-Aviv, 2001); Shuki Shtauber, *Israelis in Berlin* (Tel-Aviv, 2017) [all in Hebrew].

[10] Maya Unger, "A Berlin Mix," *Spitz*, August 2013 [Hebrew], https://bit.ly/3MslaUg

"We are the third and fourth generation post the Holocaust [...] if re-education exists, they are the ones who have mostly been re-educated. In a way ... they deserve credit for that as well," says another, but the directors undermine the comment with the visuals showing a German café in the 1930s. Then it morphs into young hip contemporary youngsters to highlight the fact that the space is the same and the past is not entirely separate from the present. The perception of the past in the present also enters into some of the monologues: "You are looking at a woman sunbathing naked in the park. You're looking at ... a river in the middle with fish, swans, absolute serenity! You say 'Goddamn, Hitler won the war!'" Another speaker comments bitterly that "My family came from here, I could have been living here in this serenity, but I just don't feel at home."

Sometimes the past appears in nightmares that invade cool contemporary Berlin: "On my first night in Berlin, I was traveling with girlfriends, I dreamed a Nazi came into our room, I woke up screaming, completely terrified." This incident is screened from within the bricks, which now enters her mind to visualize the incident and her inner fears. The frame focuses in close-up on the terrified face of a young woman, the squeaking sound of a door opening as the light from outside falls slowly on her face in the dark room. As the camera pans towards the door, a silhouette of a Nazi officer in uniform appears at the door. The animation enables the viewers to experience her nightmare, hence strengthening the acting out of the past.

Other Israelis protest against the spirit of change and the notion that both peoples should move on. "What do you mean 'enough?' there is no such thing as 'enough!' they need to ... I mean there is no ... what do you mean 'we have heard enough?' We're talking about the murder of a third of the Jewish people here!" says an Israeli as parts of the Holocaust memorial in Berlin are screened by the robot. "You can twist it whichever way you like. For me a German is a Nazi! A German is Nazi! Go, live there and wait for them to decide to kill all the Jews again. Then we'll see," says another as the frame focuses on a young man in a contemporary bar. He leans his head on his hand, where a number has been tattooed: the past and the present blend.

The Germans

Research had shown that post-World War II generations in Germany deal with the past in very complex ways. Some confront their families about the past, express guilt and shame (for actions they did not commit), and want to atone. In 2011, descendants of Nazis visited the Knesset and proclaimed that even their deepest apologies could not make up for the acts of the past. They emphasized their dedication to the fight against antisemitism. *March of Life* is a

German movement of third-generation Nazi offspring who want to atone for their families' crimes by commemorating the Holocaust and establishing strong ties to Israel. Some have moved to Israel to correct wider historical injustices through interpersonal acts of benevolence, and have even converted to Judaism and established a Jewish family in Israel.[11] On the other hand, there are young Germans who deny the facts, accept the silence of the elder generation, and choose to be indifferent to the past and to avoid dealing with it. Others embellish the familial past, trying to cling to every shred of evidence that can prove their families were "decent" even though they were Nazis.[12]

"On the one hand the relationship between Israelis and Germans is based on curiosity. On the other hand, it's obvious they are both 'troubled' about the past. You can say it's a love-hate relationship," states a young woman as the movie titles appear. Another dares to break a taboo: "I learned my first Holocaust jokes from Jews, from Israelis. For example, 'What is the difference between a pizza and a Jew? A pizza doesn't scream when you put it in the oven.'" This joke is shouted out from within the bricks. The camera zooms in to show people standing and looking at a young baker putting something into a big oven complex that looks like a crematorium. Black smoke pours out of the chimney. Even if she says she learned the joke from an Israeli, this does not change the uncomfortable feeling of hearing a joke like that from a German. She completely ignores the fact that black humor has a lot to do with the person telling the joke. The fact that this scene with this visualization appears in the movie only highlights the abnormality of the situation between young Israelis and Germans.

Other interviewees also express attitudes that remain extremely problematic to the Jewish ear, such as "We have had enough of the Holocaust." Director Eisner says that the interviews with Germans often indicated that they were fed up with the topic: "an attitude that says 'Okay, okay, but we

---

[11] Arik Bender, "Tzatzaei nazim baknesset: ne'avek b'antishemiyut" ["Nazi Descendants in the Knesset: We Will Fight Anti-Semitism"], *NRG*, November 22, 2011, https://bit.ly/3CuCLX5; Itay Ilany, "K'she tzatzaei hanazim sharim hatikva berap lifney nitzolim" ["When Nazis' Descendants Sing Hatikva Rap-Style in Front of Survivors"], *YNet News*, December 18, 2016, https://bit.ly/3CVxJVc; Liron Nagler-Cohen, "Shovrim Shtika: Nazi Descendants Sing Hatikva" ["Breaking the Silence: Nazis' Descendants Sing Hatikva"], *YNet News*, August 16, 2016, https://bit.ly/3yBNSwc; Eli Somer and Yael Agam, "Personal Action as Collectivist Reconciliation: Children of 'Aryan' Citizens of Nazi Germany Living in Israel," *Dapim: Studies on the Holocaust*, 2015, http://dx.doi.org/10.1080/23256249.2015.1026670

[12] See examples in other studies in Steir-Livny, *Remaking Holocaust Memory*, 191–199; 203–205.

Figure 7.1 2nd World War 3rd Generation *(Elad Eisen, Gil Laron, and Shahar Madman, 2013)*

didn't do it.'" He suggests young Germans are beyond blame.[13] This is captured in a comment of a young German in the movie who says "O.K. We understood. It wasn't good, but we have had enough." The animation shows a girl on her doorstep getting ready to go to school holding her father's hand. Her schoolbag drags on the floor to symbolize the past she must carry on her shoulders. The young girl looks at them with a sad face. This is the director's way of subverting "Holocaust fatigue" by reminding her and other young Germans what she hopes to forget.

The directors also combat this fatigue by devoting the last part of the movie to a German interviewee who criticizes German society: "If someone doesn't believe that there is nothing Nazi going on in Germany at the moment, he is deeply mistaken, uninformed and not connected to what's going on in reality. We still got Nazis, and worse, we've got Nazi beliefs: 'We don't trust foreigners that are taking our jobs away … or even 'Jews have too much power in Germany…', and 'We shouldn't beat ourselves up because of the past.'" As he speaks, everything that the robot worked so hard to arrange topples down. The frame trembles, the colors merge, frames from past monologues swirl into the frame and disappear quickly, the bricks fall out of their compartments on the robot and damage it, all the voices of the interviewees blur, and everything is ruined.

The final German interviewee repeats themes that appeared in *German Shepherd*: "I'm not ashamed of the fact that Germans did it, I'm ashamed of the fact that humans did it and I don't think it is a specific German characteristic, that Germans have a tendency to murder Jews, a genetic disposition for killing Jews, I don't think that exists. It is humans who have a disposition

---

[13] Toker, "The Y Generation."

for killing other humans." This is apparently the director's overall conclusion. Eisen admits it is universal: "The Germans did not have a particular gene that made them do what they did—they were human beings, and humans have a tendency to do bad things to other people. We have to learn from that."[14] In the last part of the movie, there are no scenes of destruction. The last comment is voiced against a black background. It takes the movie from the Israeli-German arena to a universal arena, and as in *German Shepherd*, this has the effect of ending the journey towards reconciliation on a more pessimistic note.

ISRAELIS MOVING TO GERMANY IN *SKETCHES FROM MÜNCHEN* AND *COMPARTMENTS*

Sketches from München is based on rapid sketches that director Shahaf Ram (aka Jack Tml) drew in Munich which were adapted to a movie about relationships, break-ups, childhood memories, and thoughts about the way the Holocaust influences the third generation. In the movie Ram talks in the first person to his ex-girlfriend. He tells her that whereas in Israel he is a "nobody," the Germans consider him a highly talented artist. He has been invited to Munich, all expenses paid, his work is being shown in a famous gallery, and the organizers expect 14,000 people to attend ("They treat me like a superstar. A great artist from Israel"). But the past is always there, preventing him from being another successful artist in Germany.

The movie was made in Ram's senior year at Bezalel Academy of Arts and Design in Jerusalem, for a "video diary" course. It was based on his feelings when he was invited to show his work in a large art gallery in Munich. He stayed there for two weeks and toyed with the idea of leaving Israel and moving there. Initially, he had no idea that he would be assailed by memories from the Holocaust. For him, Germany was simply a European country. Nevertheless, he did not tell his grandfather he was going because he knew he would not approve. The movie is a testimony to his emotional journey to Munich. He wrote the text, which is read by an actor (Eliad Landau) in the voiceover.

The black and white drawings are non-mimetic. The movie does not attempt to mimic the real but rather to evoke, by sharing Ram's feelings as a Jewish-Israeli in contemporary Germany. This journey into his subconscious becomes increasingly turbulent as his postmemory intensifies. The movie opens with a drawing of a train, one of the strongest Holocaust images, and the protagonist's voiceover telling his ex-girlfriend

---

[14] Toker, "The Y Generation."

Figure 7.2 Sketches from München *(Shahaf Ram, 2013)*

that he hopes she "survives." This choice of words suggests that they separated, but the verb "survive" associated with the train carriages also hints at the past. While displaying sketches he made of Munich's old town, he talks about the way it resembles Jerusalem, which makes him feel "a little bit at home." However, this homely feeling cannot be felt fully, because it is blocked by the past his grandfather experienced, and he didn't. Ram talks about the things his grandfather told him when he was a child, which gradually come back to his thoughts and dreams. In the animation, while commenting that "When I was 14 my grandpa took me to his place of birth," the body of a young man becomes a coffin and the old man struggles to drag it on the ground. Thus, before explaining that his grandfather is a Holocaust survivor, the animation indicates that it changed Ram's life as a young boy. He was dragged into death, which has become an integral part of his body and his identity. The pair are visualized at the top of a black mountain that appears in the middle of the frame, like black lava thrusting out of the ground. Grandfather and grandson stand on top of it, looking very small. This huge black mountain does not convey a sense of victory but rather highlights the insignificance of human beings when faced with the power of nature and evil forces. It recalls the mountain of ashes in the Majdanek concentration and extermination camp. This visualization skirts the transition from "ashes to renewal" that characterizes so many Zionist cultural texts. Instead, the ashes not only remain, but also influence the young Israeli generation that was born long after the Holocaust.

Dina Wardi suggested that in families of Holocaust survivors, one child always functions as a "memorial candle" for the dead. That child is expected—implicitly or explicitly—to act as a link between the traumatic past that must be remembered, the present, and the future.[15] *Sketches from München* shows that this term applies to the third generation as well. Ram is not a subject for his grandfather but an object through which the past is commemorated. He says that his grandfather always stressed the importance of Israel, the fact that "we" have no other place in the world, and that Israel is our revenge against Hitler. "He also told me that he survived because he was never closely attached to his family. When he felt bad, he simply got up and left and never thought about anyone."

His grandfather's explanation of how he survived deviates completely from canonical Zionist stories of survival rooted in solidarity and the importance of family connections. As his grandfather speaks, the frame shows one hand letting go of another hand and the inside of a train carriage. The train is moving so that it is not clear whether it is the grandfather who escapes or Ram who is on the train in contemporary Munich, since he has only partially integrated his grandfather's Holocaust lessons. He is in Munich, where he is adulated, feels a bit at home, and because he was able to break up with his girlfriend ("You are a prison, I love you, I hate you"), and leave Israel. Nevertheless, he fails to escape since the memories still haunt him: "You are a prison. One big prison. Six million Jews crowded together, waiting for the Messiah to save them." Thus, the prison is not just his intimate relationship but also Israel as a state (which in 2013 reached a population of six million) and the prison of the Holocaust memories of six million Jews. These are the three prisons he wants to escape from. He was able to leave his girlfriend and Israel but could not run away from the Holocaust memories that engulf him in Munich. His voiceover becomes more anxious as he uses the third person to describe his postmemory, in which the borders are not made up of walls, watch towers, or barbed wire, but collective memories—"an existential fear that grows with us from kindergarten until the swearing-in ceremony in the IDF." As he talks, the animation shows a man's feet running away that then morph into a man trying to get out of what looks like a black blanket, which covers and suffocates him as he struggles with it.

In Israeli collective memory, the trauma of the Holocaust is not derived solely from the events of World War II. The sensitive relationship between Israel and the Arab nations, the decades-long Jewish-Israeli-Palestinian conflict, the threat of annihilation, the continuing terrorist attacks, intifadas, and the politicization of the Holocaust, have all contributed to creating an

---

[15] Wardi, *Memorial Candles*, 14.

atmosphere of constant vigilance, and ongoing anxiety. For example, a 2015 survey found that 43 per cent of all Jewish-Israelis believe that a second Holocaust could be perpetrated by the Palestinians.[16]

Ram highlights the way the existential fears of the past are blended with the problematic security situation of the present ("walls of bodies of Jews in the Holocaust and fallen IDF soldiers […] electric barbed wire fences from grandfather's world." In these scenes, he talks about the transgenerational transfer of the trauma to the biological third generation (himself), but also makes the point that not all those who experience this "existential fear" are biological descendants of survivors. All Jewish-Israelis who are educated in the Israeli school system learn about the Holocaust from childhood. In so doing, he echoes research that extends the definitions of the second generation and third generation beyond the biological.[17]

His voice becomes even more staccato, as though he is in a trance or a nightmare, while the animation shows the Germans expected to attend the gallery opening staring at him. "The lights in the hall blink and I'm crawling up the wall, spitting out color, spitting blood." The animation makes no attempt to illustrate this hallucination and simply depicts a group of attendees wandering through the gallery. They do not seem threatening at all. As the horror and blood of the past overtake him, he cannot see contemporary Germans who are simply interested in his work.

His identity crisis takes on yet another perspective when he discusses his name, which the Germans cannot pronounce. Instead, they use the name he invented when he was seventeen, "and that's fine." But he does not say what this name is. In the dark, a small boat enters a harbor. Did he come home? Ram asks himself if the name he invented "is not more real than the one Mom and Dad gave me? And who said I cannot choose who I want to be?" His trance reaches its peak at the end of the movie when he states that in Israel (unlike in Munich) he is a nobody. Apparently, he has made his decision. The animation is compiled of very short rapidly blended shots including an orthodox Jew, Ram himself banging his head against a wall, the sound of glass breaking, a hand clutching a door that looks like the door of a cattle car, and a tower, like in the fairytales he described while he was walking through the old city of Munich. His image is seen high up on the tower, as he yells "I cut the umbilical cord, I avoided the camera, the electrified fence, and crossed the border. I've won. Bye Pitz (his ex's nickname)." The visuals nevertheless

---

[16] Idith Zertal, *The Nation and Death* (Tel-Aviv: Dvir, 1993) [Hebrew]; Daniel Bar-Tal, *Living with the Conflict* (Jerusalem: Carmel, 2007) [Hebrew [; Daniel Bar-Tal, "Why Don't You Want Peace?," *Haaretz*, September 2, 2016, 54–56.

[17] Liat Steir-Livny, *Remaking Holocaust Memory*, VII, 22–23.

continue to subvert his monologue, including hissing at the end of a TV broadcast or the static from a broken microphone as his image jumps from the tower window, as though he were committing suicide. In the course of the jump, his image turns into a white angel-like figure with wings. The message seems to be that reality cannot contain these mixed feelings. The boat had not reached port and living in the prison of collective traumatic memories is impossible. The moment he frees himself of the prison of memories is also apparently the moment of his demise, or does he break free and fly away? Ram leaves this question deliberately open.[18]

A similar take on the transgenerational transfer of the trauma, both personal and collective, appears in *Compartments*, which is based on the experiences of third-generation director Koffler. The movie tells the story of Neta, a young Israeli woman who was taught by her second-generation Holocaust survivor father never to forgive the Germans. As an adult, Neta meets Martin, a German her age who is visiting Israel. They fall in love, and she decides to move to Berlin. Neta's father is horrified and refuses to talk to her ever again. She tries to start over in Berlin, free of Holocaust memories, only to discover that it is impossible since the memories are imprinted in Germany and within herself. *Compartments* is the first Israeli-German short animation co-production. It has won prizes at various festivals and was rated by the German Movie and Media (FBW) as "Exceptionally Valuable."[19]

Koffler graduated from the Bezalel Academy of Arts and Design in Jerusalem and works as a freelance animator and illustrator. Her first-year movie, *The List*, and her graduation movie, *Stairs to no End*, have been screened in many international festivals. Seis is an animation moviemaker, animator, and media designer from Germany. He has worked in different areas of animation production. He has directed seven animated short movies that have been screened at numerous national and international movie festivals.[20] Actor Micha Levinson plays her father's voice, and Shirley Lev, a young Israeli actor (whom herself immigrated to Berlin), is Neta's voice.[21]

Koffler and Seis created a world in which each animated character wears a wooden box containing many tiny compartments that house their memories and the symbols of their identity. The characters have control over these memories, but certain moments in their lives cause specific memories to be amplified or disappear. The compartments also include collective memories

---

[18] Liat Steir-Livny, "An Interview with Shahaf Ram," October 8, 2020.
[19] Daniella Koffler, "Compartments," *Moonfash*, October 7, 2017 [Hebrew], https://bit.ly/3ew6NSf
[20] "Compartments," https://bit.ly/3g1eXCE
[21] Koffler, "Compartments."

Figure 7.3 Compartments *(Daniella Koffler and Uli Seis, 2017)*

of events that never happened to them personally, but are an integral part of their identities because they are elements in their group's collective memory.[22]

Most of the movie consists of flashbacks. Neta, who lives in contemporary Berlin, receives a package from her estranged father. Memories surface about incidents in her life that led her there. Her voiceover describes this journey into her past as she tries to explain her complicated ties to the Nazi past, the German present, and to Martin.

"Father and I ... it's a complicated story," she begins. The camera zooms in on her compartments and transforms them into an Israeli landscape. The camera pans to create the feeling of a train traveling past bright, sunny little houses, the antithesis of the cold, dark, and snowy Germany with which the movie begins. The camera enters her father's study, where Neta, as a child in pigtails, climbs a ladder in a moment of childish mischief. The blurring of past and present is initially symbolized by the fact that her character wears a red polka-dot shirt, both as a child and as an adult.

When the child Neta opens a book she finds in her father's study, she discovers a dedication written by her father in Hebrew: "My Neta, never forget what the Germans did to Grandma and Grandpa. Don't ever forgive. Dad." As she reads the lines, the deep, resonant voice of her father intones the words. The compartments on her chest evolve into images of Auschwitz, train tracks, barbed wire, and prisoners in striped uniforms

---

[22] Tal Kantor, "Compartments," *Munfash*, October 7, 2017 [Hebrew], https://bit.ly/3MpL777

behind barbed wire, which Holocaust researcher Oren Baruch Stier refers to as "Holocaust icons."[23] In her distress, she drops the book just as her father enters the room. Seeing her shocked countenance, he hugs her tenderly and picks the book up off the floor. His compartments are a combination of personal and communal items (a guitar, books, and a glass of wine), distinctly Jewish ones (a menorah), Israeli (a symbol of the IDF), and Holocaust-related (a yellow badge). All the items are drawn in brown, as though they were integral parts of the brown wooden box. However, as he puts the book back, the bright yellow badge stands out, making the visual statement that of all the components of his personality, this one is the most dominant. Koffler states:

> I grew up in a household very similar to the one Neta, the protagonist, grows up in. Just like her, when I was eight years old, I've found a book entitled *The Horrible Secret*, with a dedication by my father, who asked me never to forgive the Germans for what they had done to my grandparents. It was a shocking experience. A large part of my connection with my father is based on an endless search for what happened to his parents.[24]

In *Compartments*, as in *Sketches from München*, the "memorial candle" is not limited to the second generation. As Neta's father puts the book back, the yellow badge falls out of the book onto the floor. Little Neta picks it up and places it in the largest compartment on her chest. From now on, she too is branded, and her life will never be the same. Like her father's badge, the bright yellow color of Neta's badge gleams in her compartment box, signifying that it is the most dominant part of her identity. While solemnity spreads over her face, her father smiles, happy that he has transferred the family trauma. From now on, postmemory[25] is not only his inheritance, but hers as well.

The animation suggests that their father-daughter life together is based on many minutes of silence and delving into books. In the study, they are portrayed as sitting next to each other: her father in a big chair reading a book and Neta in a small chair reading a book. It is obvious that he is reading and writing about the Holocaust, since his compartments change to black and white drawings mimicking well-known pictures from Nazi Germany, where Jews were forced to stand on the street with humiliating signs on their chests. "History was all around my father. It followed him like a shadow wherever he went." From the little girl's drawings, the viewers see that her name is Neta Danzing and she is in second grade. Even the name symbolizes a merging of

---

[23] Oren Baruch Stier, *Committed to Memory: Cultural Mediations of the Holocaust* (Amherst: University of Massachusetts Press, 2013), 25, 32, 45–47.
[24] Kantor, "Compartments."
[25] Hirsch, "Past Lives."

the past and present, Israel and the Holocaust. Neta is a very Israeli name. Danzig (now Gdansk) was the first city invaded by the Nazis on September 1, 1939, which began World War II.

Her father is not mentioned by name, but he acts as a symbol of the second generation who has passed the traumatic message of "never forget" on to their children, the grandchildren of Holocaust survivors. Alongside the obvious transgenerational transfer that takes place in *Compartments*, her father is not the only one acknowledged as passing down the trauma. "History was all around me too, you know," says Neta's voiceover, as the camera pans out the window. "While we were growing up, it was all around us." The camera tilts down from blue Israeli skies. It focuses briefly on a scene in which elementary school children are standing at attention with their teacher, as is the custom in Israel on Holocaust Martyrs' and Heroes' Remembrance Day when a siren blares throughout the country. Behind them, a large panel announces "Holocaust Martyrs' and Heroes' Remembrance Day." Glued to the sign are pictures of iconic figures connected to the Holocaust who are often referenced in Holocaust commemorations, such as Anne Frank, Janusz Korczak, and Hannah Szenes. All the pupils in the frame have the yellow Star of David in their largest compartments. The aesthetics epitomize the significance of growing up in the shadow of memories. As the siren sounds in the background, the camera pans from the school children, their heads bowed as they stand at attention, to a scene of elementary school children in youth movements standing at attention, then high school students standing at attention, and then to the same group as they stand at attention, this time on an educational school trip to the Auschwitz-Birkenau memorial and museum, with the sign "*Arbeit Macht Frei*" over their heads.[26] Finally, the camera shifts to a scene of these same youngsters, now no longer children but soldiers in the Israel Defense Forces. The sequence ends with the adult Neta and her father standing at attention with others in the middle of an Israeli street, as the siren sounds. Like *Sketches from München* these generations grew up with memories imprinted in their identity. Koeffler noted that for her, *Compartments* was a very efficient way to describe how Holocaust memory shapes the identity of her generation, the third generation:

---

[26] Israeli high school educational trips to the former concentration camps in Poland have taken place since the late 1980s. Each year, tens of thousands of students go on these trips. See, for example, Jacky Feldman, *Above the Death Pits Beneath the Flag: Youth Voyages to Poland and the Performance of Israeli National Identity* (New York & Oxford: Berghahn Books, 2008); Dan Soen and Nitza Davidovitz, "Youth Delegations to the Former Concentration Camps: Pros and Cons," *Holocaust Commemoration—Issues and Challenges* (Ariel, 2011) [Hebrew], https://bit.ly/3MHA5KF

> We all grew up in a state which shapes memory in canonical ceremonies and in the educational system. Some, like me, have a direct family connection to the trauma, which is transferred from one generation to the other and exceeds the limits of reasonable logic. We don't think about it in our everyday lives. It seems normal. But when you tell other people about it, especially abroad, you realize how strange and implausible it is for history to be so present in your life in the here and now.[27]

This short sequence of pans and tilts creates a complete cycle of growing up in a culture steeped in Holocaust awareness. The scene echoes Louis Althusser's notion of interpellation, which he defined as recurrent happenings embodied in major social and political institutions that turn individuals into subjects of the hegemonic ideology. Interpellation causes the subject to act (and think) according to hegemonic ideological notions that are produced by social forces rather than independent individuals.[28] Israeli scholars have argued that the indoctrination of the Holocaust in the Israeli educational system creates a "victimized awareness"[29] and "a religion of trauma."[30]

Neta and Martin first notice each other after standing at attention on the street. *Compartments* does not indicate what Martin's grandparents did during World War II. In fact, no information is provided about Martin aside from the fact that he is a young handsome German. He is the symbol of the younger generation in Germany who serves as a catalyst for Neta's transgenerational transfer of the trauma and her attempt to combat it. In *Compartments*, falling in love and moving to Berlin constitute an act of defiance, not only towards her father but towards Israeli society as a whole ("You came from the world we had to abandon"). Although the movie deals with the personal relationship between a Jewish-Israeli and a German, it actually only describes the Israeli side of the equation.

When Neta tells her father about Martin, he is shattered. Their contradictory opinions of contemporary Germany are not heard because dramatic music covers their voices, but instead are visualized through their body language and their compartments. Her father turns to her, arguing, waving his hands. Neta looks as though she is trying to explain. However, her voice cannot be heard, and the wooden box on her chest briefly displays pictures

---

[27] Kantor, "Compartments."
[28] Louis Althusser, *Al Haidiologia [About Ideology]* (Tel-Aviv: Resling, 2003 [orig. 1970]). See also Pierre Nora, "Between Memory and History on the Problem of Place," *Zmanim* 43 (1993): 13–15.
[29] Alon Gan, *From Sovereignty to Victimhood: An Analysis of the Victimization Discourse in Israel* (Jerusalem, 2014) [Hebrew], 28–35.
[30] Adi Ophir, *Working for the Present: Essays on Contemporary Israeli Culture* (Tel-Aviv, 2001) [Hebrew], 29–51, 256–280.

in color of the new, modern Berlin that contrast with her father's black and white portrayal of Nazi Germany in his compartments and the color photos of Nazi Germany all over his library. This esthetic choice highlights what animated documentary researchers see as an advantage of this genre over live action documentaries, since animated documentary can portray the depths of human emotions,[31] and provide insights into the mental states of people, fantasy, dreams, emotions, and internal worlds, thus creating heightened identification on the part of the viewers.[32]

Her father reaches for a book, probably to explain his perspective better, as the entire book is filled with pictures of Nazi Germany. Neta is shown yelling in frustration, and Martin's image covers her compartments. "He didn't even listen to a word I said, he didn't even listen, and finally he said: 'The world is against us. It was always against us. Israel is the only safe place, and you want to leave? To Germany? Leave! Go ahead. Beware, you will see your children burning in a new Auschwitz!'"

The linguistic choices used in the voiceovers are interesting. The actress playing Neta speaks English (her lingua franca with Martin) with a very pronounced Israeli accent. Her father, on the other hand, speaks Hebrew. Actor Micha Levinson's voice is very deep and dramatic. Seis, Koffler's German associate who does not understand Hebrew, called it "a voice 2,000 years old,"[33] suggesting that his voice conveys the Jewish heritage as a whole. Koffler and Seis leave his voice untranslated, and use English subtitles instead when he speaks. This choice stresses his attachment to his Hebrew identity and her attempts to create a hybrid identity for herself.

The plane she takes to Berlin is probably an El-Al (the Israeli national airline), since it has the national colors of blue and white on it, but in addition, its tail looks like the Israeli flag. The plane is directed to a transfer area to the terminal. The music is vibrant, creating an atmosphere of a new beginning. Still, the frame tells another story, since the transfer area is animated in somber colors, with a control tower in the background that looks like a concentration camp and not a fresh start.

While still in the terminal, she hears her father's voice in her head: "They have not changed a bit. You will see." She looks fearfully at the walkway leading back to the plane, the blue and white colors reflected through its window indicating that she can still go back. "They are still the same cold-blooded murderers behind the desks. Killing is easy," she hears him, her compartments change to the J stamp, marking her religion. She closes her

---

[31] Yadin, "But is it Documentary?"
[32] Honess-Roe, *Animated Documentary*, 2, 35.
[33] Kantor, "Compartments."

coat, trying to hide the mark. What takes her out of the memory bubble is the real stamp on her passport allowing her to enter Germany. "All it takes is one little stamp," her father's voice says, completely contradicting the image of the smiling courteous young German woman officer who stamps Neta's passport.

The first part of Neta's stay in Berlin is depicted as a "victory." In a sequence resembling the oft-used montages of romantic movies, which compress different scenes in the past into one sequence, she and Martin are portrayed like any other couple falling in love. The Berlin they spend time in is a modern, fun city filled with parks, flea markets, colorful graffiti, cafés, and young people. "Berlin was everything I hoped for," Neta's voiceover confirms, "I fell in love with it instantly." As she walks, enchanted, down the streets of Berlin, her largest compartment that had contained the yellow badge is now empty. Throughout her summer in Berlin with Martin, she collects new memories and stores them in her compartments. "It was a great summer," Martin agrees, "you were like a kid in a candy store."

As it gets colder, Neta's wardrobe begins to include blue items that resemble Martin's blue shirt (a coat, a scarf, a hat), as though she is trying to mask herself with his identity, engulfing her identity in a German one, but her father's voice returns to pursue her as she explores the city. When Martin is not around, and Neta strolls down the streets with her headphones on, trying to learn German, her father's voice returns. For example, as she listens to a tutorial teaching her how to say "mother" and "father," his voice intrudes: "Mutti, Mutti, wo bist du?" ("Mother, mother, where are you?") "Do you know what that means?" he says in his thundering voice. "Your grandfather screamed these words in his sleep. For years I would wake up in the middle of the night hearing him calling for his mother in his dreams in that evil language that killed her." Neta rips off her headphones in an attempt to escape the voices in her head, but his voice continues to haunt her throughout her walks in Berlin, making her look at the Berlin buildings as though images from her grandparents' pasts were displayed on them. "I couldn't get my father's words out of my mind anymore. These memories of things that didn't happen to me but were with me all the time."

But she continues to try. Neta sits on a chair holding a blue cushion as if still trying as hard as she can to embrace Martin's identity. Martin enters and hands her a package and takes the pillow away from her, symbolically not letting her take part in his identity and sending her back to her father, who sent the package. But she refuses, pushing it away: "His history doesn't have to be mine." Hilene Flanzbaum suggested that one can also apply Hirsch's postmemory to members of the third generation, who engage with places in which they never stepped foot, in traumas they never underwent.³⁴ These scenes show how Neta tries to reject her postmemory.³⁵

However, unlike *Sketches from München*, which contrasted the Germany of the past with the nice Germans of contemporary Munich, in *Compartments*, the problematic perception of Germany does not only reside in the painful postmemory of the second and third generations. In one scene, Neta is attracted to a food truck by the smell of a dish that reminds her of her childhood. As she waits for her meal, she chats happily with the seller. "It smells like my grandmother's cooking," she confides to the blond, blue-eyed young man. "Where are you from?" he asks. Neta says that she lives in the neighborhood, an answer that seems like another act of defiance towards her father, since it would kill him to hear that she is representing herself as someone from "here," from Berlin. The seller says it is indeed a nice area but very expensive, and continues to push Neta: "I mean, where are you from? What country?" When she admits that she is from Israel, he replies, "Israel is also a very rich country, yes?" Neta's face crumbles. Her smiles and confidence disappear "Why do you think so?" "Because everyone there is Jewish," he replies, thus recycling the well-worn antisemitic trope connecting Jews with money. This scene echoes what historian Deborah Lipstadt calls the "dinner party antisemite,"; "ordinary" people who do not perceive themselves as antisemites and may condemn it, but very naturally use antisemitic expressions and perceptions.³⁶ The vendor does not make the comment in a malicious way, but casually serves up his antisemitism with the plate of hot food, which somehow makes it even worse. From Neta's perspective, the dish becomes a plate of gold coins, and the seller's previously kind face now appears vicious and intimidating. Scenes of Neta as a frightened child, surrounded by antisemitic posters and Holocaust pictures, fill the frame as they take over her mind. As she stands next to the food truck, breathing heavily for the first time since she got to Berlin, the yellow badge returns to her largest compartment.

The direct translation of the movie's title in Hebrew (*Taim Redumim*) is "sleeper cells." This idiom refers to secret agents sent to live in various places and live normal lives until they are called for duty. For Koffler, personal and collective Holocaust memories are sleeper cells. People can go about their everyday lives without knowing they are there, but suddenly, they "wake" and impact the person. This title thus suggests that director Koffler is referring to

---

³⁴ Hilene Flanzbaum, "The Trace of Trauma: Third-Generation Holocaust Survivors," *Phi Kappa Phi Forum* (Spring 2012), 32–35.

³⁵ Marian Hirsch, "The Generation of Postmemory," *Poetics Today* 29, no. 1 (Spring 2008), 103–128; Marian Hirsch, *Family Frames: Photography, Narrative, and Postmemory* (Cambridge: Harvard University Press, 1997).

³⁶ Deborah E. Lipstadt, *Antisemitism Here and Now* (New York, 2019), 68–75.

the third generation in general, where even those who believe the Holocaust is a distant historical memory are affected by its echoes at certain times in the presence of a certain trigger.

Later, when Neta gets home, she tells Martin, "It is under the surface." Beneath the modern, new city, there are layers of old antisemitism that have not faded over the years. The vendor, after all, was not some carryover from the Nazi period, nor a neo-Nazi, but simply a young man of her age. Antisemitic notions have been inherited, just as her trauma has been passed down. The movie's ending is ambiguous: viewers are not told what happens to her and Martin after this incident, and it provides no closure or "happy ending." Ultimately, the moviemaker has no definitive answer to the question of whether relationships between Israeli Jews and Germans are possible.

Conclusion

"Holocaust commemoration can—and should—take many forms" writes Holocaust researcher Christine Berberich. In the last few decades, new forms of Holocaust commemoration have emerged, along with new ways of engaging with the stories of the Shoah, different perspectives on it, and its aftereffects. "Smaller-scale commemoration can be just as insight- and impactful as official talks, or the curated work found in large, dedicated museums," says Christine Berberich, who then inquires: "how can 'we' contribute to a meaningful discussion of Holocaust commemoration and, ultimately, help formulate a commemorative discourse that is both respectful and challenging, both ethically sound and pushing boundaries, and that has meaning for new generations?"[1] Animated Holocaust documentaries may fulfill such a mission.

In animated documentaries the past and the present are represented as a combination of the survivors' (or their descendants') memory and postmemory, and the directors' interpretation of them. Tess Takahashi suggested that the hybridity of animated documentaries and the fact that they question the limits of live action documentaries are emblematic of today's unstable and disjunctive world.[2] Takahashi considers animated documentaries to be "speculative documentaries" in that they explicitly explore the value of various ways of producing documentary truths that viewers tend to take for granted, such as first-person witnessing and images. In these cases, the director functions as a researcher. Speculative documentaries "may draw on the lives of actual people and historical events, they often fictionalize those stories with the intention of producing larger historical truths […] As such they present an adequate representation of the world, and critically re-imagine it."[3]

---

[1] Christine Berberich, "Conclusion," *Holocaust Studies*, 25, no. 1–2 (2019): 201–208, esp. 201, 206.
[2] Tess Takahashi, "Experiments in Documentary Animation: Anxious Borders, Speculative Media," *Animation: An Interdisciplinary Journal* 6, no. 3 (2011): 231–245, esp. 232.
[3] Ibid., 232, 234–235.

Lior Zylberman and Vicente Sánchez-Biosca defined images that depict genocides as "vectors of memory and imagination […] whose objective is to understand the past and to give it a certain intelligibility." In their view, images confirm and contest the link between what is considered (in)visible and (un)speakable since they selectively crystallize memories, interpretations, and perspectives on the past. They are carriers of historicity, which like all forms of documentation, are imprecise and incomplete.[4] Anna Clare Hunter noted that "the most appropriate narrative response is one that accepts the impossibility of its own position."[5]

Animated documentaries respect the idea that trauma can never be fully shown, understood, or told. They are aware of the limits of representation, upfront about subjectivity and reenactments, and provide an alternative way to knowing, learning, and commemorating. Animated documentaries can provide an enhanced perspective on reality by representing aspects of life that are not observational.[6] The blurring of the human and the machine, as well as the combination of first-hand witnesses and the postmemory generations, draw attention to how memory works as an assemblage of the organic and non-organic, and of the past and the present for the future.[7]

This book aimed to shed light on the representations of the Holocaust, post-trauma, and transgenerational transfer of trauma. In its analysis of the representation of the Holocaust, this volume made a crucial problem crystal clear. Animation is a versatile tool and scenes do not have to be graphic to be horrifying. Horror does not need to be shown directly.[8] However, most Holocaust animated documentaries avoid the atrocities, the hunger, the sadism, and the genocide and create "clean" versions of the Holocaust. If these movies become a source of knowledge and information about the Holocaust in the years to come, in the post-direct-witness era, the outcome will be extremely problematic.

Alona Frenkel, who survived the Holocaust as a child, once commented that she read the testimonies her mother wrote during the Holocaust, which described the horrors vividly. "I could never write like this," says Frenkel, who shuns these descriptions and prefers a much thinner depiction of the

---

[4] Lior Zylberman and Vicente Sánchez-Biosca, "Reflections on the Significance of Images in Genocide Studies: Some Methodological Considerations," *Genocide Studies and Prevention: An International Journal* 12, no. 2 (2018): 1–17.

[5] Anna Clare Hunter, "'To Tell the Story': Cultural Trauma and Holocaust Metanarrative," *Holocaust Studies* 25, nos. 1–2 (2019): 12–27.

[6] Honess Roe, "Absence."

[7] Walden, "Animation and Memory."

[8] Laszlo Nemes, director of "Son of Saul," Bogdanow Online Holocaust Event, February 9, 2021.

Holocaust. "Maybe this is why you can read my stories but hers you cannot. Most of the things written about this period are written like hers, which is why no one reads them. It is a shame, but this is how it is."[9] This attitude may have guided animated documentary directors, but the result is that the vast majority of animated Holocaust documentaries create a palatable version of the period by obfuscating reality.

This problem mirrors the debate over the Anne Frank diary. One of the claims is that the diary became so world famous, and Frank became an icon, because the diary is easy to digest since it ends before the discovery of the family's hiding place and the deportation of its occupants to Auschwitz and Bergen-Belsen. There are no harsh descriptions of the sort written by other victims and survivors: there are no ghettos or camps, no starvation, or the loss of family members in *aktions*. The diary centers mainly on the doings of the attic's inhabitants and their daily lives, and Anne's rich inner world. Readers are not asked to cope with the atrocity itself. The Holocaust is both present and absent,[10] as is the case in the vast majority of animated Holocaust documentaries. These animated documentaries that deal with the unfilmed past of the Holocaust prefer to highlight positive moments of bravery, spiritual resistance, resourcefulness, compassion, and solidarity, and hence unintentionally distort Holocaust memory. Only a few directors have dared enter the lion's den to discuss or represent the horror.

No director is to blame. They all directed their movies with the best intentions to commemorate the stories of their families or other families' narratives. If many other Holocaust animated documentaries discussed and represented horrors, there would not be any problem with expurgated movies, since the broad spectrum of topics would enable viewers to become familiarized with all sides of this enormous historical event. But since only a small number face the atrocities explicitly, the essence of the Holocaust, in this genre, simply vanishes.

A number of researchers have claimed that no words can describe trauma and that silence is the best solution, since any use of words simply minimizes the tragedy. However, the movies analyzed in this book do not adhere to this principle either. They do not choose silence but rather use words and visualizations to narrate the Holocaust, providing a sugar-coated version of the trauma based on Holocaust icons. In addition, although most movies deal with Jewish victims, their Judaism is not highlighted. There is no context of antisemitism, no clear Jewish symbols or conclusions unique to the Jewish

---

[9] Modi, Anat, "Culture Heroes—A Child," *YouTube*, October 4, 2013, https://bit.ly/3TT3aFl

[10] Dian Porat and Liat Steir-Livny, "Anne Frank," *Hyman Encyclopedia of Jewish Women*, https://bit.ly/2XrKy2v

people. A universal message is very important, but when one considers the fact that in most movies, pain, starvation, brutality, and mass murder are scarcely mentioned or visualized, the result is a cinematic genre that does not animate the Holocaust, but "unimates" it by deleting the genocide via a "soft" version.

In the last few years, Holocaust scholars have expressed their growing concern that Holocaust memory will be lost in the twenty-first century. They have raised the pressing issue of how the Holocaust should be mediated to a younger generation that may or may not suffer from Holocaust fatigue, or simply will not care about a historical event that happened so long ago. The growing number of viewers who are ignorant of the truth about the Holocaust will fail to grasp the enormity and unique aspects of this genocide.

Lawrence Langer sheds light on this problem from a different angle. He distinguishes between "commemorating" the Holocaust and remembering it. Commemorating takes place through monuments, memorials, special days, movies, et cetera. Remembering is what a person knows. He pointed out that in 2021, "commemoration is more alive than remembering (since) to remember the Holocaust, you have to be familiar with it," and most people know very little about it. "There are so many ways of avoiding the Holocaust while you think you are confronting it," he says.[11] "As far as remembrance is concerned, […] remembrance of the Holocaust means remembering one of the most horrific events in the history of mankind, and If you are not prepared to confront that, then you ignore it."[12] The lack of a tangible horror in most animated Holocaust documentaries damages efforts to continue remembering the Holocaust. The few exceptions reveal that animation is a valuable tool for depicting horrors without turning them into pornography of terror full of gruesome, graphic details and ghastly images. Animation is capable of representing horror, as shown in the movies analyzed in the fourth chapter.

By contrast, Parts Two and Three of the book show how animated documentary contributes so much to the representation of post-trauma, secondary trauma, and postmemory. Through mimetic substitution, non-mimetic substitution, and evocation, animation compensates for the limitations of live action material, straddles the boundaries between past and present, dreams and reality, recollection and hallucination.[13] It paves the way for new horizons, and offers an enhanced perspective on reality.[14]

---

[11] "Virtual Book Launch: The Afterdeath of the Holocaust," *YouTube*, March 19, 2021, https://bit.ly/3yYXFwz
[12] Ibid.
[13] Landesman and Bendor, "Animated Recollection," 356.
[14] Honess Roe, "Absence."

The analysis of movies in Parts Two and Three shows that animated documentaries point outward and inward in new ways. When they point outward, they visualize unfilmed events in the lives of the survivors, and the childhood of the descendants, thus shedding light on incidents that shaped their lives, influenced their identity, and formed their views. The movies sensitively reveal the face of post-trauma by animating unfilmed incidents from the life of the survivors after the Holocaust. They characterize postmemory by animating unfilmed incidents from the lives of the descendants; thus showing how growing up in families of Holocaust survivors has touched the descendants in so many ways. The movies show that descendants were affected in various ways and that what they experienced as children continues to follow and shape their lives and their perspectives in the present on a vast range of topics from humanity, wars, and political conflicts, to Holocaust memory and others.

Parts Two and Three of the book also stress another considerable advantage of animated documentaries; namely their ability to represent the inner world. These movies reveal not only what the survivors and the descendants say but also what they do not say—what they think, feel, dream, and are horrified by. The movies plunge into the unconscious in scenes that evoke feelings, imagination, and hallucinations. They do so by visualizing these invisible aspects of life through animation and enabling the viewers to imagine the world from the offspring's perspective.

Are the mimetic and non-mimetic visualizations an accurate description? No movie is an accurate description. It is always the subjective outlook of its creators. According to Skoller,[15] animated documentary allows for speculative and subjective imaging in situations where there are no images to express experience or states of mind otherwise. Animated documentary is a tool that enables reflexive perception and can generate deeper affective insights into the situation explored.

In a changing world, which is looking for new ways to remember, at a time when technology is developing rapidly and is paving the way for innovative paths to keep the memory alive, animated documentaries constitute a highly important case study that points to the advantages and disadvantages of new genres of commemoration, remembrance, understanding, and visualization of the past and its aftereffects on the present and the future.

---

[15] Skoller, "Introduction."

Bibliography

Aarons, Victoria, and Berger, Alan L., *Third-Generation Holocaust Representation: Trauma, History, and Memory*. Evanston: Northwestern University Press, 2017.
Adler, A. G. *Theresienstadt 1941–1945: The Face of a Coerced Community*. Cambridge: Cambridge University Press, 2017.
Adler, Jordan. "Two TJFF Docs Deserve a Wider Audience," May 17, 2018, accessed April 6, 2023, *CJN – The Canadian Jewish News*, https://bit.ly/3A2nxoS
Adorno, Theodor W. *Negative Dialectics*. London: Routledge, 2000.
Ain, Noa. "Biography," accessed April 6, 2023, https://bit.ly/39WMXd8
Alfandary, Rony. *Postmemory, Psychoanalysis and Holocaust Ghosts: The Salonica Cohen Family and Trauma Across Generations*. London: Routledge, 2021.
Althusser, Louis. *Al Haidiologia* [*About Ideology*]. Tel-Aviv: Resling, 2003.
Amir, Dana. *Bearing Witness to the Witness: A Psychoanalytic Perspective on Four Modes of Traumatic Testimony*. New York: Routledge, 2018.
Amishai-Maisels, Ziva. *Depiction and Interpretation: The Influence of the Holocaust on the Visual Arts*. Oxford: Pergamon Press, 1993.
Andenman, Nirit. "Haanimatzha meahorey Waltz im Bashir" ["The Animation behind Waltz with Bashir"]. *Ha'aretz*, June 12, 2008, accessed April 6, 2023. https://bit.ly/3EDfMM9
Anderman, Nirit. "Lesaper et hasoah bemetziut meduma" ["Telling the Holocaust in Virtual Reality"]. *Haaratz*, August 8, 2017, accessed April 6, 2023, https://bit.ly/3om8PXO
Anderman, Nirit. "Planeta aheret: seret teudi al haobssesia livnot et Auschwitz betlat meimad" ["Another Planet: A Documentary About the Obsession to Build Auschwitz in 3D]. *Haaretz*, February 1, 2017, accessed April 6, 2023. https://bit.ly/3utFiwt
Arbib, Stephen. "Holocaust Video Game Draws Criticism." *Ynetnews*, December 14, 2010, accessed April 6, 2023. https://bit.ly/3mjWiBk
Ataria, Yohay. "Mot haed be'idan haedut" ["The Death of the Witness in the Testimony Era"]. *Ma'arag* 6 (2015): 177–214.
Aviad, Yael, and Cuhenca, Diana. "The Effects of Gender and Survival Situation of the Parent Holocaust Survivor on Their Offspring: An Attachment Perspective." *The Israel Journal of Psychiatry and Related Sciences* 55, no. 2 (2018): 15–22.
Avisar, Ilan. "The Holocaust in Israeli Cinema as a Conflict between Survival and Morality." In *Israeli Cinema: Identities in Motion*, edited by Miri Talmon and Yaron Peleg, 151–167. Austin: University of Texas Press, 2011.
Barnouw, Erik. *Documentary: A History of the Non Fiction Movie*. Oxford: Oxford University Press, 1993.
Bar-On, Dan. *Bein pahad letikva: sipurei haim shel hamesh mishpahot nitsorei shoah shlosha dorot bamishpaha* [*Fear and Hope: Three Generations of the Holocaust*]. Tel-Aviv: Beit Lochamei Haghetaot and Kibbutz Hameuchad Press, 1994.

Bar-On, Dan. *Hapsychologia shel hashoah* [*The Psychology of the Holocaust*]. Ra'anana, Israel: Open University Press, 2006.

Baron, Lawrence. "The Holocaust and American Public Memory, 1945–1960." *Holocaust and Genocide Studies* 17, no. 1 (2003): 62–88.

Barsam, Richard. *Nonfiction Movie: A Critical History*. Indiana: Indiana University Press, 1992.

Bar-Tal, Daniel. *Lihyot im hasichsuch* [*Living with the Conflict*]. Jerusalem: Carmel, 2007.

Bar-Tal, Daniel. "'Why Don't You Want Peace?'" *Haaretz* (September 2, 2016): 54–56.

Bar-Yosef, Tammy. "Nazis, Dogs and Collective Memory: The Impact of the Holocaust on a Negative Attitude Towards Gogs in Jewish Society in Israel." *Yalkut Moreshet* 99, no. 16 (December 2018): 187–215.

Bastiaans, Jan. "The Kz-Syndrome. A Thirty-Year Study of the Effects on Victims of Nazi Concentration Camps." *Rev Med Chir Soc Med Nat Iasi* 78, no. 3 (July–September 1974): 573–578.

Baudrillard, Jean. *Simulakra vesimulakrum* [*Simulacrum and Simulations*]. Tel-Aviv: Resling, 2007.

Bauer, Yehuda. "Hatisa me'al Auschwitz hayta ma'ase yalduti" ["The Shallowness of the Flight over Auschwitz"[. *Haaretz*, October 6, 2013, accessed April 6, 2023, https://bit.ly/3euLEIp

Bauer, Yehuda. *Teaching the Holocaust in the Corona Era*, Zoom Conference, June 2, 2020.

Beckman, Karen. *Animating Movie Theory*. Durham: Duke University Press, 2014.

Ben Porat, Shahar. "Sipur hashoah hafach leseret animatzia" ["Holocaust Story Became an Animation Movie"]. *Mako*, April 18, 2012, accessed April 19, 2012. https://bit.ly/3lFMTUz

Ben Simhon, Kobi. "Waltz im Bashir meorer et hatraumot haredumot" ["Waltz with Bashir awakens the Traumas"]. *Ha'aretz*, February 6, 2009, accessed April 6, 2023. https://bit.ly/3fSDZ6O

Bender, Arik. "Tzatzaei nazim baknesset: ne'avek b'antishemiyut" ["Nazi Descendants in the Knesset: We Will Fight Anti-Semitism"], *NRG*, November 22, 2011, accessed April 6, 2023. https://bit.ly/3CuCLX5

Beno, Goel. "Holocaust Video Game Pulled." *Ynetnews*, December 26, 2010, accessed April 6, 2023. https://bit.ly/3zV5eCh

Bertman. Elhalal. Anat *Memorial Ceremonies at Kibbutz Lohamei Haghetaot*, 1990–2016, MA Thesis submitted to The Open University, Ra'anana, 2018.

Blatman, Daniel. "Edut al hashoah shreuia letsumet lev meyuheded" ["A Testimony About the Holocaust which Deserves a Special Attention"]. *Haaretz*, May 27, 2014, accessed April 6, 2023. https://bit.ly/2YoKBS1

Bock, Gizla. "Challenging Dichotomies: Perspectives on Women's History." In *Writing Women's History*, edited by Karen Offen, Ruth Roach Pierson, and Jane Rendall, 1–24. Bloomington: Indiana University Press, 1991.

Bondi, Ruth. "Mishakim betzel hamisrafot" ["Playing in the Shade of the Crematoria"]. *Yad Vashem*, No Date, accessed April 6, 2023. https://bit.ly/3oo2B9U

Bovekerk, "The Representation of Gas Chambers in Holocaust Movies, 1944–2013." MA Present(ed) History, Radboud University, 2013.

Bridenthal, Renate, Grossmann, Atina, and Kaplan, Marion, eds. *When Biology Became Destiny: Women in Weimar and Nazi Germany*. New York: New Feminist Library, 1984.

Brown, Adam. *Judging "Privileged" Jews: Holocaust Ethics, Representation, and the "Grey Zone"*. New York and Oxford: Berghahn Books, 2013.

Brut, Rivka. *Baezor haa'for: hakapo hayehudi bamishpat* [*In the Gray Zone: The Jewish Kapo on Trial*]. Ra'anana: The Open University, 2019.

Butchart, Garnet. "Al etica v'kolnoa t'udi: al emet mamashit v'ma'asit" ["On Ethics and Documentary Cinema: Practical Truth"]. *Takriv*, August 2015, accessed April 6, 2023. https://bit.ly/2XdICis

Caruth, Cathy. "An Introduction: Recapturing the Past." In *Trauma: Explorations in Memory*, edited by Cathy Caruth, 151–157. Baltimore: John Hopkins University Press, 1995.

Caruth, Cathy. *Unclaimed Experience: Trauma, Narrative, and History*. Baltimore: Johns Hopkins University Press, 2016.

Chaitin, Julia. "Yeladim v'nechadim shel nitzolim mitmodedim im hashoah" ["Children and Grandchildren of Holocaust Survivors Deal with the Holocaust"]. In *Yaldut b'tzel hashoah: yeladim-nitsolim vedor sheni [Childhood in the Shadow of the Holocaust: Child Survivors and Second Generation]*, edited by Zehava Solomon and Julia Chaitin, 304–336. Tel-Aviv: Hakibbutz Hameuchad, 2007.

Cholodenko, Alan. "Introduction." In *The Illusion of Life: Essays on Animation*, edited by Alan Cholodenko, 9–30. Sydney: Power Publications, 1991.

Clifford, Rebecca. *Survivors: Children's Lives After the Holocaust*. New Haven and London: Yale University Press, 2020.

Cohen, Beth. *Case Closed: Holocaust Survivors in Postwar America*. New Jersey: Rutgers University Press, 2017.

Cohen, Boaz. "The Children's Voice: Postwar Collection of Testimonies from Child Survivors of the Holocaust." *Holocaust and Genocide Studies* 21, no. 1 (Spring 2007): 73–95. https://bit.ly/3kqfiOQ (Accessed April 6, 2023.)

Cole, Tim. "Please Mind the Gap: Integrated Histories and Geographies of the Holocaust and Holocaust Memory." Paper presented at the Beyond Camps and Forced Labor Conference, Birkbeck, University of London, January 10–12, 2018.

Cole, Tim. *Holocaust City: The Making of a Jewish Ghetto*. London and New York: Routledge, 2003.

Copley, Jessica. "Modes of Representing the Holocaust: A Discussion of the Use of Animation in Art Spiegelman's *Maus* and Orly Yadin and Sylvie Bringas's *Silence*.". *Opticon1826*, no. 9 (Autumn 2010). https://bit.ly/3C5J6GB (Accessed April 6, 2023.)

Corner, John. *The Art of Record: A Critical Introduction to Documentary* Manchester: Manchester University Press, 1996.

Dallian, Wendy. "I Was a Child of Holocaust Survivors." *Vancouver Observer*, September 17, 2010, accessed September 17, 2010. https://bit.ly/3nqVn4A

Davis, Barry. "Mending 'Broken Branches.'" *The Jerusalem Post*, August 6, 2014, accessed September 6, 2014. https://bit.ly/3978bok

Dekel, Ayelet. "Overnight Stay/Übernachtung at Haifa IFF." *Midnight East*, September 18, 2010, accessed April 6, 2023. https://bit.ly/39n19Mm

DelGaudio, Sybil. "If Truth Be Told, can 'Toons' Tell it? Documentary and Animation." *Movie History* 9, no. 2 (1997): 189–199.

Des Press, Terrence. "Holocaust Laughter?" In *Writing and the Holocaust*, edited by Lang Berl, 216–233. New York: Holmes and Meier, 1988.

Diner, Hasia R. *We Remember with Reverence and Love: American Jews and the Myth of Silence after the Holocaust, 1945–1962*. New York: New York University Press, 2009.

Dreifuss, Havi (Ben-Sasson). *Relations Between Jews and Poles During the Holocaust: The Jewish Perspective*. Jerusalem: Yad Vashem, 2017.

Dunne, Alan. "A Thousand Kisses." *Behance*, accessed April 6, 2023. https://bit.ly/3zaOPt0

Duvdevany, Shmulik. "As Long as You Draw and not Movie, it's OK." *Mikan* 13 (October 2013): 50–67.

Ebbrecht, Tobias. "Migrating Images: Iconic Images of the Holocaust and the Representation of War in Popular Movie." *Shofar: An Interdisciplinary Journal of Jewish Studies* 28, no. 4 (Summer 2010): 86–103.

Ehrlich, Nea. "Animated Documentaries as Masking," *Animation Studies Online Journal* 6 (2011), accessed January 6, 2015. https://bit.ly/3Cba8MZ

Engelking, Barbara. *Such a Beautiful Sunny Day: Jews Seeking Refuge in the Polish Countryside, 1942–1945*. Jerusalem: Yad Vashem, 2016.

Ewert, Jeanne. "Art Spiegelman's Maus and the Graphic Narrative." In *Narrative Across Media: The Languages of Storytelling*, edited by Marie-Laure Ryan, 180–193. Nebraska: University of Nebraska Press, 2004.

Feldman, Jacky. *Above the Death Pits Beneath the Flag: Youth Voyages to Poland and the Performance of Israeli National Identity*. New York & Oxford: Berghahn Books, 2008.

Felman, Shoshana, "Movie as Witness: Claude Lanzmann's Shoah." In *Holocaust Remembrance: The Shapes of Memory*, edited by Geoffrey Hartman, 90–103. Oxford: Blackwell, 1994.

Felman, Shoshana, and Dori Laub. *Edut [Testimony]*. Tel-Aviv: Resling, 2008.

Figley, Charles, ed. *Compassion Fatigue: Secondary Traumatic Stress Disorders from Treating the Traumatized*. New York: Brunner/Mazel, 1995.

Fisher, Bonnie Sue, and Steven P. Lab, eds. *Encyclopedia of Victimology and Crime Prevention*. London: SAGE, 2010.

Flanzbaum, Hilene. "The Trace of Trauma: Third-Generation Holocaust Survivors." *Phi Kappa Phi forum* (Spring 2012): 32–35.

Formenti, Cristina. "The Sincerest Form of Docudrama: Reframing the Animated Documentary." *Studies in Documentary Movie* 8, no. 2 (2014): 103–115.

Fore, Steve. "Reenacting Ryan: The Fantasmatic and the Animated Documentary." *Animation: An Interdisciplinary Journal* 6, no. 3 (2011): 277–292.

Forsyth, Hardy, ed. *Grierson on Documentary*. London: Faber & Faber, 1966.

Frankel, Victor. *Man's Search for Meaning: An Introduction to Logotherapy*. (1946) Boston: Beacon Press, 1959.

Freud, Sigmund. *Meever laoneg vemasot aherot [Beyond the Pleasure and Other Works]*. London: The Hogarth Press, 1955.

Freud, Sigmund. *The Psychopathology of Everyday Life* (1901) (New York: W. W. Norton and Company, 1990).

Friedlander, Saul. *Kitsch vemavet: al hishtakfut hanazism]Reflections of Nazism: An Essay on Kitsch and Death[*. Jerusalem: Keter Press, 1985.Friedlander, Saul, ed. *Probing the Limits of Representation: Nazism and the "Final Solution"*. Cambridge and London: Harvard University Press, 1992.

Friedlander, Saul. "Trauma, Memory, and Transference." In *Holocaust Remembrance: The Shapes of Memory*, edited by Geoffrey Hartman, 252–264. Oxford: Basil Blackwell, 1994.

Friedman, Michal. "The Double Legacy of Arbeit Macht Frei." *Prooftexts* 22, nos. 1–2 (Winter–Spring 2002): 200–220.

Friedman, Michal. "Witnessing for the Witness: Choice and Destiny by Tsipi Reibenbach." *Shofar: An Interdisciplinary Journal of Jewish Studies* 24, no. 1 (Fall 2005): 81–93.

Frisch, Michael. *A Shared Authority: Essays on the Craft and Meaning of Oral and Public History*. Albany: State University of New York Press.

Gamzou, Assaf. "Third-Generation Graphic Syndrome: New Directions in Comics and Holocaust Memory in the Age after Testimony." *The Journal of Holocaust Research* 33, no. 3 (2019): 224–237. https://bit.ly/392BLeI (Accessed April 6, 2023.)

Gan, Alon. *Korbanutam Umanutam [From Sovereignty to Victimhood: An Analysis of the Victimization Discourse in Israel]*. Jerusalem, 2014.

Geis, Deborah R., ed. *Considering Maus: Approaches to Art Spiegelman's "Survivor's Tale" of the Holocaust*. Alabama: University Alabama Press, 2007.

Gertz, Nurith. *Motion Fiction: Israeli Fiction in Films*. Tel-Aviv: The Open University Press, 1994.

Gertz. Nurith. *Makhela aheret: nitzoley shoah zarim v'aherim* [*A Different Choir: Holocaust Survivors, Aliens and Others in Israeli Cinema and Literature*]. Tel-Aviv: Am Oved and Open University, 2004.

Gertz, Nurith, and Gal Hermoni, Gal. "Bein Levanon lehirbat Hiza'a over shvil shel botz" ["Between Lebanon and Hirbat Hizah There is a Trail of Mud"]. In *Traces of Days to Come: Trauma and Ethics in Contemporary Israeli Cinema*, edited by Nurith Gertz and Raz Yosef (eds), 107–30. Tel-Aviv: Am Oved and Tel-Aviv University, 2017.

Geuens, Jean-Pierre. "Pornography and the Holocaust: The Last Transgression," *Film Criticism* (1995): 114–130.

Godfrey, Mark. *Abstraction and the Holocaust*. New Haven: Yale University Press, 2007.

Goldberg, Amos. *Trauma beguf rishon: ktivat yomanim betqufat hashoah* [*Trauma in First Person: Diary Writing during the Holocaust*]. Or Yehuda: Dvir, 2012.

Goldenberg, Myrna, and Amy H. Shapiro, eds. *Different Horrors, Same Hell: Gender and the Holocaust*, Seattle: University of Washington Press, 2013.

Gonshak, Henry. *Hollywood and the Holocaust*. Maryland: Rowman and Littlefield, 2015.

Grabovaski, Jan. *Rescue for Money: Paid Helpers in Poland, 1939–1945*. Jerusalem: Yad Vashem, 2008.

Grabovaski, Jan. *Hunt for the Jews: Betrayal and Murder in German-Occupied Poland*. Bloomington: Indiana University Press, 2013.

Greenspan, Henry. "Lives as Text: Symptoms as Modes of Recounting in the Life Histories of Holocaust Survivors." In *Storied Lives: The Cultural Politics of Self-Understanding*, edited by George C. Rosenwald and Richard L. Ochberg, 14–65. New Haven: Yale University Press, 1992.

Greif, Gideon. *We Wept without Tears: Testimonies of the Jewish Sonderkommando from Auschwitz*. New Haven: Yale University Press, 2014.

Griff, "Bettine Le Beau—A Lucky Girl." *Vimeo*, 2015, accessed April 7, 2023. https://vimeo.com/118019503

Gross, Jan Tomasz. *Neighbors: The Destruction of the Jewish Community in Jedwabne*. Poland. Princeton: Princeton University Press, 2001.

Gross, Jan Tomasz, and Irena Grudzińska-Gross. *Golden Harvest*. New York: Oxford University Press, 2012.

Gross, Larry, John Stuart Katz, and Jay Ruby, eds. *Image Ethics: The Moral Rights of Subjects in Photographs, Film, and Television*. New York: Oxford Univ. Press, 2000.

Grynberg, Michal, ed. *Words to Outlive Us: Voices from the Warsaw Ghetto*. New York: Metropolitan Books, 2002.

Hájková, Anna. *The Last Ghetto: An Everyday History of Theresienstadt*. New York: Oxford University Press, 2020.

Hajkova, Anna. "A Conversation on Anna Hajkova's 'The Last Ghetto: An Everyday History of Theresienstadt.'" *UMass Amherst*, March 9, 2021.

Haltof, Marek. *Screening Auschwitz: Wanda Jakubowska's The Last Stage and the Politics of Commemoration*. Evanston: Northwestern University Press, 2018.

Harding, Louette. "Real Lives: Bettine Le Beau 'I Kidded Myself that There was an Angel Looking After Me.'" *Mail Online*, January 28, 2013, accessed April 6, 2023. https://bit.ly/3zzWvFv

Hazan, Yoram. "Dor sheni lashoah: musag besafek" ["The Second Generation of the Holocaust: A Questionable Concept"], *Sihot: Israel Journal of Psychotherapy* 1 (1987): 104–108.

Hedgepeth, Sonja M. and Saidel, Rochelle G., eds. *Sexual Violence against Jewish Women During the Holocaust*. Waltham: Brandeis University Press, 2010.

Heinemann, Marlene E. *Gender and Destiny: Women Writers and the Holocaust*. New York: Greenwood Press, 1986.

Herman, Judith. L. *Trauma vehachlama* [*Trauma and Healing*]. Tel-Aviv: Am Oved, 1994.

Hight, Craig. "Mockumentary: A Call to Play." In *Rethinking Documentary: New Perspectives, New Practices*, edited by Thomas Austin and Wilma de Jong, 204–216. Berkshire: Open University Press, 2008.

Hirsch, Joshua. "The Pawnbroker and the Posttraumatic Flashback." In *Afterimage: Film, Trauma and the Holocaust*, 85–110. Philadelphia: Temple University Press, 2003.

Hirsch, Marianne. "Past Lives, First Memories in Exile." *Poetics Today* 17, no. 4 (1996): 659–667.

Hirsch, Marianne. *Family Frames: Photography, Narrative, and Postmemory*. Cambridge: Harvard University Press, 1997.

Hirsch, Marianne. "The Generation of Postmemory." *Poetics Today* 29, no. 1 (Spring 2008): 103–128.

Hirsch, Marianne, and Leo Spitzer. "Gendered Translations: Claude Lanzmann's Shoah." In *Gendering War Talk*, edited by Miriam Cooke and Angela Woollacott, 3–19. Princeton: Princeton University Press, 1993.

Hoffman, Eva. *After Such Knowledge: A Mediation on the Aftermath of the Holocaust*. London: Vintage, 2004.

Holocaust Educational Trust, "Bettine Le Beau, 1932–2015." Accessed April 6, 2023. https://bit.ly/3ztcDs6

Honess Roe, Annabelle. "Absence, Excess and Epistemological Expansion: Towards a Framework for the Study of Animated Documentary." *Animation: An Interdisciplinary Journal* 6, no. 3, (2011): 215–231.

Honess Roe, Annabelle. *Animated Documentary*. London: Palgrave Macmillan, 2013.

Horowitz, Sara R. *Voicing the Void: Muteness and Memory in Holocaust Fiction*. Albany: State University of New York Press, 1997.

Huyssen, Andreas. "Of Mice and Mimesis: Reading Spiegelman with Adorno." In *Visual Culture and the Holocaust*, edited by Barbie Zelizer, 28–44. London: Rutgers University Press, 2001.

Ilany, Itay. "K'she tzatzaei hanazim sharim hatikva berap lifney nitzolim" ["When Nazis' Descendants Sing Hatikva Rap-Style in Front of Survivors"]. *YNet News*, December 18, 2016, accessed April 6, 2023. https://bit.ly/3CVxJVc

Insdorf, Annette. *Indelible Shadows: Film and the Holocaust*. Cambridge: Cambridge University Press, 2003.

Jucovy, Milton E. "Telling the Holocaust Story: A Link between the Generations." *Psychoanalytic Inquiry* 5 (1985): 31–50.

Kangisser Cohen, Sharon and Dalia Ofer, eds. *Starting Anew: The Rehabilitation of Child Survivors of the Holocaust in the Early Postwar Years*. Jerusalem: Yad Vashem Publications, 2019.

Kansteiner, Wulf. "Digital Memory With and Beyond the Holocaust." *Playing the Holocaust – Part 1, Digital Holocaust Memory*, November 11, 2020, accessed April 6, 2023. https://bit.ly/3ip8Hms

Kantor, Tal. "Taim edumim" ["Compartments"]. *Munfash*, October 7, 2017. https://bit.ly/3MpL777

Kapel, Liran. "Nyosha—Behind the Scenes." *YouTube*, October 23, 2012, accessed April 6, 2023. https://bit.ly/39mj31K

Kaplan, Marion. "Gendering Holocaust Studies Looking Back and Forward." *YouTube*, March 14, 2021 accessed April 6, 2023. https://bit.ly/2XzAQj2

Kępiński, Antoni. "The So-called 'KZ-Syndrome': An Attempt at a Synthesis." *Medical Review Auschwitz*, August 21, 2017, accessed April 6, 2023. https://bit.ly/3QDaliy

Keren, Nili. "Mahane hamishpahot beAuschwitz-Birekenau" ["The Family Camp in Auschwitz-Birkenau"]. *Yad Vashem*, No Date, accessed April 6, 2023. https://bit.ly/3D4c0Yj

Kerner, Aaron. *Movie and the Holocaust: New Perspectives on Drama, Documentaries, and Experimental Movies*. London: Bloomsbury, 2001.

Kidron, Carol. "Hahavnaya hahevratit shel hador hasheni lashoah" ["The Social Construction of Second-Generation Survivors: Support Group Narratives of Wounded Carriers of Memory"]. In *Yaldut b'tzel hashoah: yeladim-nitsolim vedor sheni* [*Childhood in the Shadow of the Holocaust: Child Survivors and Second Generation*], edited Zehava Solomon and Julia Chaitin, 261–285. Tel-Aviv: Hakibbutz Hameuchad, 2007.

Kidron, Carol. "Anthropology of Memory: Researchers' Discourse." *Dapim leheker hashoah* 23 (2010): 287–291.

Klein, Hillel. "Hipus nitzolei hashoah ahar mashma'ut v'zehut" ["The Survivors' Search for Meaning and Identity"]. In *Nazi Concentration Camps: Lectures and Discussions at the 4th Yad Vashem International Historical Conference of Holocaust Researchers*, edited by Israel Gutman and Rachel Manber, 543–553. Jerusalem: Yad Vashem, 1980.

Kobi, Niv. *Look Back into the Future*. Tel-Aviv: Olam Hadash, 2014.

Koffler, Daniella. "Haker et hayozer: ra'ayon im Ayala Sharut" ["Meet the Creator: An Interview with Ayala Sharut for her Upcoming movie 'Broken Branches'"]. *Moonfash*, May 1, 2015, accessed May 5, 2015. https://bit.ly/3k5kk3k

Koffler, Daniella. "Hamasa lehanfashat hashoah: chelek aleph—mul hayam shpuru shel Saul Oren" ["The Holocaust Animation Journey—Part I: 'Facing the Sea': The Story of Saul Oren"]. *Moonfash*, April 19, 2020, accessed April 6, 2023. https://bit.ly/3D34Gfl

Koffler, Daniella. "Taim Redumim" ["Compartments"]. *Moonfash*, October 7, 2017. Accessed April 6, 2023. https://bit.ly/3ew6NSf

Kraemer, Joseph A. "*Waltz with Bashir* (2008): Trauma and Representation in the Animated Documentary." *Creativeclay Animations*, April 3, 2017, accessed May 3, 2017. https://bit.ly/3Ef5gYP

Kremish, Joseph. "Actions by the Council to Aid the Jews (Zagota Council) in Occupied Poland." *Yad Vashem*, accessed April 6, 2023. https://bit.ly/3AsF0bb

Kucia, Marek. "The Meanings of Auschwitz in Poland, 1945 to the Present." *Holocaust Studies* 25, no. 3 (2019): 220–247.

LaCapra, Dominic. *Writing History, Writing Trauma*. Baltimore: Johns Hopkins University Press, 2000.

Lahav, Yael and Zehava Solomon, eds. *Restoration of Memory, Treatment of Mental Trauma*. Tel-Aviv: Resling, 2019.

Landesman, Ohad and Roy Bendor. "Animated Recollections and Spectatorial Experience in *Waltz with Bashir*." *Animation: An Interdisciplinary Journal* 6, no. 3 (2011): 353–370.

Landsberg, Alison. *Prosthetic Memory: The Transformation of American Remembrance in the Age of Mass Culture*. New York: Columbia University Press, 2004.

Landsman, Ohad. "Waltz im Bashir" ["Waltz with Bashir"]. *Takriv*, No Date, accessed April 6, 2023. https://bit.ly/2LE43ie

Langer, Lawrence. "Redemptive and Unredemptive Holocaust Memory." In *The Afterdeath of the Holocaust*, 37–61. London: Palgrave Macmillan, 2021.

Laub, Dori. "Bearing Witness on the Vicissitudes of Listening." In *Testimony: Crises of Witnessing in Literature, Psychoanalysis and History*, edited by Shoshana Felman and Dori Laub, 57–74. London: Routledge, 1992.

Lester, Anita. "D"Noch Am Leben (Still Alive)." *Vimeo*, accessed April 6, 2023. https://vimeo.com/263945041

Levi, Primo. *Hashokim vehanitzolim* [*The Drowned and the Saved*]. Tel-Aviv: Am Oved, 1991.

Levin, Itamar. *Mi'ba'ad la'dmaot: humor Yehudi that hashilton hanatsi* [*Through the Tears: Jewish Humor under the Nazi Regime*]. Jerusalem: Yad Vashem, 2004.

Levin, Itamar. *Kapo beAllenby* [*Kapo on Allenby*]. Jerusalem: Yad Ben Zvi, 2015.

Levkovitz, Inbar. "Bein hosen vepgiut: nizolei shoah mizdaknim beisrael" ["Between Strength and Venerability: Aging Holocaust Survivors in Israel"]. *Hebrew Psychology*, April 18, 2012, accessed October 1, 2018. https://bit.ly/3zfqlip

Levy, Primo. *If This Is a Man* (1947). Tel-Aviv: Am Oved, 1989 [Hebrew translation].

Liebman, Stuart, ed. *Claude Lanzmann's Shoah: Key Essays*. Oxford: Oxford University Press, 2007.

Lingford, Ruth, and Tim Webb. "Silence: The Role of the Animators." In *Holocaust and the Moving Image: Representations in Movie and Television since 1933*, edited by Toby Haggith and Joanna Newman, 173–174. London and New York: Wallflower, 2005.

Lipstadt, Deborah E. *Antisemitism Here and Now*. New York: Schocken, 2019.

Loshitzky, Yosefa. "Holocaust Others: Spielberg's *Schindler's List* versus Lanzman's *Shoah*." In *Spielberg's Holocaust: Critical Perspectives on* Schindler's List, edited by Yosefa Loshitzky, 104–118. Bloomington: Indiana University Press, 1997.

Loshitzky, Yosefa. *Identity Politics on the Israeli Screen*. Austin: University of Texas Press, 2002.

Mandel, Naomi. *Against the Unspeakable: Complicity, the Holocaust, and Slavery in America*. Charlottesville: University of Virginia Press, 2007.

Marrison, Kate. "Why Call of Suty: WWII Struggled to Show the Horrors of the Holocaust." *Playing the Holocaust—Part 1, Digital Holocaust Memory*, November 11, 2020, accessed April 6, 2023. https://bit.ly/3ip8Hms

Martinez, Victoria. "Afterlives: Histories of Survivors of Nazi Persecution in Sweden." Linkopig University, accessed April 6, 2023. https://bit.ly/3QFmRhM

Marwell, David. *Mengele: Unmasking the "Angel of Death"*. New York: W. W. Norton & Company, 2020.

McGlothlin, Erin. "'When Time Stands Still': Traumatic Immediacy and Narrative Organization in Art Spiegelman's *Maus* and *In the Shadow of Two Towers*." In *The Graphic Novel: Critical Approaches*, edited by Samantha Baskind and Ranen Omer-Sherman, 94–110. New Brunswick: Rutgers, 2008.

Melamed, Laliv. "Book Review: Waltzing with Bashir: Perpetrator Trauma and Cinema." *Historical Journal of Movie, Radio and Television*. September 5, 2014. https://bit.ly/3fSErSy

Meyers, Oren, Neiger Motti, and Zandberg Eyal. *Communicating Awe: Media Memory and Holocaust Commemoration*. Basingstoke: Palgrave Macmillan, 2014.

Michman, Dan. "Particularist and Universal Interpretations of the Holocaust: Complex Relationships." *Moreshet* 17, no. 100 (December 2019): 223–243.

Milner, Iris. *Kirey avar* [*A Torn Past*]. Tel Aviv: Am Oved, 2004.

Modi, Anat. "Culture Heroes—A Child." *YouTube*, October 4, 2013, accessed April 6, 2023. https://bit.ly/3lHgMnj

Mollica, Richard F. *Textbook of Global Mental Health: Trauma and Recovery: A Companion Guide for Field and Clinical Care of Traumatized People Worldwide*. Cambridge: Harvard Program in Refugee Trauma, 2011.

Morag, Raya. *Waltzing with Bashir: Perpetrator Trauma and Cinema*. New York and London: I. B. Tauris, 2013.
Munday, Rob. "German Shepherd." Accessed April 6, 2023 https://bit.ly/3TgaR7V/
Nagler, Eva. *Massacre on the Baltic*, 1995.
Nagler-Cohen, Liron. "Shovrim Shtika: Nazi Descendants Sing Hatikva" ["Breaking the Silence: Nazis' Descendants Sing Hatikva"]. *YNet News*, August 16, 2016, Accessed April 6, 2023. https://bit.ly/3yBNSwc
Nichols, Bill. *Representing Reality: Issues and Concepts in Documentary*. Bloomington: Indiana University Press, 1991.
Nichols, Bill. *Introduction to Documentary*. Indiana: Indiana University Press, 2001.
Noack-Mosse, Eva. *Last Days of Theresienstadt*. Madison: University of Wisconsin Press, 2018.
Nora, Pierre. "Between Memory and History on the Problem of Place." *Zmanim* 43 (1993): 13–15.
Novick, Peter. *That Noble Dream: The "Objectivity Question" and the American Historical Profession*. Cambridge: Cambridge University Press, 1988.
Ofer, Dalia, and Lenore J. Weitzman. *Women in the Holocaust*. New Haven: Yale University Press, 1998.
Ofer, Dalia. "The Past That Does Not Pass." *Yalkut Moreshet* (2010): 7–39.
Olga, Gershenson. "Meta-Memory: About the Holocaust in New Israeli Video Art." *Jewish Film & New Media* 6, no. 1 (2019): 67–90.
Ophir, Adi. *Avodat Hahove* [*Working for the Present: Essays on Contemporary Israeli Culture*]. Tel-Aviv, 2001.
Ostrower, Haya. *L'lo humor hayinu mitabdim* [*Without Humor We Would Have Killed Ourselves*]. Jerusalem: Yad Vashem, 2009.
Ouza, Anna. "In Search of Memory: The Legacy of Auschwitz in Photography and Art", MA in Sustainable Heritage Management, Aarhus University, accessed April 6, 2023. https://bit.ly/3iol4PY
Oz-Salzberger, Fania. *Israelis, Berlin*. Tel-Aviv, 2001.
Perl, Adi. "Proyect metziut meduma matzia levaker bebeit Ana Frank" ["A Virtual Reality Project Suggests to Tour Anne Frank House"]. *Geektime*, May 5, 2015, accessed April 6, 2023. https://bit.ly/3FcI2TA
Pilling, Jayne, ed. *Animating the Unconscious*. London and New York: Columbia University Press, 2012.
Porat, Ben. "Holocaust Story. Conference Future of Holocaust Testimonies lll—Nyosha—Animated Movie Based on Holocaust Survivor Testimony." *YouTube*, June 1, 2014, accessed April 6, 2023. https://bit.ly/2Z2nAEr
Porat, Dan. *Bitter Reckoning: Israel Tries Holocaust Survivors as Nazi Collaborators*. New Haven: Harvard University Press, 2019.
Porat, Dina. *Café haboker b'reach ha'ashan* [*Smoke-Scented Morning Coffee*]. Jerusalem: Yad Vashem, 2011.
Portelli, Alessandro. "What Makes Oral History Different." In *The Oral History Reader*, ed. Robert Perks and Alistair Thomson, 63–74. London: Routledge, 1998.
Posner, Gerald. *Mengele: The Complete Story*. New York: Cooper Square Press, 2000.
Prager, Brad. *After the Fact: The Holocaust in Twenty-First Century Documentary Film*. London: Bloomsbury, 2015.
Raskin, Richard. *Seven Minutes in the Warsaw Ghetto and With Raised Hands—A Movie Ebook*. Arhus: Arhus University Press, 2013.

Raskin, Richard. "An Interview with Johan Oettinger on *Seven Minutes in the Warsaw Ghetto*." *Short Film Studies Journal*, no. 4.2 (October 2014): 191.

Raskin, Richard. "Art and the Holocaust: Positioning *Seven Minutes in the Warsaw Ghetto*." *Short Movie Studies* 4, no. 2 (2014): 223–226.

Reich, Gila'd. "Model veanti model beyetzug hashoah" ["A Model and an Anti-Model in Holocaust Representation"]. *Takriv*, No Date, accessed April 6, 2023. https://bit.ly/3F6GOcF

Renov, Michael. *The Subject of Documentary*. Minnesota: University of Minnesota Press, 2004.

Revell, Anna. *Josef Mengele: Angel of Death: A Biography of Nazi Evil*. Amazon Digital Services LLC, 2017.

Rhodes, Gary D. and John Parris Springer. *Docufictions: Essays on The Intersection of Documentary and Fictional Moviemaking*. Jefferson: McFarland, 2006.

Rittne, Carol and John Roth, eds. *Different Voices: Women and the Holocaust*. St. Paul: Paragon House, 1993.

Roberts, Geoffrey, ed. *The History and Narrative Reader*. London: Routledge, 2001.

Rosen, Ilana. "Personal Historical Narrative Shaping the Past and the Present." *European Journal of Jewish Studies* 3, no. 1 (2009): 103–133.

Rosenfeld, Alvin. *The End of the Holocaust*. Bloomington and Indianapolis: Indiana University Press, 2013.

Rosenthal, Perihan Aral, and Stuart Rosenthal. "Holocaust Effects in the Third Generation: Child of Another Time." *American Journal of Psychotherapy* 34, no. 4 (1980): 572–580.

Rozenbaum, Ron. *Hitler: masa el shorshei haro'a* [*Hitler: A Journey to the Roots of Evil*]. Tel-Aviv: Matar, 1999.

Rozenkrantz, Jonathan. "Colourful Claims: Towards a Theory of Animated Documentary." May 6, 2011, accessed May 10, 2011. https://bit.ly/3ht2fKH

Sagi-Schwartz, Abraham, Marinun H. van IJzendoorn, and Marian J. Bakermans-Kranenburg. "Does Intergenerational Transference of Trauma Skip a Generation? No Meta-Analytic Evidence for Tertiary Traumatization with Third Generation Holocaust Survivors." *Attachment and Human Development* 10, no. 2 (June 2008): 105–121.

Sand, Shlomo. *Hakolnoa kehistoria: ledamyen velevayem et hameah haesrim* [*Movie as History: Imagining and Screening the Twentieth Century*] Tel-Aviv: Am Oved and Open University Press, 2002.

Saxton, Libby. "Shneihem sonim et Spielberg" ["They Both Hate Spielberg"]. *Mita'am* (December 2007), 106–124.

Saxton, Libby. *Haunted Images: Movie, Ethics, Testimony and the Holocaust*. London and New York: Wallflower Press, 2008.

Schweitzer, Ariel. "Archiv, bidyon, ta'amule: America bemilhama" ["Archive, Fiction, Propaganda: America in War"]. *Takriv*, accessed April 6, 2023. https://bit.ly/2ZQ6GJJ

Sechrduti, Ya'aoba. *Nigun hagoral: hasoah bacomics 1942–1958* [*The Playback of Destiny: Holocaust in Comics 1942–1954*]. Tel-Aviv: New World, 2019.

Segev, Tom. *Hamillion hashvi'i: haisraelim vehashoah* [*The Seventh Million: The Israelis and the Holocaust*]. Jerusalem: Keter, 1991.

Shamah, David. "Animated Holocaust Movie uses Spielberg Online Witness Archive." *The Times of Israel*, April 18, 2012, accessed 19 April 2012. https://bit.ly/3nPsf7i

Shandler, Jeffrey. *Holocaust Memory in the Digital Age: Survivors' Stories and New Media Practices*. Stanford: Stanford University Press, 2017.

Shapira, Anita. "Hashoah: zikaron prati v'zikaron tziburi" ["The Holocaust: Private Memory and Public Memory"]. In *Yehudim Yeshanim, Yehudim Hadashim* [*New Jews, Old Jews*], 103–186. Tel-Aviv: Am Oved, 1997.

Shargal, Dvorit. "Waltz with Bashir." Accessed April 6, 2023. https://bit.ly/3SZMr2L
Shenhav, Yehuda. "Identity in a Postnational Society." *Theory and Criticism* 19 (2001): 5–16.
Shmotkin, Dov, Shrira Amit, Shira C. Goldberg, and Palgi Yuval. "Resilience and Vulnerability Among Aging Holocaust Survivors and Their Families: An Intergenerational Overview." *Journal of Intergenerational Relationships* 9, no. 1 (2011): 7–21.
Shtauber, Shuki. *Israelim Beberlin* [*Israelis in Berlin*]. Tel-Aviv: Yedioth Aharonot, 2017.
Sipe, Dan. "The Future of Oral History and Moving Images." In *The Oral History Reader*, 2nd ed., edited by Robert Perks and Alistair Thomson, 379–388. London: Routledge, 2006.
Skoller, Jeffrey. "Introduction to the Special Issue Making It (Un)real: Contemporary Theories and Practices in Documentary Animation." *Animation: An Interdisciplinary Journal* 6, no. 3 (2011): 207–214.
Slavin, Marit. "Bnei adam zochrim gam havayot shelo havu" ["People Also Remember Events They Did Not Experience"]. *Walla*, June 12, 2005, accessed June 13, 2005. https://bit.ly/3zeOepX
Sliwa, Joanna. "Jewish Humour as a Source of Research on Polish-Jewish Relations." In *Jews and Humour*, edited by Leonard Greenspoon, 67–82. West Lafayette: Purdue University Press.
Soen, Dan, and Nitza Davidovitz, Nitza. "Masaot noar lemahanot haricuz lesheavar: bead veneged" ["Youth Delegations to the Former Concentration Camps: Pros and Cons"]. *Holocaust Commemoration—Issues and Challenges*. Ariel, 2011. Accessed April 6, 2023. https://bit.ly/3MHA5KF
Somer, Eli, and Yael Agam. "Personal Action as Collectivist Reconciliation: Children of 'Aryan' Citizens of Nazi Germany Living in Israel." *Dapim: Studies on the Holocaust* (2015): 81–100.
Steir-Livny, Liat. "Interview with Prof. Dina Porat." April 10, 2002.
Steir-Livny, Liat. *Two Faces in the Mirror: The Representation of Holocaust Survivors in Israeli Cinema*. Jerusalem: Eshkolot-Magnes, 2009.
Steir-Livny, Liat. "Faith in the Face of Hell." In *A Holocaust Crossroads: Jewish Women and Children in Ravensbrück*, edited by Irith Knebel, 205–220. London: Vallentine Mitchell, 2010.
Steir-Livny, Liat. *Har hazikaron yizkor bimkomi* [*Let the Memorial Hill Remember*]. Tel-Aviv: Resling, 2014.
Steir-Livny, Liat. "From Victims to Aggressors: Cultural Representations of the Link Between the Holocaust and the Israeli-Palestinian Conflict." *Interactions: Studies in Communication and Culture* 7, no. 2 (September 2016): 123–136.
Steir-Livny, Liat. "An Interview with Ayala Sharot." August 5, 2016.
Steir-Livny, Liat. *Is It O.K. to Laugh about it? Holocaust Humour, Satire and Parody in Israel Culture*, London: Vallentine Mitchell Press, 2017.
Steir-Livny, Liat. "An Interview with Daniela Sherer." June 20, 2019.
Steir-Livny, Liat. "An interview with Hadar Huber." September 26, 2019.
Steir-Livny, Liat. "An Interview with Richard Goldgewicht." October 7, 2019.
Steir-Livny, Liat. "An Interview with Shirly Pershkulnik." November 3, 2019.
Steir-Livny, Liat. "An Interview with Anita Lester." November 8, 2019.
Steir-Livny, Liat. "An Interview with Anita Lester." November 8, 2019.
Steir-Livny, Liat. *Remaking Holocaust Memory: Documentary Cinema by Third-Generation Survivors in Israel*. Syracuse: Syracuse University Press, 2019.
Steir-Livny, Liat. "An Interview with Rubi Gat." January 20, 2020.
Steir-Livny, Liat. "An Interview with Eitan Rozenthal." April 9, 2020.
Steir-Livny, Liat. "An Interview with Eliav Lilty." April 14, 2020.

Steir-Livny, Liat. "An Interview with Daniela Koffler." May 19, 2020.
Steir-Livny, Liat. "An interview with Johan Oeslinger." June 3, 2020.
Steir-Livny, Liat. "An Interview with Shahaf Ram." October 8, 2020.
Stier Oren, Baruch. *Holocaust Icons: Symbolizing the Shoah in History and Memory*. New Brunswick: Rutgers University Press, 2015.
Stier Oren, Baruch. *Committed to Memory: Cultural Mediations of the Holocaust*. Amherst: University of Massachusetts Press, 2013.
Strøm, Gunnar. "The Animated Documentary." *Animation Journal* 11 (2003): 46–63.
Takahashi, Tess. "Experiments in Documentary Animation: Anxious Borders, Speculative Media." *Animation: An Interdisciplinary Journal* 6, no. 3 (2011): 231–245. See, 234.
Tercatin, Rossella. "Brain Structure Change in Holocaust Survivors Hereditary, Study Finds." *The Jerusalem Post*, July 4, 2019, accessed April 7, 2023. https://bit.ly/3rTzVGq
Toker, Ina. "The Y Generation Makes Holocaust Movies." *YNET*, April 24, 2017, accessed April 7, 2023. https://bit.ly/3Vmpvwh
Tomkins, Yonathan. "Sherut hamiluim shel Donald duck: Animatzia Meguyeset bezman milhemet haolam hashniya" ["Donald Duck in Reserve: Animation Propaganda During WWII"]. *Slil* 2 (2008), 5–27. Accessed April 7, 2023. https://bit.ly/3tFrKgL
Turim, Maureen. *Flashbacks in Film*. London: Routledge, 1989.
Tydor-Baumel Schwartz, Judy. *Double Jeopardy: Gender and the Holocaust*. London: Vallentine Mitchell, 1998.
Unger, Maya. "Mix Berlinayi" ["A Berlin Mix"]. *Spitz*, August 2013, accessed April 7, 2023. https://bit.ly/3MslaUg
Van den Heede, Pieter. "Playing the Holocaust: Online Roundtable Panek Contribution: Towards Productive Moments of Historical Revelation." *Playing the Holocaust—Part 1, Digital Holocaust Memory*, accessed April 7, 2023. https://bit.ly/3ip8Hms
Vice, Sue. "British Representations of the Camps." *Holocaust Studies* 22, no. 2–3 (2016): 303–317.
Walden, Victoria Grace. "Animation: A Different Way of Looking at the Past." *Animation Studies* 2.0, 26 November, 2014, accessed November 1, 2015. https://bit.ly/3C39AbO
Walden, Victoria Grace. "Animation: Textural Difference and the Materiality of Holocaust Memory." *Animation Studies Online Journal*, December 31, 2014, accessed February 2, 2015. https://bit.ly/3k293Re
Walden, Victoria Grace. "'A Potted History of Games', Playing the Holocaust—Part 1, Digital Holocaust Memory." November 11, 2020, accessed April 7, 2023. https://bit.ly/3ip8Hms
Walker, Janet. *Trauma Cinema: Documenting Incest and the Holocaust*. Berkeley: University of California Press, 2005.
Wang, Horng-luen. "Mind the Gap: On Post-National Idea(l)s and the Nationalist Reality." *Social Analysis: The International Journal of Anthropology* 46, no. 2 (2002): 139–147.
Ward, Paul. "Animated Realities: The Animated Movie, Documentary, Realism." *Reconstruction: Studies in Contemporary Culture* 8, no. 2 (2008). Accessed June 1, 2010. https://bit.ly/3z0yPK0
Ward, Paul. "Animating with Facts: The Performative Process of Documentary Animation in the Ten Mark (2010)." *Animation: An Interdisciplinary Journal* 6, no. 3, 296.
Wardi, Dina. *Nosei habotam* [*Memorial Candles*]. Jerusalem: Keter, 1990.
Warren, Charles, ed. *Beyond Document: Essays on Nonfiction Film*. Hanover and London: University of New England Press, 1996.
Webster, Andy. "Review: In 'Karski & the Lords of Humanity,' a Holocaust Spy." *The New York Times*, November 26, 2015, accessed April 7, 2023. https://nyti.ms/3l34pTr

Wells, Paul. "The Beautiful Village and the True Village: A Consideration of Animation and the Documentary Aesthetic." In *Art and Animation*, edited by Paul Wells, 40–45. London: Academy Editions, 1997.

Wells, Paul. *Understanding Animation*. London and New York: Routledge, 1998.

White, Hayden. "The Historical Text as Literary Artifact." In *Tropics of Discourse: Essays in Cultural Criticism*, edited by Hayden White, 221–236. Baltimore: Johns Hopkins University Press, 1978. Republished in Geoffrey Roberts, ed., *The History and Narrative Reader*. London: Routledge, 2001.

Widmann, Tabea. "Responsibility at Play? Memory Cultures and Digital Games." *Playing the Holocaust—Part 1, Digital Holocaust Memory*. Accessed April 7, 2023. https://bit.ly/3ip8Hms

Wiesel, Elie. "Art and the Holocaust: Trivializing memory." *The New York Times*, June 11, 1989, accessed October 2, 2010. https://nyti.ms/3z96rFz

Winston, Brian. "The Tradition of the Victim in Griersonian Documentary." In *New Challenges for Documentary*, edited by Alan Rosenthal, 269–287. Berkeley: University of California Press, 1988.

Winston, Brian. *Lies, Damn Lies, and Documentaries*. London: British Movie Institute, 2000.

Winston, Brian. "'Ça va de soi': The Visual Representation of Violence in the Holocaust Documentary." In *Killer Images: Documentary Film, Memory and the Performance of Violence*, edited by Joram Ten Brink and Joshua Oppenheimer, 97–119. London: Wallflower, 2012.

Winston, Brian, Gail Vanstone, and Chi Wang. *The Act of Documenting: Documentary Film in the 21st Century*. London: Bloomsbury Academic, 2017.

Wisse, Ruth. *No Joke: Making Jewish Humour*. Princeton: Princeton University Press, 2013.

Yadin, Orly. "But is it Documentary?" In *Holocaust and the Moving Image: Representations in Film and Television since 1933*, edited by Toby Haggith and Joanna Newman, 168–172. London and New York: Wallflower, 2005.

Yair. Gad. *Ahava ze lo praktish* [*Love Is Not Practical*]. Tel-Aviv, 2015.

Yaron, Oded. "Aim hegia hazman lemishakim al hashoah?" ["Is it Time for Holocaust Games?"]. *Haaretz*, October 3, 2013, accessed April 7, 2023. https://bit.ly/3mdrjqR

Yerusalmy, Yosef Haim. *Zakhor: Jewish History and Jewish Memory*. Seattle and London: University of Washington Press, 1996. (Original Tel-Aviv, 1982).

Young, James E. *Writing and Rewriting the Holocaust: Narrative and the Consequence of Interpretation*. Bloomington: Indiana University Press, 1988.

Young, James E. "Toward a Received History of the Holocaust." *History and Theory* 36, no. 4 (1997): 37–39.

Zandberg, Eyal. "Critical Laughter: Humor, Popular Culture and Israeli Holocaust Commemoration." *Media, Culture & Society* 28, no. 4 (2006): 561–579.

Zandberg, Eyal. "'Ketchup is the Auschwitz of Tomatoes': Humor and the Collective Memory of Traumatic Events." *Communication, Culture & Critique* (2014): 1–16.

Zdesilaw, Ryn. "The KZ-Syndrome and its Evolution through the Generations." *Medical Review Auschwitz: Medicine Behind the Barbed Wire Conference Proceedings* (2018): 85–92.

Zertal, Idith. *Hauma vehamavet* [*The Nation and Death*]. Tel-Aviv: Dvir, 1993.

Zimmerman, Moshe. *Al Tig'u li bashoah* [*Do Not Touch my Holocaust*]. Haifa: Haifa University Press, 2002.

Ziv, Avner. "Psycho-Social Aspects of Jewish Humour in Israel and in the Diaspora." In *Jewish Humour*, edited by Avner Ziv, 47–76. New Brunswick: Transaction Publishers, 1998.

Zylberman, Lior and Vicente Sánchez-Biosca. "Reflections on the Significance of Images in Genocide Studies: Some Methodological Considerations." *Genocide Studies and*

Prevention: An International Journal 12, no. 2 (2018): 1–17."'Silence' by Orly Yadin & Sylvie Bringas." *AnimatedDocumentary.com*, No Date, accessed June 1, 2015. https://bit.ly/3C7ySFS

"'German Shepherd' Intro—Director Nils Bergendal." *YouTube*, September 23, 2014, accessed April 7, 2023. https://bit.ly/3RX9IBa

"Jiří Trnka." *A Medium Corporation*. Accessed July 1, 2015. https://bit.ly/3k5BwFR

"'Nyosha' by Liran Kapel and Yael Dekel." *AnimatedDocumentry.com*, No Date, accessed April 7, 2023. https://bit.ly/3Cs8ExP

"A Bird at the End of the World: The Story of Yehudith Yegermann." *YouTube*, April 16, 2020, accessed April 7, 2023. https://bit.ly/3EmFzFV

"A Goodluck Charm from Grandma: The Story of Abraham Appelbaum." *YouTube*, April 16, 2020, accessed April 7, 2023. https://bit.ly/3EpqLq8

"A Piece for Dinner: The Story of Yehudith Ashriel." *YouTube*, April 16, 2020, accessed April 7, 2023. https://bit.ly/3CgvDfd

"A Thousand Kisses." Accessed April 7, 2023 https://bit.ly/3CfT8Fr

"A Thousand Kisses." Accessed April 7, 2023 vimeo.com/258300600

"A Trip to the Other Planet." Official website. Accessed April 7, 2023 https://bit.ly/3A8WZmP

"Aaron Razel—The Holy Hunchback." *YouTube*, March 31, 2019, accessed April 7, 2023 https://bit.ly/2Xe8cUv

"About." *Daniela Sherer*. Accessed April 7, 2023 https://bit.ly/2Z42PrY

"Animated Documentary, by Annabelle Honess Roe." *Studies in Documentary Movie* 9, no. 1 (2015): 92–94.

"Anne Frank's Diary—An Animated Feature Movie." *YouTube*, May 3, 2020, accessed April 7, 2023. https://bit.ly/3k1UGfF

"Az'akat emet" ["A True Alarm"]. *Dyukan* (July 14, 2017): 36–40.

"Biological Toll on Brain Function of Holocaust Survivors Revealed." *Neuroscience*, July 1, 2019, accessed April 7, 2023. https://bit.ly/3RXMPxq

"Body Memory" (Ülo Pikkov, 2011, 9 min., Estonia). *YouTube*, November 21, 2012, accessed April 7, 2023. https://bit.ly/3B8k9Ky

"Body Memory." *Nukumovie*. Accessed April 7, 2023. https://bit.ly/3Fgszlx

"Broken Branches." Accessed April 7, 2023. https://bit.ly/3QN75l6

"Clinical Practice Guideline for the Treatment of Posttraumatic Stress Disorder (PTSD) in Adults (2017)." *Post Traumatic Stress Disorder*, APA. Accessed April 7, 2023. https://bit.ly/3xj66Sw

"Concentration Camp Syndrome." *APA Dictionary of Psychology*. American Psychological Association. Accessed April 7, 2023. https://bit.ly/3quZ7Ch

"Conference Future of Holocaust Testimonies lll—Nyosha—Animated Movie Based on Holocaust Survivor Testimony." *YouTube*, June 1, 2014, accessed April 7, 2023. https://bit.ly/3tQOLgY

"Donald Duck—Der Fuehrer's Face | eng sub." *YouTube*. Accessed April 7, 2023. https://bit.ly/3tCTanv

"DSM-5 Criteria for PTSD." National Center for PTSD, US Department of Veterans Affairs, accessed April 7, 2023. https://bit.ly/2vOFuZK

"Esther and the Officer: The Story of Esther Miron." *YouTube*, April 16, 2020, accessed April 7, 2023. https://bit.ly/3zm0PrO

"Eva Kor: The Holocaust Survivor who Forgave the Nazis | BBC Ideas." *YouTube*, February 20, 2020, accessed April 7, 2023. https://bit.ly/3DaoNZo

"Eva Kor," The Forgiveness Project, accessed April 7, 2023. https://bit.ly/3RJ97Us

"German Shepherd en DocumentaMadrid 2015." *YouTube*, June 8, 2015, accessed April 7, 2023. https://bit.ly/3TeiSdG

"German Shepherd." *Vimeo*, No Date, accessed April 7, 2023. https://vimeo.com/79479302

"German Shepherd." Accessed April 7, 2023. https://bit.ly/3SZcJCe

"Grandma Mimi." *Facebook*, May 8, 2016, accessed May 8, 2016. https://bit.ly/3z3Z5Di

"Hitler e l'Olocausto raccontato con i Lego." *YouTube*, January 22, 2015, accessed April 7, 2023. https://bit.ly/3kqVPhj

"I Survived the Holocaust Twin Experiments." *YouTube*, September 16, 2017, accessed April 7, 2023. https://bit.ly/3UhpcT8

"In Front of the Sea—The Story of Saul Oren." *YouTube*, April 16, 2020, accessed April 7, 2023. https://bit.ly/2WwcsyV

"Jan Karski." *Yad Vashem*, accessed April 7, 2023. https://bit.ly/3mjHWBh

"Karski & The Lords of Humanity." *Facebook*. Accessed April 7, 2023. https://bit.ly/3FcSAlR

"Karski and the Lords of Humanity." *Kickstarter*. Accessed April 7, 2023. https://bit.ly/3a2Azsc

"Kol Nidrei—The Story of Moshe Kaptain." *YouTube*, April 16, 2020, accessed April 7, 2023. https://bit.ly/3A93XYa

"Kol Nidrei—The Story of Moshe Kaptain." *YouTube*, April 16, 2020, accessed April 7, 2023. https://bit.ly/3A93XYa

"Luck: The Story of Israel Kleinmann." *YouTube*, April 16, 2020, accessed April 7, 2023. https://bit.ly/3l1zffw

"Mahadura Rishona" [First Edition]. *Facebook*, May 4, 2016, accessed May 4, 2016. https://bit.ly/398XD82

"Making of Eyes." *YouTube*, April 23, 2012, accessed April 7, 2023 https://bit.ly/3oxros2

"Mother's Dream: The Story of Miriam Woodislivasky." *YouTube*, April 16, 2020, accessed April 7, 2023. https://bit.ly/3CjjIgC

"My Good Fortune in Auschwitz." Accessed April 7, 2023. https://vimeo.com/142921363

"Nana." *Alikelner*, accessed April 7, 2023. https://bit.ly/3D4wtwc

"Noch Am Leben (Still Alive)." A. D. Lester, *Vimeo*, accessed April 7, 2023. https://bit.ly/3L8oG5J

"Nyosha." *Vimeo*. Accessed April 7, 2023. https://vimeo.com/43928582

"Nyosha Presented by SFJFF." *YouTube*, October 1, 2013. https://bit.ly/3Ctq2SV

"Orly Yadin and Sylvie Bringas's Silence." *Opticon1826*, no. 9, Autumn 2010. Accessed April 7, 2023. https://bit.ly/3C8YJNH Accessed 2 February 20215.

"Our Story: 12 Short Movies About the Human Spirit in the Holocaust." *YouTube*, April 16, 2020, accessed April 7, 2023. https://bit.ly/3tKQSmh

"Overnight Stay." *My Hero Films Community*, accessed April 7, 2023. https://bit.ly/3CxstUF

"Prof. Yehuda Bauer: The Distortion of Holocaust History." *YouTube*, May 6, 2020, accessed April 7, 2023. https://bit.ly/3C29Rf8

"PTSD—How Do You Recognize a Post-Traumatic Reaction? Post Trauma Signs and Treatment Methods." Dr. Tal Center. Accessed April 7, 2023. https://bit.ly/3qBg2Dm

"PTSD Post-Traumatic Stress Disorder Symptoms, Diagnosis and Treatment." *Tamir Institute for Psychotherapy*. Accessed April 7, 2023. https://bit.ly/3d7dQQW

"PTSD." *Diagnostic and Statistical Manual of Mental Disorders* (5th ed.). Arlington: American Psychiatric Publishing, 2013, 271–280.

"Red Fox—The Story of Zippora Feibelevich." *YouTube*, April 15, 2020. Accessed April 7, 2023. https://bit.ly/3hFhZdU

"Richard Goldgewicht." *A Thousand Kisses*. Accessed April 7, 2023. https://bit.ly/3zY1IXJ

"Salute Your Shorts 2018—Still Alive/Noch Am Leben." *We Are Moving Stories.* Accessed April 7, 2023. https://bit.ly/3FfbcSk

"Silence: – příběh z období holocaustu (eng, cze sub)." *YouTube*, January 31, 2009, accessed April 7, 2023. https://bit.ly/3mi0lhz

"Silence." *Yadin Productions.* Accessed April 7, 2023. https://bit.ly/3B1g8rr

"Sketches from Munich." *YouTube*, September 5, 2013, accessed April 7, 2023. https://bit.ly/3MrRl6d

"The 2000 Oscar Shortlist." Accessed April 7, 2023. https://bit.ly/3irDDm7

"The Dress." Hadar Huber. *Vimeo.* Accessed April 7, 2023. https://vimeo.com/71809187

"The Execution of Memory." *YouTube*, May 14, 2020, accessed April 7, 2023. https://bit.ly/2Xdpn8F

"The German Nurse—The Story of Elka Bernstein." *YouTube*, April 16, 2020, accessed April 7, 2023. https://bit.ly/3Cs93Aj

"The German Nurse." Accessed April 7, 2023. https://bit.ly/2Z843m5

"The Hart of New York Show with NYC Judge, David Paul, discussing the Holocaust." *YouTube*, January 22, 2020, accessed April 7, 2023. https://bit.ly/3rSvnQu

"The Progressive Nature of Concentration Camp Syndrome in Former Prisoners of Nazi Concentration Camps—Not Just History, but the Important issue of contemporary medicine." *Journal of Psychiatric Research* 75 (April 2016): 1–6.

"The Sand Mine." Accessed April 7, 2023. https://bit.ly/3Ek8HOf

"The Springman and the S.S. (1946)—B&W/14:18 Mins." *YouTube*, August 17, 2016, accessed April 7, 2023. https://bit.ly/2Xh1CMY

"Victim of Nazi Twin Experiments in Auschwitz | DW Documentary." *YouTube*, January 26, 2020, accessed April 7, 2023. https://bit.ly/3daT16U

"Virtual Book Launch: The Afterdeath of the Holocaust". *YouTube*, March 19, 2021, accessed April 7, 2023. https://bit.ly/3EbYfIs

"Waltz with Bashir." Israeli Cinema book. Accessed April 7, 2023. https://bit.ly/3g63odh

"Why a Holocaust Survivor Forgave the Nazis | The Girl who Forgave the Nazis." *YouTube*, November 27, 2018, accessed April 7, 2023. https://bit.ly/3xj9Jb8

"Yehudit—English Subtitles." Cinema and Animation Department, Tel-Hai College. *YouTube*, December 30, 2015, accessed January 1, 2016. https://bit.ly/3tMQcNy

Filmography

A Thousand Kisses (Richard Goldgewicht, 2017).
A Trip to the Other Planet (Israel, Tom Kless, 2014).
Another Planet (Amir Yatziv, 2017).
Bettine Le Beau—A Lucky Girl (Martin O'Neill and Andrew Griffin, 2015).
Broken Branches (Ayala Sharot, 2014).
Compartments (Daniella Koffler and Uli Seis, 2017).
Dear Fredy (Rubi Gat, 2016).
Eva Kor: The Holocaust Survivor who Forgave the Nazis (Anna Humphries and Amelia Chiew, 2020).
Facing the Sea—The Story of Saul Oren (Horenfeld) (Daniella Koffler, 2020).
German Shepherd (Nils Bergendal, Sweden, 2014).
Grandma Mimi (Shirley Prishkolnik, 2016).
I Was a Child of Holocaust Survivors (Ann Marie Fleming, 2012).
Karski and the Lords of Humanity (Slawomir Grünberg, Poland, 2015).
Kishon (Eliav Lilty, 2017).
Kol Nidrei (Shira Meishar, 2020).
Luck: The Story of Israel Kleinmann (Anat Kosty, 2020).
My Good Fortune in Auschwitz (Reber Dosky, 2012).
Nana (Ali Kellner, Canada, 2017).
Noch Am Leben [*Still Alive*] (Anita Lester, 2017).
Nyosha (Liran Kapel and Yael Dekel, 2012).
Overnight Stay (Übernachtung, Daniela Sherer, 2009).
Red Fox—The Story of Zippora Feibelevich (Daniella Koffler, 2020).
2nd World War 3rd Generation (Elad Eisen, Gil Laron, and Shahar Madmon, 2013).
7 Minutes in the Warsaw Ghetto (Johan Oeslinger, 2012).
Silence (England, Silvie Bringas and Orly Yadin, 1998).
Sketches from München (Shahaf Ram, 2013).
The Dress (Hadar Huber, 2013).
The German Nurse (Daniella Koffler, 2020).
Yehudith (Daniel Geron, 2015).

Index

2nd World War 3rd Generation, 198–204
7 Minutes in the Warsaw Ghetto, 103, 122–8

A Bird at the End of the World (film), 31–2
A Piece for Dinner (film), 31–2
A Thousand Kisses, 37, 53–8, 225
A Trip to the Other Planet, 9, 137, 161–7
Aharoni, Noa, 119
Another Planet, 65, 86, 95–102
Appelbaum, Avraham, 32
Arnon, Yehudit, 24–31
Assouline Travilio, Natalie, 5
Auschwitz-Birkenau, 9, 24–5, 27–9, 32, 34, 41, 45, 65, 72–3, 75, 86–101, 108, 112, 115–16, 118–21, 135, 139, 142, 154, 156–9, 162–7, 175–8, 193, 209, 211, 213, 219
Austria, 20, 82, 85

Baltic Sea, 104, 108
Ben Shemen Youth Village, 146–9, 151
Bergendal, Nils, 171, 181–2, 185
Berlin, 53–8, 65, 67–8, 70, 137–8, 142–4, 182–4, 200–1, 208–16
Bettine Le Beau – A Lucky Girl, 37, 48–52
Bornstein, Elka, 45–8
Brdečka, Jiří, 4
Bringas, Silvie, 6, 66, 69, 70, 137
Broken Branches, 137, 144–52, 157
Budapest, 75–7, 82, 84, 154–5

Cardon, Jacques Armand, 4
Charm from Grandmother (film), 31–2
Chiew, Amelia, 103, 113, 137
Compartments, 198–9, 208–16
Czechoslovakia, 4, 24, 73, 75, 77, 79, 87

Danube, 76
Dark Side, The, 5
Dear Fredy, 66, 73–5, 103, 112, 115–18
death march, 45, 89, 104, 106, 108–9, 159
Dekel, Yael, 37–9, 42–4
Dosky, Reber, 65, 90–1
Dress, The, 65, 86–90

Eichmann, 72, 100, 162–4, 179
Eisen, Elad, 200, 204
Eisenstein, Bernice, 174–81
Esther and the Officer (film), 31–2
Everything's for You, 5

Facing the sea—The story of Saul Oren, 65, 86, 92–4
Feibelevich, Zippora, 31–6
Fleming, Ann Marie, 17, 171, 174–5, 177, 180–1
Folman, Ari, 171, 186–9, 191–6

Gat, Rubi, 5, 65, 73–4, 116–7
Genis, Maxim, 97–9
German Nurse – The Story of Elka Bornstein, The, 37, 45–8
German Shepherd, 72, 171, 181–5, 203–4
Germany, 20, 23, 45, 53, 55, 59, 62, 67, 142, 145, 154–5, 157, 177, 181–5, 200–1, 203–16
Geron, Daniel, 20, 26
Giron, Daniel, 24–31
Goldgewicht, Richard, 37, 53, 55–7
Gordonia Zionist youth movement, 145
Grandma Mimi, 20–4, 32, 35
Greif, Gideon, 100–2
Griffin, Andrew, 37, 48–9

Gross, Yoram, 4–5
Grünberg, Slawomir, 103, 128–9

Haber, Natalia (Nettie), 53–8
hard labor, 45, 81–2
Hirsch, Fredy, 66, 73–5, 103, 112, 115–18
Hitler, 55, 57, 125, 153, 156, 166, 201, 206
Huber, Hadar, 65, 87–9
Huber, Haya, 87–90
Humphries, Anna, 103, 113, 137
Hungary, 76, 82–4

I was a child of Holocaust survivors, 17, 171, 174–81, 183–4

Jolsva labor camp, 75–7

Kapel, Liran, 37–40, 42–4
Kapel, Nomi (Nyosha), 37–45
Kaptain, Moshe, 110–11
Karski and the Lords of Humanity (film), 103, 122, 128–31
Karski, Jan, 128–31
Ka-tzetnik (Yehiel De-Nur), 161–7
Kellner, Ali, 65, 82–86
Kishon, Ephraim, 75–80, 137, 152–6
Kishon, 65, 75–80, 137, 152–6
Kleinmann, Israel, 80–2
Koffler, Daniella, 20, 31–3, 35–6, 38, 46, 65, 80, 92–3, 198, 208–10, 213, 215
Kol Nidrei, 103, 110–11
Kor, Eva, 111–15, 156–9
Krakow ghetto, 58, 80
Krakow, 58, 80
Kristallnacht, 20–4

l'Empreinte [*Imprint*] (film), 4
Lanzmann, Claude, 9–10, 68, 129–30, 154
Laron, Gil, 198, 203
Le Beau, Bettine, 48–52
Lester, Anita, 103–10, 137, 159–61, 198–9
Lilty, Eliav, 65, 77–80, 137
Lodz, 129
London, Yaron, 75–6, 154

Madmon, Shahar, 198
Maus II: And Here My Troubles Began, 5
Maus: A Survivor's Tale, 4–5

Mauthausen, 80, 82
Meishar, Shira, 103, 111
Melk, 80, 82
Meyer, Hajo, 90–2
Miron, Esther, 32
Mother's Dream (film), 31–2
My Good Fortune in Auschwitz, 65, 86, 90–2

Nagler, Sonia, 104–10
Nagler, Eva, 104–10, 159–61, 198–9
Nana, 65, 82–6
Noch Am Leben, 103–10, 137, 159–61, 198–9
Nyosha, 37–45, 123

O'Neill, Martin, 37, 48–9
Oren, Saul, 92–4
Overnight Stay, 37, 58–62

Palestine (The Land of Israel), 48, 145, 148–9
Paul, David, 181–5
Pérák a SS [*Springman and the SS*] (film), 4
Pershkolnik, Shirley, 20–24
Pictures from my Life, 5
Plaszow, 80, 82
Poland, 37, 58, 63, 80–2, 103, 110, 128, 145, 147, 151–2, 162, 176, 198
Prague, 73, 116
Prishkolnik, Shirley, 20–1

Ram, Shahaf, 198, 204–5, 208
Raskin, Richard, 122–8
Ravett, Abraham 5
Rechter, Michla (Michal), 145–52
Red Army, the, 32, 85, 163
Red Fox – The Story of Zippora Feibelevich, 20, 31–6
Reiner, Vera, 82–6
Ross, Tana, 65–73, 137–44, 184, 196

Sabotage, 112, 119–22
Sagiv, Miriam (Mimi), 20–4
Sarah/ The Seventh Match (film), 4
Schindler's List (film), 83, 127, 184
Sharot, Ayala, 137, 145–52, 157
Sherer, Daniela, 37, 58–60, 62–3
Shoah (film), 9–10, 68, 129–30, 154
Silence, 6, 65–73, 137–44, 184, 196

Sketches from Munich, 198, 204–8, 210, 215
Spiegelman, Art, 4–5
Star of David, the, 21, 25, 42, 71, 77, 84, 91, 211
Steinberg, Irene, 58–63

Theresienstadt, 65, 69–75, 115, 138–42
Trnka, Jiří, 4

USSR, 47, 110

Wajcblum Heilman, Anna, 119–22
Wajcblum, Esther (Estusha), 119–22
Waldmann, Moses, 53–8
Waltz with Bashir, 1, 8, 129–30, 137, 167, 171, 186–96
Warsaw, 37, 40, 122–30, 184, 194

Yad Vashem, 20, 31–3, 35, 45, 80, 87, 93, 102
Yadin, Orly, 6, 11, 66–7, 69–72, 137, 139, 143–4, 175, 196, 213
Yatziv, Amir, 65, 95–101
Yehudit, 20, 31, 24–32
yellow badge, 42, 74, 154, 178, 210, 214–15
Yellow Star Houses, 82

EU representative:
Easy Access System Europe
Mustamäe tee 50, 10621 Tallinn, Estonia
Gpsr.requests@easproject.com